Jared Savage is an investigative reporter for the *New Zealand Herald* who has won journalism awards every year since 2010, including twice being named as the best reporter in the country. He lives in Tauranga with his wife and two young children.

D1616962

GANG LAND

JARED SAVAGE

HarperCollins*Publishers*

HarperCollins*Publishers*
Australia • Brazil • Canada • France • Germany • Holland • Hungary
India • Italy • Japan • Mexico • New Zealand • Poland • Spain • Sweden
Switzerland • United Kingdom • United States of America

First published in 2020
by HarperCollins*Publishers* (New Zealand) Limited
Unit D1, 63 Apollo Drive, Rosedale, Auckland 0632, New Zealand
harpercollins.co.nz

A catalogue record for this book is available from the National Library of New Zealand.

ISBN 978 1 7755 4162 2 (pbk)
ISBN 978 1 7754 9193 4 (ebook)
ISBX 978 1 4607 8500 3 (audiobook)

Cover design by Design by Committee
Cover photo by Brett Phibbs
Typeset in Sabon LT Std by Kirby Jones

Printed and bound in Australia by McPherson's Printing Group
The papers used by HarperCollins in the manufacture of this book are a natural, recyclable
product made from wood grown in sustainable plantation forests. The fibre source and
manufacturing processes meet recognised international environmental standards, and carry
certification.

For the Savage tribe – Rebecca, Harry and Lucy.

CONTENTS

INTRODUCTION

A 'SOURCE' IN JOURNALISM is someone who will talk to a reporter when they're not supposed to. Developing a network of sources is as essential to a journalist as a keyboard.

The truth is out there, but there are increasingly sophisticated ways of burying it. Every professional organisation has a PR department that is very skilled at brushing inconvenient truths under the carpet. As for the *Official Information Act*, it sometimes seems to exist only to drive journalists mad. You make a request. You wait. You wait, and wait, and eventually you get told that the information can't be revealed.

That's where sources come in.

But it's not always clear why *they* want to talk to *us*. There's a risk it'll get them into serious trouble.

Sometimes they do it because they have an axe to grind, but even then it's still a story if the information can be corroborated. Sometimes people like having their achievements in the news. Sometimes it's simply because they like the reporter. But at the heart of it, I think, is their belief in the public's right to know.

The first glimpse I was ever given into the criminal underworld was through a source. This person rang me when I was sitting in an Auckland bus on the way to work.

It was March 2009. I'd recently joined the *New Zealand Herald* as a 26-year-old crime reporter, after three years at the

Herald on Sunday, a sister paper with a separate newsroom. Working for a Sunday newspaper in a competitive market is hard graft for a journalist; you can't rely on the news of the day, you've got to dig out yarns that will hold until the end of the week. You hope.

A lot of my digging meant days loitering around the Auckland District Court. I'd trawl through dozens of charge sheets – which included the defendant's name and details and a brief description of their alleged offence – until I found something that seemed as though it might be a yarn. Then I'd hang around until that defendant appeared in court. I'd also nag people for help: court staff, Crown prosecutors, defence lawyers, police officers, even criminals.

The first time I went to court, back in 2006, I'd asked a defence lawyer where representatives of the media could sit. He'd pointed me to a wooden box in the middle of the room.

I started walking towards it and was nearly there before I realised the joke. *I* was the punchline. The laughing lawyer had sent me to the dock, where defendants stand to face their accusers. It sums up how many lawyers feel about reporters.

But simply turning up and asking for help ('Is there a suppression order?' 'What does propensity evidence mean?' 'Can you please check the next court date?') meant I soon became a familiar face.

I made mistakes, and I'm sure plenty of people came to loathe me. I learned that nothing is ever black and white, although it can often seem that way printed in a paper. But over time, other people came to trust me. We'd chat about what was happening around the traps; they might tip me off about an arrest or an intriguing trial about to start. Sometimes it was as simple as a steer in the right direction.

Eventually these relationships grew to the point where we might catch up for coffee down a side street, or maybe for a couple of beers in a quiet bar. If not, I made a point of calling these people nearly every week, just to shoot the breeze and perhaps ask if there was anything new worth chasing. Some have even become good friends.

Quite by accident, or at least not by cynical design, I was learning a very valuable skill for a journalist: how to cultivate sources.

The source who rang me when I was on the bus in March 2009 had an important story that they genuinely believed the public had a right to know. They suggested I get to the Auckland High Court quick-smart. A significant methamphetamine dealer was being sent to prison, likely for a very long time, and the source hinted that the case involved some very interesting details.

I had never written about methamphetamine or organised crime before. What I heard in the courtroom that day was fascinating. The guy in the dock was a geeky-looking Chinese man with a cool nickname, 'Four-Eyed Dragon'. The amounts of money he'd made through selling meth were staggering. (He appears in Chapter 2.)

There were no other reporters in the courtroom, and I couldn't quite believe my luck as I walked back to the *Herald* offices with the facts of the scoop scribbled down in my notebook. It was my first front-page story for the *Herald*, a splash in the Saturday edition, which exposed how Asian crime syndicates were laundering drug profits through Auckland's SkyCity casino.

It was my entrée into New Zealand's growing obsession with methamphetamine, and the colourful characters who inhabit the criminal underworld. Reporting on that hidden world was addictive. I was hooked.

* * *

Since then I've had a front-row seat at one of the most gripping true-crime dramas ever to hit the country.

I've learned about interception and surveillance warrants, fizzes, undercover agents, controlled deliveries, ContacNT capsules and the *Criminal Proceeds (Recovery) Act*. I've collected thousands of pages of trial transcripts and witness statements and hundreds of photographs from court files. I've attended countless press conferences, and filled notebooks with scribbled interviews or snatched conversations. When accused criminals were released on bail I staked out their homes with *Herald* photographers in tow; some of the hard work of those photographers is republished in these pages.

I've also spent a fair bit of time with crooks.

I fondly remember tracking down 'Uncle' Paul Szeto at his home. The story was that Szeto, who was facing money-laundering charges, had been given the privilege of living in a Housing New Zealand property on Auckland's North Shore. With three flash cars parked outside: two Mercs and a Porsche.

With *Herald* photographer Greg Bowker in tow, I went to interview him at his second home in Mission Bay. It was surrounded by a high fence with a large dog behind it.

Bowks snapped Szeto when he came outside for a cigarette. The 60-year-old promptly marched over to have a word. He was a small, thin man, wearing a canary-yellow T-shirt and running shorts. His face was contorted by the effort of keeping calm, but his eyes were angry.

He soon switched into victim mode, lifting his T-shirt to show me the scar from his recent liver transplant. When that didn't dissuade us from pursuing him, he tried another tack: he promised to feed me information for other stories.

His pitch was a masterclass. He started by dropping a little hint, then tried to wheedle information out of *me*. He claimed to be a police informant, and from the way he was acting, it wasn't a stretch to imagine him feeding intelligence to the police in order to curry favour – and take out a rival.

We met for coffee the next day, but he stopped returning my phone calls when we splashed his face across the front page of the *Herald*. (Uncle Paul appears in Chapter 4.)

And then there was Danny Crichton. 'DC' had strong links to two local gangs as well as members of the Asian criminal world. He was facing serious jail time on meth charges, but managed to secure bail by using a valuable stolen war medal as a bargaining chip.

During one of his appearances at the High Court, I slipped my business card to an associate of his in the public gallery. To my surprise, I got a phone call from Crichton that evening. He felt he hadn't received enough credit for helping ensure the safe return of the war medal, and wanted to talk.

We arranged to meet at his home on Mount Albert Road, Auckland. I was led into a dark room at the back of the house. During the medal caper, Crichton had been publicly labelled by one of his rivals as a 'rat' or 'nark': probably the worst insult a career criminal could receive. He wanted to set the record straight, and held forth with my tape recorder running. (The story features in Chapter 2.)

Sitting at the table with DC was an older man with long, wild hair. It wasn't until near the end of the interview, when Crichton referred to 'Waha', that I realised who he was: Waha Saifiti, a legendary figure in the underworld. (He appears in Chapter 1.)

I've also spent a lot of time with the cops who go after the crooks. By their very nature, they're mistrusting of everyone – especially reporters.

But I respect and admire their work. Their ingenuity and persistence are utterly amazing and go largely unseen. New

Zealand is very fortunate to have such a determined group of detectives serving in what is now known as the National Organised Crime Group.

The only people who will disagree are the crims behind bars.

* * *

Gangland: The Evolution of New Zealand's Underworld attempts to illustrate the subtle shifts in the multi-million-dollar enterprise of organised methamphetamine trafficking – and the investigative techniques employed by the police in response.

Organised crime is about one thing and one thing only: making money. In the 1970s and 1980s, organised crime in New Zealand was small beer. Those making money from crime lived locally. The illicit commodities they sold, such as cannabis and stolen property, were sourced locally. Their networks and customers were local too. Back then, organised crime was a corner dairy.

But then smart criminals started to look overseas in order to expand their business across the country. Members of motorcycle gangs such as the Head Hunters were among the first to recognise the fortunes to be made from methamphetamine, a drug that was just becoming popular in New Zealand in the late 1990s. Meth soon became the hard drug of choice, ensnaring thousands upon thousands of users.

The influence of these motorcycle gangs grew alongside that of Asian organised crime syndicates, which controlled the flow of the drug, or the main ingredients needed to cook it, from source countries, including China.

Both groups were entrepreneurs who became experts at international trade. There were huge profit margins and millions of dollars to be made. And there was no need for a price war, because there was more than enough to go round.

The offshore connections provided a huge boost to the local drug economy in the early 2000s. The corner dairy was now a chain store. As an economic model, methamphetamine was a New Zealand success story.

Then the world moved in. Since around 2015, multinational criminal enterprises have been setting up base in New Zealand, flooding the market with the country's favourite drug at cut-throat prices that are shaking up the laws of supply and demand.

The immigration policy of our dear friend Australia has meant that members of *their* gangs, such as the Comancheros and the Mongols, have been able to move into the neighbourhood, and jostle for business alongside the local motorcycle clubs, the Asian syndicates and others. And all these competitors *mean* business. There are more firearms on our streets now than ever before, as criminals arm themselves to the teeth for protection and intimidation.

As well as the Australian and Asian groups, we now have Mexican cartels sending meth and cocaine to our shores. In response, the US Drug Enforcement Administration – the guys who brought down El Chapo – have set up offices in Auckland and Wellington. NZ *Narcos*.

Once upon a time, a few ounces of methamphetamine were a big deal to the police – before a massive 95-kilo bust in 2006 (covered in Chapter 2). That blew everyone's mind, and held the record for the biggest meth haul for a decade.

But these days, busts of 100 kilos are routine. Customs officials and drug cops don't get out of bed for anything less. There have been two 500-kilogram shipments stopped in the past four years (2016 to 2020), as well as many others in the 200 to 400-kilogram range.

Organised crime in New Zealand has evolved from a local dairy to the branch office of a corporate giant. This is a global business now. The criminal underworld is fluid, constantly trying to stay a step ahead of law enforcement in a never-ending game of cat-and-mouse.

This book has tried to capture the fundamentals of this subtle evolution in a collection of 12 of the most intriguing cases I've covered as reporter. The brutal execution of a husband and wife; the undercover cop who infiltrated a casino VIP lounge; the midnight fishing trip that led to the country's biggest cocaine bust; the gangster who shot his best friend in a motorcycle shop ... These stories go behind the headlines and open the door to an invisible world – a world where millions of dollars are made, life is cheap, and allegiances change like the flick of a switch.

1

BREAKING BAD BEGINS: THE BIRTH OF 'P' IN NEW ZEALAND

1996–2003

BEFORE WALTER WHITE, there was William Wallace. His story was New Zealand's very own version of *Breaking Bad*, the hit TV show about a suburban high-school teacher whose knowledge of chemistry makes him a skilled manufacturer of methamphetamine.

A diagnosis of cancer turned White to the dark side. Bill Wallace, too, had a kind of mid-life crisis. In 1994, at 54, Wallace was made redundant from Air New Zealand after 20 years of loyal service as an industrial chemist. It was a crushing blow to a hard-working guy, and Wallace suddenly found himself consigned to the scrapheap.

Some men sink into bitterness when told they're surplus to requirements. But the bespectacled Wallace got busy.

He rolled up his sleeves and bought an electroplating shop in Otahuhu, the industrial heart of Auckland, working long hours to support his family.

Four years later, he sold the business at a tidy profit. He could now enjoy retirement with his wife Beverley.

A classic-car enthusiast, Wallace splurged $63,000 on a Brabham, the Formula One car made famous by world champion Sir Jack Brabham. Paid for in cash. So was the $143,000 that it cost him to repair and restore a pair of Italian De Tomaso racing cars to their former glory.

An industrial unit in Avondale with a mortgage of $100,000 was paid off in cash deposits too. A stone wall built around the Wallaces' Mount Albert home cost $100,000: again, paid in cash. There were holidays to Fiji, and to Australia for 'Opera in the Outback'; when booking one of the trips to Fiji, Beverley Wallace gave the travel agent a plastic bag containing $13,000 in bundles of $50 and $100 notes. Informed she'd paid too much, Beverley told the agent to keep the balance as a down payment on another holiday they might take in the future.

Life was good.

After selling the electroplating business, Wallace purchased another commercial premises, but registered the property in someone else's name. He was seen coming and going from the building, in Portage Road, New Lynn, surreptitiously. It was the new office for his *true* business. Wallace had big expansion plans.

The upstairs room was fitted with three-phase electricity, powerful extractor fans and three large dessicators, glass jars used in science experiments to dry out a liquid substance. There were industrial scales and handbasins for washing up. Shelves along the walls held containers full of strange powders and chemicals – ephedrine, hydrochloric acid, red phosphorous – none of which had any use in electroplating.

Over five days in June 1997, Auckland's drug squad detectives would dismantle the premises and log their findings as evidence. Among their other discoveries were a book called *Secrets of Methamphetamine Manufacture* and $157,582 stuffed into a biscuit tin.

There would be some dispute among detectives as to whether Wallace's was the very first clandestine meth lab uncovered in New Zealand. But his sophisticated setup certainly marked a turning point for the local drug scene.

A new drug had arrived, and it was here to stay.

* * *

Police had been used to making busts for cannabis, and commonly hauled in users or dealers of harder drugs such as heroin, LSD, cocaine and ecstasy. But in 1996, the Auckland drug squad started hearing about methamphetamine: how easy it was to purchase, and how popular it had quickly become on the streets.

Criminal informants passed on the name William John Wallace. He was a known associate of the Highway 61 motorcycle gang; they brought their bikes into his electroplating shop.

Police quickly launched Operation Surf. Tracking devices planted in Wallace's car led the police to the Portage Road laboratory in New Lynn, where hidden cameras were soon trained on the exits to see who was coming and going.

Police were also granted a search warrant, giving them the authority to break into the laboratory, and collect more evidence.

They were able to prove that Wallace was in possession of chemicals and equipment typically used in the manufacture of methamphetamine, but Operation Surf didn't arrest him or seize anything just yet. Instead, detectives used the new evidence to apply to a High Court judge for a warrant to conduct covert surveillance in May 1997.

This surveillance, using hidden cameras and listening devices, was an investigative tool then in its infancy. Detectives – and the judges who granted interception warrants – were still coming to grips with the new technology.

Over the course of the next week, detectives listened in to Wallace's private phone conversations, and patiently transcribed what was said.

Wallace had an enthusiastic discussion with an accomplice about his success, when the equivalent of three days' work was completed in six hours. There was no point hurrying, Wallace said in one conversation, because he had enough methamphetamine and raw ingredients to last a lifetime.

His plan was to survive the next few months without getting caught by the police, then get out of the game. It didn't work out that way.

When Operation Surf broke down Wallace's door the following month, they found enough chemicals to manufacture more than $5 million worth of methamphetamine. It was an astronomical figure, but actually quite conservative: Wallace supplied Highway 61 members at a much cheaper bulk rate.

After his defence lawyers failed to have the surveillance evidence thrown out, Wallace pleaded guilty to manufacturing and supplying methamphetamine since December 1995. Methamphetamine was only a Class B drug at the time, with a maximum penalty of 14 years in prison.

Wallace appeared before Justice Giles at sentencing in November 1998. 'You seem to have taken great pride, Wallace, from the fact that with your skill and knowledge as a chemist, whilst it had taken you some years, you had got the process of manufacturing methamphetamine right,' said the judge. 'I do not accept that your involvement in this business was out of some form of misguided professional desire to develop the perfect system for the manufacture of this proscribed drug. You knew what you were doing and you knew it was wrong.'

He gave Wallace a sentence of 10 years' imprisonment.

Bill and Beverley Wallace also admitted to money laundering, one of the first such cases in New Zealand history.

Money laundering was a relatively new offence, added to the *Crimes Act* in 1995, to fulfil New Zealand's obligations as a signatory to the United Nations Convention Against Illicit Traffic in Narcotic Drugs and Psychotropic Substances 1988. A forensic analysis of the Wallaces' financial affairs revealed unexplained income – racing cars, real estate, holidays, the $100,000 stone wall – of $1,057,812.50.

'Bucket loads of cash' was how Justice Giles bluntly translated the legal term 'unexplained income'. Financial gain 'bordering on avarice and greed', he said, was their motivation for manufacturing significant quantities of a 'pernicious and dangerous drug known to cause huge human suffering'.

He continued: 'I have no doubt at all that all of you would have been sitting pretty, in a reasonably secure financial position which other New Zealanders might never achieve.'

* * *

The Portage Road bust came before methamphetamine was common in New Zealand, and before it became inextricably linked in the public's mind with violent crime.

Meth was not a new drug. In 1887, a Japanese chemist in Germany was researching a man-made alternative to the ephedra plant, which had been used in Chinese medicine for centuries.

Nagai Nagayoshi identified the plant's active chemical as ephedrine, which he was able to extract as a stimulant. Six years later, ephedrine was synthesised into amphetamine.

The next step was taken in 1919 by another Japanese scientist, Akira Ogata, who used red phosphorus and iodine to reduce ephedrine to a crystallised form. It was the world's first batch of methamphetamine.

At first, both amphetamine and methamphetamine were drugs created without a purpose in mind. But in time, both stimulants were used to treat different maladies such as nasal congestion, asthma and the sleep disorder narcolepsy, and as a general 'pick-me-up' pill.

By the time World War II started, the energising effects of the drug were well known. Tablets of methamphetamine were distributed to soldiers on both sides of the conflict to ward off fatigue. Strong doses were reportedly given to kamikaze pilots before their suicide missions.

By the 1950s, methamphetamine was being prescribed as a diet aid and to fight depression. Easily available, it was used as a stimulant by college students, truck drivers and athletes. Over the next decade, use of the drug spread, and in 1970, the United States Government made most uses of methamphetamine illegal.

A black market was born, with motorcycle gangs soon controlling the production and distribution of the drug. Regulations around the sale of ephedrine, the precursor used to make methamphetamine, were tightened in the 1980s. So meth cooks turned to another precursor, pseudoephedrine, which was readily available as the active ingredient in many cold and flu medicines.

The drug's popularity in the United States took off in the 1990s, and it was around the same time that it first turned up on New Zealand's shores.

The country did not have a history of widespread hard-drug use. There was some heroin smuggled into the country in the 1980s, and a smattering of LSD and ecstasy in the dance scene, but homegrown cannabis was the drug of choice for most New Zealanders.

All of that changed with meth arrived. (No one is entirely sure how the drug was first introduced to New Zealand, although an American bikie gang was rumoured to be involved.) Meth was something else entirely.

The powdered form can be dissolved in water and injected into the bloodstream, or snorted like cocaine.

But in New Zealand, it's always been more common for users to *smoke* the drug. Crystalline granules, almost like small shards of ice, are heated over a naked flame in a glass pipe or hollowed-out lightbulb, allowing the user to inhale the wispy smoke for their next euphoric high.

Meth – or 'P', short for pure – cut across the social divide. It wasn't just the poor and downtrodden passing a pipe around but also university students, white-collar professionals in downtown office blocks, and the rich and successful living in leafy suburbs.

Easy to see why. It's one hell of a drug. The science of consuming P is that when the methamphetamine hits the brain, it stimulates the reward centre, releasing dopamine in an intense rush that lasts around a minute. The heart races, breathing quickens, the body sweats or shivers. An extended high follows, for as long as eight hours, during which users feel energised, invincible, attractive and very, very awake.

This intensely pleasurable rush is a joy that users wish would last forever. They want to do it all over again, and again. They want it more than anything. They will do anything to get it. And when they get it, they get addicted.

The rush doesn't last. Eventually, the ugly stuff kicks in: anxiety, aggression, paranoia, and an insatiable urge to pick at invisible bugs crawling on the skin, creating open wounds known as 'meth sores' that scab, then scar. Later on, extreme weight loss. Rotted teeth. Exhaustion, to the point where they can't get out of bed without a hit.

But by then, their tolerance has grown. They need more and more of it, but it does less and less, meaning the withdrawal grows worse and worse.

Not all addicts are the same. But all addicts' stories follow a similar, depressingly narrow path.

When a 36-year-old woman shared her story with the *New Zealand Herald* in 2019, it read like a blueprint for meth addiction.

> The first time that I smoked meth it was like the best thing that ever happened to me. It was mind-blowing. It was mind-opening. I felt like I could conquer the world. I felt like I had energy for days. But you never get that again.
>
> At the height of my addiction I would wake up and use. Even during pregnancy I used. I couldn't stop using. When I went to the hospital and I was being monitored, my friend turned up and had gear. Even though I was in labour and even though I knew I was risking my child, I said to him, have you got a puff? And he said yes, so we went into the toilets and I got high.

At the peak of her addiction she was spending anything from $250 to $800 a day on the drug.

> For many years I would prostitute for money to get gear and then when my addiction got worse or when my habit got bigger I stopped doing it for money and just prostituted for the gear itself.
>
> I lost all my teeth and I was very anaemic.
>
> The last time I smoked it I felt horrible. My mind was scattered. I felt like I lost myself. I felt guilty. I felt suicidal. I felt horrible …

* * *

Just three years after the discovery of Bill Wallace's laboratory, it was clear New Zealand was facing a methamphetamine crisis. Persistent warnings from frontline police to their bosses in Police National Headquarters and the Beehive had gone unheeded.

P wasn't just another drug. It was the drug of choice for most New Zealand users, and the booming methamphetamine market was already transforming New Zealand organised crime to a degree that made the infamous Mr Asia drug syndicate of the 1970s pale into insignificance.

It was a problem that would occupy the thoughts of Detective Inspector Bruce Good until his retirement. He'd risen through the ranks after joining the police in 1976, and by 2000 was second in charge of what was then known as Auckland District Services. Based in Harlech House, a stark, grey, nine-storey building that loomed above its surroundings on Great South Road in Otahuhu, 'District Services' was a boring name for a police division that did very interesting work.

Within the walls of Harlech House were different specialist teams that provided support to the three main police districts across the isthmus: Auckland City, Waitemata and Counties Manukau. There was an intelligence division, an informant management team, a motorcycle gang unit, an Asian organised crime unit, and covert surveillance teams, as well as the Technical Support Unit, which installed electronic equipment like recording devices and hidden cameras inside houses, or tracking devices on cars. At the time, this was cutting-edge technology not available in every police district, which stirred some resentment among those without the same resources.

Alongside those specialist teams were drug squads of four or five detectives each, headed by a detective sergeant – experienced and hard-headed investigators like Darryl Brazier, John Sowter, Bruce Howard and Mike Beal. The drug squads would use the services of the specialist teams as needed.

Also within the walls of Harlech House, which the New Zealand Police had purchased from the Inland Revenue Department for $8.5 million, was a potentially fatal bacterium. As a result, Bruce Good's boss, Detective Inspector Maurice Whitham, contracted Legionnaires' disease, a form of pneumonia, which forced him out of the office on sick leave, and eventually into retirement.

After less than a year in the building, Good was put in charge of a relatively small division on the front line of the methamphetamine epidemic, during a period when that epidemic was morphing the criminal underworld into something completely new.

The most notorious criminals in the 1980s and '90s had been armed robbers like Leslie Maurice Green, Peter Francis Atkinson and Waha Saifiti. Wearing masks and waving pistols, they held up security vans, or robbed bank tellers and tavern tills full of cash late on a Friday or Saturday night. They were legendary figures, daring and dangerous thugs who were revered by fellow criminals and often rightly feared by the public.

But in terms of their thinking they were old-school crooks. In their view, they had a job to do and so did the police. If the cops gathered enough evidence to put them away, fair enough.

As methamphetamine first began to grip the country, armed robbery fell away. Robbing banks was a high-risk crime for a relatively low reward. Manufacturing P was a low-risk crime, with incredibly high rewards.

The millions of dollars at stake also attracted fringe players in the criminal world: the outlaw motorcycle gangs.

Rival New Zealand gangs had warred with each other since the 1970s. By the 1990s, the tit-for-tat violence was easing, as previously rebellious young men with patches on their backs mellowed with age, and the ranks were not being replenished with younger members. Older, wiser heads knew what gang warfare meant: constant pressure from the police and always looking over your shoulder.

There was a kind of ceasefire, which left the various gangs in a stalemate. Nobody could move; all the territories were already divvied up. As long as no one made an aggressive foray onto someone else's turf, gang violence – which had once made front-page headlines and energised politicians looking for votes in election year – remained in check.

And then along came P. The market was so immensely profitable that it was now smart business for enemy gangs to get along, rather than warring and attracting unwanted attention. Surveillance jobs recorded members of rival gangs – the Hells Angels, Highway 61, the Head Hunters, the Mongrel Mob, Black Power – visiting one another at home.

The Auckland chapter of the Hells Angels, set up in 1961, was the first official chapter outside the United States. Savvy and risk-averse, the Angels were rumoured to have been the first to manufacture methamphetamine in New Zealand, and were supposedly taught the recipe by their US brothers.

The conviction of the chapter's sergeant-at-arms, Andrew 'Ses' Sisson, in 1999, for conspiracy to manufacture methamphetamine and money laundering, was one of the rare occasions when an Angel has been caught in the illicit trade. When Operation Shovel, led by Detective Sergeant Darryl Brazier, raided Sisson's 3-hectare property in Dairy Flat, north of Auckland, police found $97,000 buried in one spot, and a recipe for methamphetamine in another. A search of Sisson's rented house turned up another $18,000 in cash and 49 grams of methamphetamine, worth about $49,000.

There were other items of interest: brochures on counter-surveillance, military-standard night-vision goggles, counter-surveillance photographs of police officers, and a restricted police document about the Highway 61 gang.

* * *

A fierce rival of the Hells Angels, Highway 61 was among the first gangs to take control of the methamphetamine trade – first through William Wallace, then through former bank-robber Peter Francis Atkinson.

Atkinson, nicknamed 'Pete the Terrorist', has a criminal record that started in 1981 with a conviction for possession of heroin. It's probably the tamest on his rap sheet. He soon graduated to armed robberies, and grew notorious for brandishing a Magnum pistol and firing warning shots at police officers who gave chase. He earned his 'Terrorist' moniker by blowing up a lawyer's car with a stick of dynamite.

Prison was where Atkinson mixed and mingled with some of New Zealand's worst criminals, and initially learned of the next big thing in the underworld. He became one of country's first and best meth cooks, teaming up with Kelly Raymond Robertson, a senior Highway 61 member who handled the distribution side through his bikie networks.

Their lucrative business eventually unravelled in 1999 because of Operation Asphalt, another Brazier investigation, and thanks to the courage of a sex worker who testified against them and was placed into the witness protection program. Both men were convicted of methamphetamine offences, and 55-year-old Atkinson was sentenced to 12 years in prison.

Robertson, who was known as 'Bad News Brown', would go on to be convicted of killing Kevin Weavers, president of his Highway 61 chapter. He was charged with murder after stabbing Weavers in the leg at the gang's headquarters in September 2003, but convicted of the less serious offence of manslaughter.

The death of Weavers caused a rift within Highway 61 from which the gang never recovered, losing members and influence within the criminal fraternity. Instead, it would be another gang that consistently featured in intelligence reports coming across Bruce Good's desk: the Head Hunters.

* * *

If the Hells Angels were respected by other gangs, then the 'Heads' were feared. Their propensity for violence was extreme.

Even so, before the rise of meth, they were only in the middle of the underworld pecking order, and posed no danger to the wider public. The sight of them riding their motorcycles, with a flaming-skull logo on the patch of their leather vests, was comparatively rare. All that changed within a few short years, when members started enjoying the money, power and influence that came with the explosion of the meth scene.

But how did a middling gang manage to muscle their way in to take control of the lucrative new P market?

One answer came in the terrifying form of senior member William Hines. The guy had form. Better known simply as 'Bird', Hines was convicted in 1991 of kidnapping a man at gunpoint, and torturing him with pliers and an electric drill in a garage because of a supposed debt.

The victim refused to give evidence – it's reasonable to expect this was out of fear of retribution – but the jury still reached a guilty verdict. Justice Robertson sent Hines to prison for four years. 'You just take the law into your own hands and use whatever is necessary to get what you perceive is your entitlement,' he told Hines.

It was an accurate description. Five years later, Hines and two other Head Hunters confronted an undercover police officer and held him at knifepoint. Again, Hines was convicted of kidnapping and jailed for 12 months.

Then, in 2000, Hines got caught in the middle of one of Bruce Good's first big meth investigations, codenamed Operation Flower. His two partners in crime were former bank robber Waha Saifiti and budding meth cook Brett Lionel Allison.

Better known as 'Donut', Allison had spiralled into a life of drug addiction from the age of 14. By the time he was 40, he had racked up about 30 convictions, including a three-and-a-half-year prison lag for growing weed in Northland. But there was nothing in his criminal record to suggest what was to come next.

Somehow, Donut obtained an online recipe for methamphetamine when the internet was in its infancy; through trial and error, he taught himself how to cook it. Word of his newfound skills spread and he was soon being handsomely rewarded for his work.

The long-time sickness beneficiary enjoyed the fruits of his labour, and would stay for days, sometimes a week at time, at expensive hotels around Auckland. Colourful characters would visit at all hours of the night, with Allison racking up huge bills for room service and alcohol consumption. Whenever concerns were raised by staff, Allison sauntered into reception and pulled out a wad of cash to settle the bill, before moving on to the next hotel. It was common knowledge that he always walked around with $10,000 or $15,000 in his pocket.

Word reached the police too, and Darryl Brazier was put in charge of Operation Flower. A surveillance team followed Allison to a factory in Lorien Place, East Tamaki, where the now-accomplished meth cook had set up his clandestine lab. He had leaned on the reluctant owner, an acquaintance who had agreed to his demands to let him stay for 'a few days'. Allison stayed for months. On the rare occasions when the owner visited, he could smell what he thought was paint thinner wafting down from the upstairs room where Allison spent most of his time.

At first, drug squad detectives staked out Lorien Place to watch who was coming and going from the suspected meth lab, but they were soon replaced by video cameras hidden on adjacent properties.

The neighbours gave permission for the police to do so, but only on the condition that their identities – and the footage, which, if viewed, would reveal the location of the cameras – were never revealed.

They were scared of retribution – and with good reason.

Among the various criminals caught on camera was Waha Saifiti. Born in Samoa, Saifiti was in his late 40s and the father of seven children aged between one and 30 at the time of Operation Flower. Charming, intelligent and a committed family man, Saifiti had led a double life by accumulating 60 convictions dating back to 1966.

Most were for minor offences such as receiving stolen goods, although prison sentences in 1972 – six years for aggravated robbery – and 1992 – four and a half years for theft (of money) and stealing a vehicle – revealed a darker, potentially dangerous streak.

This second conviction was for his part in the robbery of $480,000 from a security van, the most money ever taken in a New Zealand heist at the time; the proceeds were never found. He was also suspected of having pulled the strings in the robbery of $202,500 from the Birkenhead branch of the Bank of New Zealand the previous year, although charges were never laid against him.

These daring crimes turned Saifiti into a legend in criminal circles.

But on his release from prison on parole, Saifiti moved on to a *new* way of making money. He even claimed to have joked about it with a former police officer: he was waiting in line at a bank and bumped into the retired officer, who was surprised to learn Saifiti wasn't 'eyeing up' the place. 'I sell amphetamines now,' Saifiti later boasted that he'd told the ex-detective. 'It beats robbing banks, I tell ya.'

Saifiti's bragging was recorded by a listening device, hidden somewhere inside the lounge of the bungalow he was renting in Grey Lynn. It had been installed in September 2000, after Saifiti was repeatedly spotted at Allison's clandestine lab on Lorien Place. Police suspected they were working together.

Officers hid in a van parked within range of the rented bungalow, recording conversations onto audio tapes and noting any passages that might be of evidential value. Weeks and weeks of drug-fuelled ramblings and whispered discussions were recorded onto 120 audio tapes.

One unfortunate officer, Sergeant Jason Mackie, was assigned the task of transcribing the tapes, listening and rewinding repeatedly to ensure he was accurately copying what had been said, and by whom. It was a nightmare of a task: television and radio in the house generated ambient noise and electronic feedback, and individual speakers were at different distances from the recording device. Conversations in which people spoke over each other were common, and they often spoke ambiguously, or in code, in an effort to disguise what they were talking about in case the police were listening in. It was frequently difficult to work out who was speaking, but over time Mackie became more familiar with their voices.

It took him 1000 hours over six months to produce a transcript. It was 860 pages long.

In one taped conversation, Saifiti was overheard saying: 'three ways – he makes it, we split it'. Based on this comment, the police theory was that Saifiti and Bird Hines supplied pseudoephedrine and other ingredients to Brett Allison, who cooked batches of meth. The product was then split between Saifiti and Hines, who sat atop their own supply networks.

Police also learned that two of Hines's fellow Head Hunters, David 'Tunner' Dunn and another who can't be identified for legal reasons, had been brought on board as 'managers' to distribute the drugs to their own networks. Saifiti was the 'chief executive' of the operation, which the Crown prosecutors later dubbed 'the Methamphetamine Makers Co Ltd'.

Over the course of the six-week Flower investigation, the police estimated that Allison manufactured at least 19 ounces (curiously, meth wholesalers always supply in ounces, not grams).

In 2000, pure meth sold for between $20,000 and $25,000 an ounce. Drug dealers lower down the supply chain would break up the ounce to sell by the gram, for around $800, and meth users could then buy a 'point' – 0.1 grams of meth crystals – for $100 to place in their glass pipe and smoke.

In little over a month, Allison had manufactured drugs worth more than $500,000 at street value.

Yet according to bugged conversations, Waha Saifiti and Bird Hines had received only 1 or 2 ounces to sell on. They were getting concerned about Allison's abilities as a cook, and suspected Dunn and the other Head Hunter were 'eating cheese off their plate'. An agitated Saifiti ranted about people 'leaving the planet', of 'punching dents in c****', of holding people under the water and cutting off noses.

'Rest assured, we will not be made to look like fools here,' said Saifiti. 'We will just whack anybody who needs to be whacked ... Whack him straight on the spot.'

In October 2000, Allison moved his clan lab – as was common practice – out of the East Tamaki factory to an unknown location. Police decided to wrap up the investigation. They believed they had enough evidence, and it was time to stop any more meth from hitting the streets.

Detectives found 73 grams of methamphetamine in Waha Saifiti's home, but Allison and his new hideaway were nowhere to be found.

Eight days later, armed police surrounded a panel-beater's garage on Great North Road in the West Auckland suburb of Kelston. The surrounding streets were cordoned off and a nearby secondary school was placed in lockdown for fear of an explosion from the lab.

After several hours of negotiations, Donut Allison came out peacefully.

He belligerently refused to take his clothes off for the decontamination showers set up outside. Instead, he sat in the back seat of a police car, dripping wet, as he was taken back to Harlech House to be charged. The officers travelling with him later reported feeling queasy and getting headaches, due to the chemical fumes emanating from Allison.

Inside the garage was what an ESR scientist would later describe as 'by far' the biggest meth lab she had seen in New Zealand. It took five days to dismantle all the equipment, which included two 1000-litre plastic containers, or Bailey tanks, holding 1500 litres of liquid between them. When the chemicals were drained off, nearly 6 ounces of methamphetamine sludge were left behind.

The five main players in Operation Flower denied the meth manufacturing and conspiracy charges and fiercely contested the evidence, in particular the transcripts of the bugged conversations. Poor old Sergeant Mackie was heckled and jeered at from the dock and accused of manipulating the evidence at their trial in 2003. But, after 11 weeks of evidence and two and a half days of deliberation, the jury found Saifiti and Allison guilty of manufacturing methamphetamine. The jury could not reach a verdict for Hines on the manufacturing charge, although he and David Dunn were convicted of conspiracy to supply.

In sentencing the five members of the drug conspiracy, Justice Williams rightly observed that methamphetamine was a 'pernicious, addictive drug capable on one hand of causing immense harm and degradation to its users and on the other producing very considerable profit'.

Operation Flower had uncovered a commercial meth operation on a scale that showed a high level of organisation and involved substantial quantities of the drug.

As the principal cook, Allison was sentenced to 10 years' imprisonment, closely followed by nine and a half years for Saifiti, while Hines and Dunn received sentences of seven and six years respectively. The High Court judge noted that they had been sentenced on the basis that methamphetamine was a Class B drug at the time of their offending, although Parliament had since elevated it to Class A status.

The higher classification, which now carried a maximum sentence of life imprisonment, reflected the public's concern over the harm the drug was causing in the community. Clan labs had been unknown just a few years earlier, said Justice Williams, but now – six years after William Wallace was arrested for running the country's first known clan lab – ESR scientists visited one every week.

'From being rare in this country only a few years ago with most of the drug being imported,' he said in his judgment, 'its manufacture in New Zealand is now widespread … People manufacture with no care for the human misery they cause, simply for greed.'

But in the eyes of police on the front line, the elevation of methamphetamine to a Class A controlled drug, as well as the force's establishment of specialist clan lab teams, was too little, too late. Their warnings about meth had gone unheeded for years, and vast profits had now transformed organised crime in New Zealand in a way that could never be reversed.

Operation Flower had opened a window onto the criminal underworld's tight stranglehold on the meth trade. Yet it was only a hint of what was to come.

As Waha Saifiti was heard saying on the wire: 'He who controls the oil, controls the world.'

2

WORKING THE WIRE: THE DRUG CATCHER WHO BECAME A POLICE RAT

2006

BILLY FUNG HAD A choice to make. He had only two options, and neither was appealing: risk spending the rest of his life far from home in a New Zealand prison, or rat out his drug partners to the cops.

Drug squad detectives had watched the 41-year-old since he flew into Auckland from Hong Kong on 14 March 2006, purporting to be there on business. As he handed over his passport at Auckland International Airport – revealing his full name, Kai Lok Fung – he was setting in motion a process that would allow police to listen in to every phone conversation he thought was private.

Suspicious of Fung's story, Customs staff rifled through his luggage and found paperwork linking him to the Jacob Plastic and Epoxy Company of Hong Kong, which they suspected to be a shadow company for a drug-smuggling syndicate.

They contacted Detective Inspector Bruce Good – now working for the imaginatively renamed Auckland Metro Crime and Operation Support (AMCOS) – who convinced a High Court judge to grant an interception warrant for Fung's mobile phone. This was the starting point of Operation Major.

By 2006, new technology meant new, easier methods of surveillance. No longer did police need to sneak inside the houses and cars of suspected criminals to plant audio devices, or tap their landlines, resulting in the kind of poor-quality audio recorded at Waha Saifiti's home during Operation Flower. They now had a back door into the digital world of mobile devices.

Staff at AMCOS called it 'working the wire'. They even got team polo shirts made with the motto stitched into a logo.

New software allowed the tapped phone calls to be directly routed from the telco providers, such as Vodafone and Telecom, to the newly established Crime Monitoring Centre at Police National Headquarters in Wellington, then to the desktop computers in the AMCOS offices in Auckland. Each conversation was recorded and logged as an easy-to-use digital file. No more bulky physical reels to copy and store, no more risk of damage every time officers rewound or fast-forwarded the tapes. And no more endless recordings of people snoring, dogs scratching or refrigerators humming on hidden listening devices.

The technology brought the New Zealand police into the 21st century, and would provide crucial evidence in courtroom trials in the years to come. Professional criminals were practised at throwing away disposable 'burner' phones every few days, or speaking in coded phrases, but there was always someone – usually lower down the chain of command – who let something slip.

Little more than suspicion tied the Jacob Plastic and Epoxy Company of Hong Kong to drug shipments. Billy Fung was the one lead the head of Operation Major, Detective Sergeant Scott Steedman, and his deputy Detective Sergeant Mike Beal had to follow.

As well as listening to Billy Fung's phone calls, Operation Major tracked his movements across town with rotating surveillance squads. The day after his arrival in Auckland, Fung rented office space in Albert Street from the East Asia Company, a reputable Chinese consultancy in downtown Auckland, and registered his own business, Isaac International Trade Company, based at the address.

Over the following days, Fung opened a bank account with ANZ, obtained an Inland Revenue number for tax purposes, and sought a client code from Customs to import goods. He took every step necessary to create the illusion of a legitimate trading company.

After just eight days in New Zealand, he flew back to Hong Kong to make the company's first business deal.

A month later, on 22 April 2006, the *Provider* sailed from China to New Zealand with a 20-foot freight container on board, addressed to Fung's newly established business, Isaac International Trade Company. According to the bill of lading faxed to Customs, there were 879 cartons of plastics inside the container, sent by Jacob Plastics and Epoxy Company, the Hong Kong business that had triggered police interest in the first place.

As soon as Fung flew back into Auckland on 10 May, Operation Major was granted a new interception warrant for his mobile phone and waited for the *Provider* to deliver the goods.

Three days later, the ship docked at the Port of Tauranga. Customs pulled aside the Isaac container and took it to a secure warehouse on the docks, where it was opened in private.

Large white plastic sacks were piled inside. Each sack was painstakingly opened by Customs officials. Inside were ... granules of a rubber compound.

But the shipping container was also packed with more than 1000 metal tins. Inside was ... green paint.

An X-ray machine failed to identify anything suspicious, so every single one of the paint cans had to be searched by hand. Each and every step had to be meticulously documented and photographed in case officers came across a tin that would be needed as evidence.

The lid of each tin was popped off, then a wooden stick pushed into the paint until it reached the bottom with a metallic clink. Officers opened one tin after another, stuck in their stick, and documented and photographed absolutely nothing of any use – until finally they opened one particular tin, stuck in the stick, and didn't feel it reach the bottom.

The green paint was poured out. What came out along with the paint was … a block of plastic resin in the same shade of green. They smashed it open and found a clear plastic bag of methamphetamine encased in the hard resin. It was a brilliant concealment of drugs, one of the best seen in New Zealand to this day.

The bag weighed 1 kilo, which by itself was about as much meth as an experienced detective in 2006 would ever see in a single seizure.

But then Customs and police found another resin brick, then another, then another. When the final tally was counted, 95 of the 1-kilo bags were lined up on the concrete floor: a staggering haul, almost beyond comprehension.

On that day – 19 May 2006 – Operation Major had, in one swoop, scooped up three times the amount of meth stopped by police and Customs across the entire previous year. In fact, 95 kilos was more than all the meth ever seized in New Zealand up to that point.

This mind-blowing discovery shattered the myth – ignorantly perpetuated in Wellington's corridors of power – that P was a passing fad, and that the drug's popularity had been grossly exaggerated by a headline-hungry media.

Three days later, a second shipment arrived on board the *Prosperity*. Hidden inside hundreds of sacks of cement were 154 kilograms of pink ContacNT granules, a Chinese cold and flu remedy whose active ingredient was pseudoephedrine.

Pseudoephedrine was now a Class C controlled drug in its own right. Police had worked out that meth cooks were hiring people as 'pill shoppers' to go from pharmacy to pharmacy buying up packets of Sudafed and similar products. So Helen Clark's government had banned most over-the-counter sales of products containing pseudoephedrine. Pharmacists could sell only a limited number of pills containing the drug, and had to keep a register of customers who bought them. But, as a perverse, unintended consequence, the restrictions were creating a new opportunity for local Asian crime figures with ties to China.

While ContacNT was never sold in New Zealand, it was freely available in China. The profit margins were incredible. A packet of 100 ContacNT pills cost just a few dollars in China. In New Zealand, a 'set' of pseudo – 10 packets, or 1000 pills, weighing just 223 grams – sold on the black market for between $8000 and $10,000.

To gather the 154-kilo pseudoephedrine mountain found on the *Prosperity*, thousands and thousands of packets of ContactNT would have been purchased in China. Someone would have removed the capsules from their blister packs, painstakingly unscrewed each plastic capsule shell by hand, then tipped out the pink contents to repackage.

This vital pipeline of easily purchased pseudoephedrine had made Asian organised crime figures increasingly influential in their new homeland.

The *Prosperity* shipment provided enough pseudoephedrine to manufacture another 43 kilograms of meth, on top of the 95 kilograms of finished product found in the *Provider* shipment. It was so much methamphetamine that if every single person in Auckland had wanted to try a 'point' of P, there would have been enough to go around.

* * *

The massive haul came as a shock even to the drug squads who worked on the front line every day. The sophistication of the criminal syndicate behind the shipment – let alone the near-genius technique used to smuggle the drugs in – was like nothing anyone at Harlech House had ever seen. This level of organisation was very different from the methods they were used to: putting drugs in courier bags and firing them off in a scattergun approach, hoping one got through; or exploiting hapless human drug couriers sitting nervously on planes; or even the homegrown manufacturing the Head Hunters controlled in Auckland.

Bruce Good was left with a nagging feeling that he and his staff had badly underestimated the sleeping giant of the New Zealand underworld: Asian organised crime.

Police had been aware of elements of organised crime in the Asian community in New Zealand since the late 1980s. From behind a façade of legitimate commerce, the groups had run a range of illegal businesses, from money laundering, drug importation and prostitution to credit-card fraud, extortion and paua smuggling.

In many respects, they had been small-time players. But suddenly, it seemed, they were a crucial link to a huge, untapped drug source.

It was tempting, of course, to call a press conference and trumpet the success story of stopping nearly $150 million of meth from being sold on the streets. Yet Billy Fung was only a middle man. Police knew they had a window of opportunity to land a big fish or two, not just a minnow like Fung.

But that window was narrow, and closing fast.

They didn't know who was behind the shipment, nor its ultimate destination. Detectives couldn't even prove that Fung, their one lead, was actually involved in drug smuggling. Although his signature was all over the paperwork, any half-decent defence lawyer could raise reasonable doubt as to his guilt.

An operational decision was made to proceed with a 'controlled delivery' of the methamphetamine shipment: the container was carefully repacked and delivered to its destination as if nothing had been found.

Surveillance teams waited patiently as Fung directed the unloading of the container into three secure storage units in Penrose. Police swooped, caught him red-handed and hauled him in.

Sitting opposite Detective Jane Scott in one of the sterile interview rooms at Harlech House, Fung was given his choice: a possible life sentence in prison, or cooperation with the police.

It was a fork in the road. Which direction to take? Stay staunch and do the time? Or act out of self-interest and squeal?

It wasn't actually a dilemma Fung agonised over. He flipped in a matter of minutes.

It's unlikely that his conscience was pricked by the memory of his training in Presbyterian theology. When it came to the crunch, Fung had little incentive to stay loyal to the shadowy figures who'd paid him only $10,000 to do their dirty work. He agreed to work with the police in exchange for a lenient prison sentence.

Operation Major now had a rare and valuable asset: an inside man who could lead them to the bigger players.

Under the close care of police, Fung carried on as if nothing were wrong. He kept in touch with higher-ranking members of the syndicate to draw them deeper into Operation Major's trap. He received calls from a man in China known only as 'Raymond' about what he was to do next.

On 19 May, Fung was told the next step would take place in three days' time.

He was ordered to stash 20 of the 1-kilo meth parcels inside a rubbish bag, place them in the boot of a rental car, then drive to the carpark of the St Lukes Shopping Centre in Sandringham. He hid the keys inside a wheel arch and walked away at around 3pm, then called Raymond to confirm that the car was in position.

About 45 minutes later, syndicate members Deng Guo Wei and Fan Li arrived in another car. The younger of the two men, 31-year-old Fan, approached the rental car left by Fung, rummaged around for the keys and retrieved the rubbish bag full of meth, then he and 46-year-old Deng left.

It was a classic dead drop – a method more common to spycraft. None of the players had to meet each other face to face, presenting less chance that they would be caught in possession of a large amount of drugs, or that they would be able to identify other members of the syndicate if they were nabbed by police.

Classic, except that Detective Sergeant Mike Beal had switched the meth with 19 bags of harmless white granules that looked quite a lot like the real thing. Fifty grams of actual crystal methamphetamine were stored inside a 20th package – laced with a marking powder and an electrical device that let off a signal when the bag was opened. The sample of real methamphetamine was in the first bag within reach, in case Fan and Deng decided to check the product, while the marking powder would taint the hands of whoever opened it. It's a useful piece of evidence when a defendant tries to claim someone else had their hands on the gear.

Surveillance teams followed Fan Li and Deng Guo Wei – nicknamed 'Spare Ribs' – back to an address in the expensive suburb of Kohimarama, on the other side of Auckland. Fan Li, who had lived in New Zealand since he was 13, rented the property under a fake name solely for the purposes of drug dealing.

It was the closest thing to a criminal safehouse Beal had ever seen. When the police raided it, the only personal belongings in the entire place were found in the master bedroom of Fan Li, alongside his false passport.

The other rooms revealed the elaborate organisation of the criminal syndicate. Video monitors were set up in the lounge, playing a live feed from the security cameras on the outside of the house. One room housed money-counting machines and $50,000 in cash. Another room contained drugs – among them, the 20-kilogram drug placebo. Alongside them were loaded firearms, including pistols and a knock-off AK-47, modified to full automatic mode, meaning someone holding the weapon could empty the magazine simply by holding down the trigger.

In yet another room, a row of mobile phones was plugged in and charging, each labelled with a geographic location in Chinese characters. These were dedicated 'job phones', to be used to contact one person about a specific task – say, an incoming shipment – then destroyed once the job was done.

The still-active phones were a treasure trove of intelligence. Records on the phones led Operation Major to Fan and Deng's bosses, Pan Wei Feng and Chen Ming Chin, number one and two respectively in the New Zealand arm of the drug-dealing syndicate. Between them, in the space of just a few months, the well-educated pair had remitted $550,000 back to China, where they had legitimate business interests. Chen ran a company in China supplying polyurethane floor paint, the same substance used to cover the 95 resin bricks in the paint tins.

As the detectives began the slow and careful process of analysing thousands of pages of shipping, travel and business records, they noticed a familiar pattern. A foreign national would arrive in New Zealand and register a company, open bank accounts and post office boxes, and apply for IRD and GST numbers. That individual would then return to China and engage with Customs brokers to clear shipments of goods to New Zealand, returning just before the freight containers arrived to supervise the unpacking of the drugs hidden inside. It was exactly the same modus operandi Billy Fung had used to bring in the Isaac shipments.

All the evidence pointed towards a sobering fact: there had been four other shipments in the 12 months before the two lots of illegal cargo were stopped in May 2006. Most galling of all, the fourth shipment had actually been examined by Customs officials but waved through. The concealment had been too good.

The buzz of stopping the country's largest ever drugs shipment through an innovative and fluid investigation was tempered as Bruce Good and his detectives realised how much they still didn't know about Asian organised crime. Their $150 million drug bust was clearly just the tip of the iceberg.

Watching the tradecraft of these crooks – their complex business structures, ingenious smuggling techniques and elaborate counter-surveillance measures – made AMCOS determined to raise the bar even higher in response.

* * *

Six months after his arrest, Billy Fung was sentenced to 15 years in prison, after quickly pleading guilty to one charge of importing a Class A drug. His cooperation with police was suppressed at his High Court hearing, in order to protect the fair-trial rights of his four co-accused, although Justice Lynton Stevens made a veiled reference to 'mitigating features' in giving Fung a generous 40 per cent discount on his sentence.

Nearly two years later, in July 2008, Fung was a key witness in the Crown case against Chen Ming Chin, Deng Guo Wei, Fan Li and Pan Wei Feng, who denied a range of serious criminal charges made against them. Each took to the witness stand to plead ignorance of the drug shipments, or employed a 'cut-throat' defence by blaming the co-conspirators sitting beside them in the dock.

While under cross-examination, Pan became so enraged by the probing questions of one lawyer that his bail was revoked. His implausible explanations for the incriminating evidence laid out before him in detail were deemed so utterly ridiculous that jurors openly laughed.

Their verdicts, however, were no laughing matter. Guilty ... guilty ... guilty ... guilty. Pan and Chen were convicted of the most serious charge – importing a Class A drug – while Deng and Fan were found guilty of possession of a Class A drug for supply. The maximum penalty for importation or manufacture was life imprisonment.

Early in her sentencing remarks, Justice Patricia Courtney made it clear that she agreed with the jury's verdicts.

No one had ever received a life sentence for methamphetamine charges. The drug had been upgraded to a Class A drug only in 2003. Justice Courtney pointed out that in the past 20 years, only two sentences of life imprisonment for drug offending had been upheld in the Court of Appeal.

Both cases were for importing heroin, in far smaller amounts than the quantities seized in Operation Major.

Justice Courtney was guided by a 2005 judgment by the Court of Appeal, *R v Fatu*, which set out four bands of sentencing for the manufacture, supply and importation of methamphetamine. The highest category of offending, Band 4, was defined as the manufacture or importation of 'large commercial amounts' of 500 grams or more, where someone could expect a sentence of between 12 years and life.

The 95-kilogram haul of meth in the first Isaac shipment alone was nearly 200 times more than the 500-gram starting point. Operation Major was in a league of its own.

'The extraordinary scale of the operation,' said Justice Courtney, 'the level of planning, the potential damage to the community and the local economy as a result of this level of drug importation is so significant that I cannot view it as anything less than being within the most serious of cases for which the maximum penalty is prescribed.

'In the last 10 years or so the drug-dealing scene in New Zealand has altered with the emergence of methamphetamine as the drug of choice for importers and manufacturers. A veritable flood of methamphetamine makes its way across our borders each year. Its users quickly become addicted and the drug has a devastating effect on the personality and function of almost all who use it.

'It leads to the destruction of relationships, serious domestic violence, street violence and gang violence. There have been cases in which methamphetamine use has been directly implicated in instances of murder, lending truth to the Court of Appeal's observation about the activities of major drug dealers being equated with murder because they pose just as serious a threat to society.'

Chen Ming Chin and Pan Wei Feng became the first people sentenced to life imprisonment on methamphetamine offences.

Deng Guo Wei and Fan Li were imprisoned for 17 years and 19 and a half years respectively.

Inevitably, an appeal was lodged against the record-breaking prison lags – but dismissed by the Court of Appeal, with the panel of three senior judges actually increasing the sentences for both Deng and Fan to 25 years. What a backfire.

Only Billy Fung was granted a reprieve. His 15-year sentence was cut even further, to 10 years, as the Court of Appeal did not think the original discount had been generous enough. Choosing to work with the police turned out to be the best decision he ever made.

* * *

The AMCOS staff had learned a valuable set of lessons from Operation Major; in particular, they now had a better understanding of the dynamics between the Asian underworld figures. By watching body language at a meeting, or listening carefully to how surveillance subjects spoke to one another, the detectives became more adept at figuring out who was more senior in the hierarchy.

With limited resources and staff, the police had to be quick and clever in making decisions, such as whether to stop following one target and start running surveillance on a second. It was often a matter of reading what was unfolding in front of them, which meant taking calculated risks, such as the controlled deliveries in Operation Major. That gamble had paid off.

And yet Detective Sergeant Mike Beal was left pondering a few unanswered questions. The most obvious was how to find the entrenched network of buyers, essentially the trusted wholesalers, who purchased meth from the well-oiled importation syndicate Operation Major had foiled.

* * *

One of the players who had a cameo role in Operation Major would be the headline act in Beal's *next* investigation.

Born in Vietnam, Tac Kin Voong was 30 when he fled to New Zealand as a refugee in 1993. He moved to Australia in 2000, returning to Auckland five years later to open his own bakery. The business was sold within 12 months and Voong started a new venture as a self-employed plasterer and painter.

When his name first cropped up in Operation Major, Voong was dismissed as nothing more than a lowly foot-soldier and police brought no charges against him. He had no criminal record to speak of, just a handful of minor convictions in the late 1990s for careless driving and three for wilful trespass. The trespass convictions were for entering the SkyCity casino after being banned, most likely due to problem gambling.

His sins were evidently forgiven by SkyCity: by the time Operation Ice Age started investigating Voong in 2006, the 'painter' was running his *own* operation, and essentially living in SkyCity's exclusive VIP lounge. The lounge encouraged 'valued customers' of the casino – those who spent the most money – to keep returning by offering them free meals and alcohol, or other perks such as complimentary nights in SkyCity hotels.

When the construction of SkyCity Casino began in 1994, with its spire forever changing Auckland's skyline, anti-gambling advocates warned that casinos the world over were a cover for large-scale criminal activity, and a meeting place for people involved in organised crime. Money laundering was identified as a particular risk.

Laundering can be done in several ways. One is simply exchanging dirty cash for casino chips, then cashing them in later for a gambler's cheque. It's an imperfect tactic: doing it too often can raise suspicions among SkyCity staff.

Another method is to pump money straight into poker machines, which work on a mathematical calculation that the casino will eventually keep 12 per cent of the takings. Therefore, by spending enough time – and money – you can eventually recoup up to 88 per cent of the cash gambled, which criminals see as a low rate of tax on their illicit gains.

For hours on end, the 47-year-old Voong sat playing the pokies in SkyCity's VIP lounge, or even paid people to sit on the slot machines all day to wait for the jackpot.

In the space of just six months, July to November 2006, Voong's gambling turnover was more than $10,860,000. Not bad for a plasterer. He even earned the nickname 'Mr Casino'.

If Voong wasn't gambling, or smoking cigarettes, he was on his mobile phone. Thousands of conversations were exchanged between Voong in the VIP lounge and his suppliers, as well as his dealers, such as right-hand man Yihua Luo, better known as Joey Dai.

Voong was always very careful talking on the phone and deliberately kept at least one step removed from the physical delivery of the methamphetamine. The distribution was rapid and well synchronised, in order to minimise the length of time the drugs were in each person's possession and lower the risk of being caught.

Sometimes the deals took place inside the casino building. On one occasion, Voong handed a Louis Vuitton bag full of cash to a go-between, who went down into the underground carpark, brazenly returning with a bag of drugs.

Voong was bugged in October 2006 asking Hung Trung Kha, a Vietnamese associate, to take money to Voong's girlfriend's place. When the police pulled over Kha's BMW on Remuera Road at four the next morning, they found a P pipe, 80 grams of methamphetamine, $95,000 in cash (again in a Louis Vuitton bag) ... and a heavily tattooed gangster sitting in the front passenger seat.

Daniel William Crichton, 40, was a staunch standover man in Auckland criminal circles, and not to be messed with. A former Black Power member who had left the gang after a dispute over a woman in which shots were fired, Crichton was now linked to the Head Hunters and had close ties with Waha Saifiti.

In December 2007, while in custody following his arrest with Kha, Crichton's notoriety would skyrocket when, thanks to his knowledge of the criminal underworld, he became aware of the identity of two thieves who had just carried out a daring heist. Days earlier, 95 medals had been stolen from National Army Museum in Waiouru, in an operation that took a mere four minutes. Through Saifiti, Crichton arranged for the safe return of a George Cross medal. In time all the medals – including nine Victoria Crosses – were given back and the culprits apprehended.

He was given bail as a reward for his role in the treasures' safe return: a decision that outraged the public when it became known. He also gained a nine-month discount on his lengthy prison sentence, when he was sentenced alongside his business partner Kha.

They'd made an odd couple: the diminutive Asian man and the large Maori with facial tattoos, tooling around together in a late-model BMW. But their relationship was a good illustration of how organised crime in New Zealand had evolved. The Asian crime networks could smuggle methamphetamine and pseudoephedrine into the country as importers, and the homegrown gangs had the contacts and grassroots distribution networks to sell the meth on to the end user.

It was a business relationship in which differences were set aside to make money. *Lots* of money.

* * *

By December 2006, Kha and Crichton were in custody, but Operation Ice Age had yet to close the net on Mr Casino himself. That month, detectives raided the Know All Group, a small foreign exchange on Victoria Street, directly opposite SkyCity casino.

Tac Kin Voong regularly gambled and socialised in the VIP lounge with the foreign exchange's manager. And police had listened in when the manager and Voong's right-hand man Joey Dai started talking about sending money 'to the other side'.

What Mike Beal and his team found inside the 40-square-metre Victoria Street premises remains the biggest haul of cash ever seized by police under a single search warrant. They discovered $185,028 stuffed inside the drawers of a desk at reception, and another $320,000 inside a safe in a bedroom. In a small backpack on the bedroom floor, $89,410, and $499,980 in five separate packages under the bed. Stacked on a shelf in a dresser, $450,000, and $359,740 in a wardrobe. To top it off, three packages totalling $549,720 behind a fax machine. In total: $2,453,878.90.

Financial analysis of the money-shop's accounts found no evidence of any legitimate business. The discovery of so much cash being funnelled overseas through a business dedicated to illegal financial transfers was another indication of just how much organised crime in New Zealand had developed.

* * *

But Tac Kin Voong wasn't the only VIP high roller who came to the attention of police that year. For some time, there had been talk in Asian criminal circles of a Chinese Godfather-type character known as 'Four-Eyed Dragon'.

This mysterious individual sold meth in large amounts, 500 grams or a kilo at a time, but he never touched the commodity he was selling. Instead, he gave orders to a crew of between six and eight people at any given time, who were responsible for keeping the meth safe, weighing, bagging and delivering it as well as collecting cash or debts.

Four-Eyed Dragon was also security-savvy. To thwart police surveillance, he used a prepaid mobile phone for just two or three days at a time before changing numbers, destroying the handset or giving the phone to a random stranger. This made it difficult for police to obtain up-to-date information for High Court interception warrants.

Four-Eyed Dragon would work 24 hours a day, for up to four days at a time, before crashing in his waterfront apartment in Auckland's Viaduct Harbour. His luxury pad was just a short walk down Hobson Street from SkyCity casino, where he spent most of his time in the VIP lounge, rubbing shoulders with the likes of Tac Kin Voong.

Through an informant, police knew that his real name was Zhou Ri Tong. He was an even more prolific gambler than his rival, Mr Casino. The 41-year-old Zhou was one of SkyCity's top five players, according to records held by the Department of Internal Affairs, which monitors casinos' compliance with gambling laws.

In just three months, between November 2005 and February 2006, his turnover was $9.3 million. In the 12 months prior, it was $8.55 million. Zhou was making a lot of money from methamphetamine, and it was Detective Sergeant Lloyd Schmid's job to prove this in Operation Manu, which began in October 2006.

Schmid was the officer in charge of the newly established Organised Crime Unit for Auckland City, one of the 12 police districts across the country.

The Auckland Organised Crime Unit was completely separate from AMCOS, but it wasn't long before Schmid and his team, including young detectives Stu Hunter and Josh McAllum, were working under the same roof anyway. Operation Manu needed a separate computer and an office, which could be locked for security reasons, neither of which could be guaranteed at the old Auckland Central Police Station, so Schmid's team shifted to a spare office in Harlech House and ran at the same time as Operation Ice Age.

Like the parallel investigation into Tac Kin Voong, Operation Manu relied heavily on the new phone-tapping technology. It was still very unfamiliar to the detectives: Stu Hunter finished the electronic investigation course at police college on a Friday, then started surveillance of Zhou on the Monday.

Over the next two months, Stu and others would listen to a mind-numbing 13,500 phone calls: a record number in a single investigation. And as in Operation Ice Age, the vast majority of the conversations were in a foreign language – Mandarin, Cantonese or Hokkien – all of which had to be translated immediately. It wasn't just to gather evidence for any eventual courtroom trial, but also influenced decisions that had to be made quickly, such as urgent surveillance of the next drug deal.

Manu's three main targets were Zhou, a 24-year-old English-language student known as 'Visa' (real name Zhong Wei), and a Tauranga man named Alan Clinton McQuade, who had connections with two bikie gangs, the Mongrel Mob and the Outcasts, in the Bay of Plenty and Waikato areas.

This was how the supply chain worked: when Zhou needed methamphetamine, he called Visa, who in turn contacted a man in China called Xiao Pang. Xiao's man on the ground in Auckland was Chen Huang, another young English-language student who controlled the stockpile of drugs. Bugged conversations indicated the stockpile could be as large as 30 kilograms at any one time.

Once the deal was authorised by the mastermind Xiao, Chen Huang alerted Visa, who would pass the message on to Zhou. He also rented an apartment in the Scene Three complex on Beach Street, just a stone's throw from the Auckland High Court, used solely for exchanging cash and drugs. Sometimes the deals were done in the yum cha restaurant downstairs.

On 31 October 2006, Alan McQuade was photographed leaving the Scene Three apartment with a brown paper bag under his arm. He then drove south from Auckland in his Nissan Skyline.

The police tailed him from a distance down State Highway 1 until he pulled into the Rangiriri Hotel carpark, about 50 kilometres north of Hamilton. A search of the vehicle found 13 ounces of methamphetamine, some cannabis, 133 ecstasy tablets, $2000 cash – and a baton, presumably for protection and/or debt collection.

A week later, on 7 November, the police started homing in on Visa – Zhong Wei – who drove a flamboyant red Chrysler Crossfire. A covert warrant gave them authority to open Zhong's safety deposit box at the ASB Bank on Albert Street in Auckland.

When the stacks of cash inside were spread on the table, the detectives counted $558,400. No wonder he was called Visa.

Two days later, the police intercepted a series of phone calls between Zhong and Di Wu, one of Zhou Ri Tong's lieutenants, concerning a 17-ounce deal. Zhong made the calls during breaks in his English lessons. Curiously, his teacher was Lloyd Schmid's wife, blissfully unaware of her student's extracurricular activities.

Later that night, detectives Natasha Bryce and Stu Hunter discarded their civilian clothes to don police uniforms, as well as borrow a marked car from the Auckland Central Station. Knowing Zhong was on his way to deliver the goods to Di Wu, the pair flashed their lights and sirens when they saw his distinctive Chrysler sports car on Great North Road.

Zhong pulled over near the Grey Lynn shops and stepped out of the vehicle, but became antsy when the detectives beckoned him to approach. A scuffle broke out when Zhong tried to walk back to his car; things escalated when Hunter wrested him to the ground and Bryce tried to cuff his hands.

The roar of an engine cut through the noise of the crowd that had gathered. Stu Hunter turned to see the Chrysler Crossfire zoom down Great North Road towards the Auckland Zoo. An opportunistic thief had seen that the two police officers had their hands full with Zhong Wei and had stolen the valuable sports car – with, the police believed, a substantial amount of methamphetamine stowed inside.

The ensuing pursuit ended in a crash near the St Lukes Shopping Centre. The drunken driver did a runner, but was pulled down by a police dog.

A drug squad detective was sent to Auckland City Hospital to take a formal statement from the young car thief, in order to confirm that the Crossfire did not belong to him and that he had taken the car in a split-second decision.

Thinking he was being asked to confess, the thief decided to exercise his right to silence by swearing at the officer.

He soon changed his tune when informed of the 18 ounces of Class A drug found inside the car, and the threat of a maximum sentence of life imprisonment.

Another 18 ounces of meth were found in Zhong Wei's apartment, as well as $38,000 in cash. Visa was awash with the stuff: on top of the $38,000 plus the $558,400 in the safety deposit box, an audit of his financial records showed he had transferred $1,566,136 back to China in just a few months.

Two of the three main targets in Operation Manu were now locked up, leaving just Four-Eyed Dragon – Zhou Ri Tong – who quickly moved on to a new supplier following the arrest of Zhong Wei.

* * *

Zhou was placed under 24-hour surveillance in the lead-up to the termination of Operation Manu. There was no love lost between the two rivals. To the mirth of the detectives listening in, Zhou and Voong slagged each other off in taped conversations.

But with so much money at stake, it was almost inevitable they would form a business relationship while mingling in the casino VIP lounge. At least one deal between Zhou and Voong was arranged through their lieutenants, with the exchange taking place in the casino's basement carpark.

For a while, the police thought Zhou had realised he was being watched and skipped town. The surveillance teams couldn't get eyes on him, and he wasn't answering phone calls and messages from his associates. It was complete radio silence until Zhou's phone sparked into life again. He'd been sleeping off the effects of staying awake for three days straight, as he was in the habit of doing. And where else would Zhou be when the police finally caught up with him, but in the VIP lounge of the casino? Operation Manu wound-up with Zhou's arrest, which took place shortly after Tac Kin Voong's arrest at the conclusion of Operation Ice Age in December 2006.

In May 2010, Voong was convicted of eight counts of supplying a Class A drug, two of conspiracy to supply and two of possession of a Class A drug for supply. In sentencing the 47-year-old to 18 years in prison, Justice Patrick Keane described Voong as the 'heart and directing mind' of a group distributing methamphetamine in wholesale ounce amounts.

The High Court judge compared 'Mr Casino' with Zhou Ri Tong, who was sentenced to 15 years by Justice Rhys Harrison in March 2009. He called Zhou an 'extremely active and prosperous wholesaler'.

Zhou received a shorter sentence than Voong on account of his pleading guilty, saving the taxpayer the considerable cost of a High Court trial.

'You planned carefully and cynically to make huge financial gain from the misery of others. You knew the risks, Mr Zhou, and now you must pay the price,' Justice Harrison told him. 'In that respect it is of concern that much of your dealing was transacted through the medium of the VIP lounge or the basement carpark at the SkyCity Casino. You used both as offices.'

The judge then took the unusual step of ordering that his sentencing notes be sent to SkyCity chief executive Nigel Morrison. Through the company's lawyer, Morrison assured the public that the casino had 'zero tolerance' of criminal behaviour. He said they were now sharing more intelligence on their customers with the police and the Department of Internal Affairs, whose national compliance manager told the *New Zealand Herald*: 'I would be extremely surprised if this happened again.'

Yet only a few years later, the drug squad would again be forced to focus on the SkyCity VIP lounge and the millions of dollars flowing through the casino (that investigation will be looked at in Chapter 6).

* * *

Looking back on 2006, Detective Inspector Bruce Good was justifiably proud of what the three big operations run out of Harlech House had achieved. New Zealand was now clearly part of the global drug market, no doubt because of the seemingly insatiable local demand for methamphetamine, which sold at prices that were among the world's most profitable.

The record-breaking seizures in Operation Major were particularly significant. But despite this success, Good remained perturbed. The syndicate behind Operation Major was just one of five Asian groups the police believed were importing drugs into the country. That syndicate's first four shipments had slipped past the border unnoticed. And the huge bust in Operation Major had had virtually no effect on the street price and availability of P – no more than a blip for a matter of weeks.

New Zealand's biggest drug bust, and the two operations that followed it, had only scratched the surface of a massive methamphetamine trade.

P was overwhelming the justice and health systems. New Zealand was drowning in methamphetamine, and it felt like everyone had buried their heads in the sand.

3

GRANITE, SKULL AND ROCKY: AN EXECUTION IN TAURANGA

2006–2007

A MISSING-PERSON FILE IS a blank canvas for police. There's no dead body to raise the alarm and provide clues to the killer's identity; there's often not even any evidence to suggest foul play has been involved. Sometimes the missing person just doesn't want to be found.

Hours and hours of scarce police manpower can be wasted on someone who's run away from home, is trying to start over in a new town or is simply addled by drugs or alcohol. But each and every missing-person file has to be taken seriously, just in case the worst has happened.

When the file of Grant Trevor Adams landed on the desk of the Tauranga Criminal Investigation Branch in the winter of 2006, it didn't take detectives long to conclude the 29-year-old was most likely dead. Nicknamed 'Granite', Grant Adams had links to the Head Hunter and Filthy Few motorcycle gangs, and touted himself in the underworld as a meth cook.

He was no angel, but Granite never forgot to phone home on important dates. So when he missed Mother's Day, Christmas, Easter and – unthinkable to his family – his daughter's birthday, his mother contacted the Henderson Police Station near her home in West Auckland.

Six months had passed since she last heard from her son. In October 2005, Adams had phoned her from Napier. His phone had not been used and his bank accounts remained untouched since December.

The file was sent down to police in Hawke's Bay. A few months went by and the file was bounced back north, this time to Tauranga, where Adams had recently moved without telling any of his family.

Granite Adams was a large man with one hell of a temper. Every three months or so, as if keeping a regular appointment, Adams would commit a crime, most often an assault, which would attract the attention of police.

By December 2006, there was nothing in the police intelligence system to show any police contact with Adams for 12 months. To the two detectives working the case, Senior Sergeant Greg Turner – better known as 'Turbo'– and his second-in-charge Detective Sergeant Lew Warner, it most likely meant he was no longer alive.

They started sketching on the blank canvas. Over the next few months, in and around other investigations that cropped up, Warner and his squad of detectives knocked on doors. They visited everyone Adams knew – criminal associates, people he'd lived with, neighbours, friends and casual acquaintances.

Nobody knew anything about the vanishing act, or if they did, they weren't saying. Despite the hours and hours of shoe-leather police work, there was not a single suspect to look at more closely.

But then a new addition to the Tauranga CIB received a phone call out of the blue. And, incredibly, it would be the first step in unravelling an international drug-smuggling ring, run from inside New Zealand's toughest maximum-security prison.

* * *

After years of making life miserable for gang members and drug dealers in Auckland, Detective Sergeant Darryl Brazier moved to Tauranga in 2007 to enjoy a better lifestyle and create some distance between himself and the Head Hunters. Since the Operation Flower days, 'DB' had kept digging into the gang's involvement in the meth trade, and had rolled from one investigation onto the next.

Some of the Heads had taken exception to his interference in their business plans. It had got to the point where Brazier was forced to drive home from Harlech House by a different route each night, and to carry a police firearm everywhere he went, after rumours that the Head Hunters had put a price on his life. Brazier had joked he had friends who would do it for half the money on offer.

The hard-nosed detective had been loath to give an inch, but staying in AMCOS wasn't worth the stress. A rare opportunity to transfer to Tauranga came up – and it ended up giving his new colleagues the break they needed on the Granite file.

His reputation had preceded him. On learning of his arrival in town, a member of the Tauranga criminal fraternity called him and asked for a meeting to talk about drug dealing.

Brazier readily agreed. Every detective knows that criminal informants – fizzes – are the lifeblood of any investigation. The conversation soon turned to the missing-persons case of Grant 'Granite' Adams.

The informant made mention of a man called 'Lifer' – Brett Michael Ashby, a 49-year-old who had served a 10-year sentence for importing commercial quantities of drugs in the 1980s. Since then, Ashby had kept out of trouble with the police and had started an earthworks business.

It had been successful enough to allow him to purchase a large new home on a lifestyle block in rural Ohauiti, on the outskirts of Tauranga. But according to Brazier's new acquaintance, Ashby was also cooking significant amounts of methamphetamine, and had fallen out with Grant Adams before his disappearance.

This was the first time Ashby's name had been mentioned in connection with Adams. In fact, it was the first time Tauranga police had become aware that the former drug importer with serious criminal connections was even living in their city.

Armed with this new information, Greg Turner successfully applied to a High Court judge for an interception warrant under the *Misuse of Drugs Act* to tap the phones of Ashby and two suspected associates named by Brazier's informant. The identity of one was never made public – but the other was a high-profile inmate in Paremoremo prison.

By now, Granite's missing-person case had been upgraded to a homicide investigation, Operation Spider. On 19 June 2007, Greg Turner held a press conference at the Tauranga Police Station and offered a reward of $50,000 for information that would help police solve the case.

'It would be fair to say we are offering a reward because it is quite apparent there are a number people in the community who know exactly what happened to Granite,' Turner told the reporters.

And it was fair to say that the police had a good idea too. The $50,000 reward was just a tool to rattle a few cages and get people talking, whether they spoke to police or one another.

By listening to Ashby's phone calls, police were able to stay one step ahead of his movements, which helped the covert surveillance teams keep tabs on him. In one phone conversation, Ashby summoned an associate to meet him – not at his house or workplace, in the normal, boring way of the law-abiding, but in the furtive and really very silly way of those who live outside the law: in a cemetery on Pyes Pa Road, in the middle of the day.

* * *

Operation Spider officers watched the cemetery rendezvous from a distance, and saw a rather chubby fellow stepping out of a Ford Falcon to speak with Ashby. The detectives were too far away to see the mystery man's face, but the registration plate on his Falcon was traced back to a Craig Brennan Cullen. Better known as 'Skull', 43-year-old Cullen lived near Bayfair Shopping Centre in Mount Maunganui, and was suspected to be neck-deep in Tauranga's flourishing meth trade.

The next morning, 21 June 2007, there was no answer when Turbo Turner and Detective Alan Kingsbury knocked on Skull's front door. The pair drove a few hundred metres down the road to park their unmarked police car, then waited.

Sure enough, a few hours later, they saw Cullen's Ford Falcon exiting the driveway. He'd been home the whole time.

A quick burst of the lights and sirens on the police car got Cullen's attention. He pulled over to the side of the road, and agreed to accompany the detectives back to the police station on Monmouth Street.

For the rest of the day, Kingsbury and Turner gently prodded and cajoled Skull into telling them what he knew. A hardened criminal, Cullen was reluctant to break the code of never cooperating with police. But the detectives sensed that he wanted to get something off his chest.

He did. He wanted to talk about Granite, the so-called missing person.

Cullen indicated that he knew what had happened to Granite and that he was willing to help. He also said that he wanted to go home and talk to his lawyer first.

By this time, daylight had given way to the evening gloom of winter. Letting a potential star witness in an unsolved homicide inquiry walk out of the interview room, without first securing a formal statement, was a major risk. Cullen could get cold feet, do a runner and abscond from Tauranga, alert the main suspect, Brett Ashby, or possibly even commit suicide in fear of what would happen.

If anything went wrong, the consequences for both detectives could be career-ending.

On the other hand, playing hardball with Cullen wasn't going to work. Turner and Kingsbury needed him onside if they wanted to solve the case, and in any event, they had no grounds to hold him at the station.

They let Cullen walk out the front door, then spent a sleepless night wondering if they'd made a huge mistake.

But Skull returned the next day with respected barrister David Bates in tow, and sat down again with Alan Kingsbury at 1.20pm to give a formal written statement that stretched to 13 pages. He told them everything he claimed to know.

* * *

Cullen said that he had first met Ashby through a mutual friend who thought the two could work together towards a common goal.

Ashby had acquired a substantial amount of ma huang, a Chinese plant, which had been dried and ground into a yellowish-brown powder. It looked like instant coffee granules. Ma huang contains ephedrine, the main precursor material used to manufacture methamphetamine.

But Ashby was unaware of how to extract the ephedrine from the ma huang, Cullen claimed. That was where *he* came in. Although Cullen wasn't entirely sure how, his job, in an experimental trial-and-error process, was to try to extract the ingredient from the plant material. He signed up on the understanding that any profits would be split.

Yet Cullen also had a chemistry problem of his own. He had a stash of ContacNT pills, the Chinese cold and flu medicine, but he was struggling to extract the pseudoephedrine from the pink granules.

And then he met Granite. Tall, aggressive and 'full of himself' was how Cullen described Grant Adams, who claimed to have experience in the chemical extraction process and promised to sort out the pseudoephedrine problem. He also made an investment into the new enterprise: a Jack Daniel's bottle filled with what he claimed was pseudoephedrine liquid, although Cullen was sceptical about the bottle's contents.

Dividing up their duties, Adams and Cullen got to work in a shed out the back of Ashby's property on Ohauiti Road. Over a two-week stretch, Cullen concentrated on the ma huang and Adams on the ContacNT.

Everyone who works in an office gets to know the truth of the saying that hell is other people. The close quarters, the annoying habits, the sight of the same old face day after day ... The walls of their 'office' – a small shed – began to close in. Cullen grew sick of Granite's belligerence and constant boasting of his links with the Auckland Head Hunters, and the pair fell out.

Adams walked away. But he continued to demand payment for the supposed pseudoephedrine in the Jack Daniel's bottle. He told friends he would collect on his debt by 'taxing' Ashby's Harley-Davidson, truck and home. (Taxing is the criminal slang for taking someone's possessions to recoup a perceived debt.) Word of the threat filtered back to Ashby. He called Cullen to a meeting at his lifestyle property, where they talked outside on the driveway.

Like Cullen, Ashby was pissed off with Granite. He was also convinced that Granite had stolen pseudoephedrine from him.

Ashby told Cullen about Adams's threat, then reached into his car and pulled out a semi-automatic, 9-millimetre, black steel Beretta handgun. He fired a single shot through a hedge into an adjacent paddock.

Cullen told Kingsbury in the interview room: 'Brett said, "I'm gonna fucken waste him" and "Nobody's gonna take anything off me." He said, "I'll kill the fucker" or "I'll shoot the fucker."'

Cullen claimed Grant Adams was lured to Ashby's home about three weeks later, in December 2005, on the pretext he would be paid the supposed debt owed to him. Cullen agreed to come along, thinking Ashby would threaten Granite, tell him to back off and forget about the supposed pseudoephedrine debt. A mutual friend, Pete 'Panther' Hughes, offered to drive Adams to the 'peace talks'.

Cullen heard the crunch of the tyres of Hughes's BMW on the driveway. His right arm was iced and strapped with cloth at the time: he had badly burned himself earlier that day, during a pseudoephedrine extraction in Ashby's shed that went wrong. When the toluene solvent he was using ignited, Cullen had grabbed the large stainless-steel pot it was in and run outside, but the blazing liquid had splashed onto the inside of his right arm, leaving a deep burn (which had healed by the time he spoke to police), as well as a mark on the doorway he had sprinted through.

While waiting for Granite to arrive, he and Ashby had discussed where they would dump the body. But Cullen doubted Ashby would go through with shooting someone in cold blood. In his mind, he wanted to believe that Ashby would only threaten Granite, not kill him.

Panther Hughes entered the garage first, followed by Adams, who started to walk around in a circle. Ashby walked the opposite way, then turned around.

No threats or warnings were uttered, Cullen told police. Ashby simply shot Adams in the back between the shoulder blades three or four times, then walked over and silenced the groaning Granite with a single bullet to the head.

Hughes stumbled outside and vomited.

Next, said Cullen, he and Ashby unfurled a rectangular rug, about 4 metres long and 2 wide, moved Adams's body onto it and rolled it up. The bundle was then wrapped in black plastic and tied with twine. Adams was a heavy man, and it took them some effort to lug his body onto the tailgate of Ashby's Holden Rodeo ute, which he'd backed into the garage. A small pool of blood, about 30 centimetres wide, was left behind on the concrete floor.

In concluding his witness statement, Cullen said he was aware of the $50,000 reward offered by police in exchange for information, but that wasn't what had motivated him to come forward. 'I don't want the reward … I can no longer live with the fact of what's happened and just want to get it sorted,' Cullen told Kingsbury. 'I just want it over.'

Two days after the interview, on Sunday, 24 June 2007, Cullen took the police to where Granite's body was buried. They drove south for nearly two hours, from Tauranga to the Wairakei geothermal power station just north of Taupo, between the western bank of the Waikato River and State Highway 1. Ashby's company, Ground Works Taupo, was contracted to provide earthworks services for the power station. Ashby had swipe-card access to the restricted industrial site.

Cullen told police the original plan had been to throw Adams's body into a geothermal steam hole. No one would ever have stumbled across his remains. But the spot Ashby had in mind was too dangerous. They got there at 10pm and it was pitch black, and they were surrounded by thick fog from the geothermal activity. One false step and it would have been *them* falling into the steam vent, not the body they were trying to dispose of.

Ashby had turned the ute back towards the power station, into what he called the 'Steam Fields', where one of his diggers was parked. He drove the 3-tonne digger a few hundred metres away from the steam pipes and down into a gully, and started excavating at the bottom of a bank.

It took about 10 minutes to dig the hole, which Cullen thought was about 2.5 metres deep, before a rope strop was tied around Adams and attached to the digger's bucket so it could lift the body off the back of the ute.

Ashby watched in silence as Cullen lowered Granite into the hole, then Ashby poured petrol over the plastic-wrapped body. Cullen claimed Ashby then pulled out a cigarette lighter to ignite a rag and tossed the rag into the pit, followed by the plastic petrol can.

Cullen and Ashby stood and watched for about 30 minutes as flames engulfed the body. It burned so brightly that the pair were scared a passing motorist on State Highway 1 might see the fire and call 111. They extinguished the blaze with dirt – by then charred bones were the only thing left of Granite – and filled up the hole.

Eighteen months after Cullen helped to bury Granite with a digger, he returned with Detective Alan Kingsbury and other police staff to point out the secret grave. A radar device, which could penetrate the ground to map what lay beneath the surface, confirmed what Cullen had told the detectives.

He had identified the location with amazing accuracy: he was out by less than a metre.

It took three days for CIB staff to carefully exhume the remains, finding every bone except 'for one of the delicate bones of the thyroid.

Detectives also set about corroborating other aspects of Cullen's story, as well as rounding up other witnesses. Records from the Wairakei power station showed that Ashby's swipe card had been used to enter the site three times between 9.57 and 11.46pm on 14 December 2005. A few hours later, at 4.22am, Ashby's credit card had been used at the Caltex petrol station in Tauriko on the edge of Tauranga, as Cullen had also told police. The receipt revealed a murderer's shopping list: a 1.2 litre bottle of Janola bleach, a box of Just Juice, a packet of Holiday cigarettes, two V energy drinks, Dettol disinfectant and a packet of bacon.

The other man at that fateful meeting at Ashby's property, Pete 'Panther' Hughes, told the police he'd been completely unaware he was driving Adams to his death. According to his statement, Hughes walked into the garage a few steps ahead of Adams, heard a 'loud bang', and turned to find that Adams had been shot. As he fled the building, Hughes saw 'something' in Ashby's hand and heard more gunshots once he was outside.

The police also interviewed a Taupo man to whom, according to Cullen, Ashby had given the 9-millimetre Beretta for safekeeping, although he'd later had second thoughts and gone back to retrieve it.

Another witness, one of Ashby's employees at Ground Works, told police about a disturbing conversation he'd had with his boss when they drove past the 3-tonne digger a few months after the murder. Ashby made a passing comment about how they should call it the 'grave digger', and when asked why, allegedly said: 'I shot the bastard and rolled him up in carpet ... I buried him deep to make him rot quicker. I poured petrol on him and burnt the bastard.'

Four days after Cullen pointed out the burial site, the Armed Offenders Squad raided Ashby's home in Ohauiti and arrested him. Police staff found the burn mark on the door of the shed from the pseudoephedrine fire that had scorched Skull Cullen, as well as chemicals such as hydrochloric acid and toluene associated with methamphetamine manufacture.

The 49-year-old Ashby appeared in the Tauranga District Court on 28 June 2007, charged with murder and manufacturing methamphetamine, although the second charge was later dropped. He was denied bail.

Cullen pleaded guilty to being an accessory to murder after the fact and was sentenced to 12 months' home detention. He received a hefty discount for cooperating with police: without his help, Granite would likely be buried in Wairakei to this day.

As for Ashby, the murder prosecution against him was heading towards a trial, and he had entered a plea of not guilty, but the case never made it in front of a jury.

Nearly two years after his arrest, Ashby died of liver cancer while at home with his family. He'd been granted bail on the ground of compassion, given his terminal illness – which was a far more dignified end than Granite received, whoever killed him. Given the evidence gathered by police, it's likely Ashby's defence at trial would have been to point the finger of blame at Skull Cullen as the real killer.

In tributes published in the family notices of the *Bay of Plenty Times* newspaper, his wife Joanne called Ashby an 'an amazing husband and father' and special friend to many people, while her brother Arthur called him a 'battler to the end'. Arthur wrote: 'If it could be beaten you were the man to do it. Mate, you were much more than a brother-in-law to me.'

* * *

The death of Brett Michael Ashby brought an end to the Adams murder investigation. But the death of Granite Adams had taken police in an entirely new direction.

Ashby's brother-in-law Arthur, who'd penned the heartfelt tribute in the *Bay of Plenty Times*, was in fact Arthur William Taylor, one of the country's most notorious and intelligent career criminals.

Once described by a Court of Appeal judge as having a better legal mind than many barristers, Taylor had been put on a path of crime after being sent to the Epuni Boys' Home as a teenage truant. He committed his first criminal offence at 16 and went on to amass another 150 criminal convictions before 2007 for fraud and dishonesty offences, burglaries, and the masterminding of armed bank robberies.

But what really made his name was an audacious prison break from Paremoremo, New Zealand's maximum-security facility, in 1998. The escape plot had been meticulously planned over the prison's phones; masks, camouflage clothing and bulletproof vests were smuggled into the prison, while equipment, including firearms, was hidden outside the walls to help Taylor and his fellow fugitives evade capture. Three inmates went on the run with Taylor, including two convicted murderers, Graeme Burton and Darren John Crowley, as well as armed robber Matthew Thompson

The escape had triggered a massive police manhunt. The fugitives spent six days on the run in Muriwai and then the Coromandel Peninsula, where they hid in the bush and hunkered down in the $2.5 million holiday home of a wealthy American businessman.

Eventually, the police caught up with them. Taylor had three years added to his sentence. It wasn't the first time he'd escaped from custody, nor would it be the last.

Seven years later, shortly after his release from prison, Taylor was again jailed for serious firearms and drugs charges.

He was being escorted under guard to a meeting at Child, Youth and Family in Wellington about the custody of his son. While the prison van was waiting in a carpark before the meeting, an accomplice approached and pointed an air pistol at the three Corrections officers to demand Taylor's release.

Taylor's freedom was shortlived. He ran down the street to a shop, where he managed to hide in the ceiling before it broke and he fell to the floor. He escaped from the shop, but was captured soon afterwards.

For the escape and the kidnapping of the prison guards, Taylor was given an extra four years in prison on top of the eight years he was doing for the drugs and firearms offences. At the sentencing in the Wellington High Court in 2007, the judge was told Taylor had spent 32 of the past 35 years behind bars.

'No course of any treatment will have any effect on you and your further offending,' Justice Ronald Young told Taylor, now 51. 'That will end when you have decided you have had enough of prison.'

The words would prove prophetic. Just a few months before the judge offered this advice, Taylor had been caught talking on the phone, plotting his next criminal move.

When the High Court allowed police investigating Granite's disappearance to intercept the communications of Brett Ashby, Taylor had been named on the same warrant, since police had suspected he was involved with his brother-in-law in methamphetamine offences.

They never actually found any evidence of that – but succeeded in stumbling upon a drug conspiracy between Taylor and another infamous Paremoremo inmate, conducted from inside the prison walls with smuggled mobile phones. The second prisoner, Ulaiasi Pulete, was an enormous Tongan and a senior member of the King Cobra gang, known to everyone as Rocky.

During a flurry of phone calls and text messages over two days in early June 2007, Taylor contacted someone known as Wayne Clarke. Taylor told Clarke to 'get his wallet out', as Taylor would be able to get hold of what everyone was looking for. The smallest amount was a 'round one' and the price was '12k'.

One of the most critical elements of any covert police investigation is 'proving product'. Drug dealers speak obliquely, so the police have to prove they're talking about methamphetamine, not 'oranges' or 'wheels' or any other innocent-sounding item, no matter how ridiculous.

To the mirth of the police listening in on this occasion, it was apparent Clarke didn't understand the code and was confused about what Taylor was offering. It sounded as if he thought it was ecstasy.

In an attempt to clear things up, Taylor said he could get 'round things – you know, the white things', 'big ones' and 'Os'.

Clarke still didn't get it. Finally an exasperated Taylor blurted out: 'They are Os of you know what, Os of P!'

In another conversation later in the day, Clarke indicated he knew some people who were after 'one of those things, maybe two', before asking Taylor to 'keep three aside'.

Taylor agreed, then sent a text with Clarke's order to Pulete. 'That was good news,' replied Pulete, who confirmed he had three 'sitting there right now'.

There were subsequent text messages in which they thanked each other, and discussed timing, delivery, payment and quality of the product.

'You're truly an angel my friend, thank you,' Taylor told Pulete.

In the end, the deal fell over. Wayne Clarke's customers were unable to cobble together enough money to complete the purchase.

Business was business. If more was needed in the future, Pulete advised Taylor that his supply was 'regular'.

Their conversations were clearly about 3 ounces of meth-amphetamine at a price of $12,000 per ounce. Taylor's role was to facilitate and negotiate the sale, while Pulete controlled the supply.

But neither was charged. By late June, just a few weeks after police intercepted the drug deal, Greg Turner and the Tauranga CIB were tied up with the arrest of Brett Ashby for murder. The offences at Paremoremo were outside Turbo's police district, so he passed the transcripts to Detective Inspector Bruce Good in Auckland.

The AMCOS drug squads at Harlech House were already drowning in their own depressing caseload. By the end of 2007, the file was handed to Detective Sergeant Mike Paki, the officer in charge of the newly formed Serious Crime Unit based at North Shore Police Station.

Paremoremo prison was inside Paki's patch, the Waitemata Police District, so Paki's team of detectives started tugging on the thread of evidence exposed by Taylor and Pulete's tapped phone calls and texts.

Born from Operation Spider – the Granite murder investigation – Operation Web uncovered a cast of almost comical characters who, amazingly, had been able to orchestrate an international drug ring from behind bars.

In May 2008, High Court judge Helen Winkelmann –
who would go on to become Chief Justice – granted Paki's
squad an interception warrant to pick up where Operation
Spider had left off: tapping Arthur Taylor's phone, as well as
Rocky Pulete's.

For the next three months, Web detectives intercepted
thousands of phone calls and text messages sent from the
smuggled mobile hidden in Taylor's prison cell, but not a
single conversation incriminated him.

The same could not be said for Rocky Pulete. A senior
member of the King Cobra gang, whose members are almost
exclusively of Pasifika heritage, the 39-year-old was almost
revered by other inmates.

He might have been immense in size, but Pulete didn't
need to rely on his imposing frame. In fact, he was something
of a gentle giant, who spent his time in prison productively.

With so much time in the company of other inmates,
Pulete carefully cultivated trusting relationships, and was
considered one of the best-connected criminals in the country.

And the Operation Web detectives listening to his calls,
Vanessa Cook and Wayne Poore, had the benefit of hindsight:
Rocky Pulete had run an international drug network from
behind bars before.

* * *

In April 2000, a large manila folder had come through the
International Mail Centre in Auckland, destined for a post
office box in the Far North town of Kaitaia. The declaration
form glued to the front stated that there was a CD-ROM
from Warsaw in Poland inside, but in fact the package
contained nearly 500 grams of speed, a cheaper substitute for
methamphetamine.

Customs and police conducted a controlled delivery to track who collected the package. It was picked up by a 24-year-old woman, with a baby in the back seat of her car.

Investigators were initially puzzled as to how a young woman with no ties to Europe had become entangled in a Polish drug syndicate. The penny dropped when the police arrested her and she revealed that her partner was Gary Victor Martin, who was sharing a cell in Mount Eden Prison with Rocky Pulete. At that time Rocky was locked up and awaiting trial for robbing the Sinners nightclub on Karangahape Road, Auckland, at gunpoint the previous year.

Inside Mount Eden Prison, members of a Polish syndicate looking for a local distribution arm were fraternising with New Zealand crooks keen to make money from drugs.

It was an irresistible opportunity for Pulete, with his ready access to mobile phones and his vast network of criminal contacts. He already lived in a world of shadows: his own defence lawyer, Roger Chambers, rather beautifully described his client as 'a spectre moving in a world of spectres'.

The remark was made at the sentencing hearing for the Sinners robbery in February 2001, at which Justice David Baragwanath imposed a prison term of 14 years, to be served at Paremoremo.

* * *

Now, halfway through his sentence, Rocky was back at it again, although not with his previous Polish partners. A number of prisoners with Chinese heritage had been transferred into Paremoremo's D Block, and Pulete, never slow to spot a networking opportunity, put a protective arm around his new wingmates. China was the number-one source country for pseudoephedrine, and anyone with connections there was a valuable business partner.

Step right up Wan Yee Chow, an enforcer from the 14K Hong Kong crime syndicate, convicted of an execution-style murder outside a karaoke bar on Auckland's Symonds Street in 2005. Known as 'Tall Man', Wan was close to Wanzhe Gui, jailed for 13 years for a particularly nasty kidnapping of a woman, in which he had demanded a $1 million ransom.

The investigation had started to sprawl in size. Each time the Operation Web detectives picked up the phone number of a different inmate by listening to Pulete's calls, they got a new interception warrant. Police officers did a double-take when they listened to Gui's conversations and analysed the phone data. Incredibly, from inside Paremoremo, Gui was calling a contact in China to arrange the purchase of ContacNT, which was then being shipped to New Zealand.

The tapped conversations between Gui and someone called 'Fourth Elder' revealed that postal workers in China were being bribed to help the packages get through. Usually around 1 kilo in weight, they were sent to the addresses of family and friends of Pulete and other Paremoremo inmates.

The recipients included a middle-aged mother from Manurewa, South Auckland. Her son was a member of the Killer Beez street gang (more on them in Chapter 10), who was incarcerated with Pulete in D Block following serious violence and methamphetamine convictions. And, as police discovered when she was arrested in a separate investigation, the woman was doing a lot more than collecting the odd parcel from her letterbox.

The woman's identity cannot be revealed: she was granted permanent name suppression when she became a witness for the police at Pulete's trial in the Auckland High Court in 2011. As she gave evidence, armed officers were there for her protection, strategically placed behind pillars in the courtroom so the jury wouldn't notice their presence.

In any case, all their attention must have been focused on the 50-year-old woman's story. It revealed that even family ties take second place to methamphetamine. Because of her heavy addiction to P, she was at her son's beck and call.

He and Wanzhe Gui, whom she knew as 'Jackie', would ring to tell her to pick up packages from China left in different letterboxes around Auckland. Once safely home in Manurewa, she would sift through the packages, stuffed with hand towels and toiletries, until she found tubes of toothpaste. She'd snip off the tops then squeeze out the pink granules, which she'd weigh and distribute into plastic ziplock bags.

Police also tracked down other parcels in which the ContacNT had been concealed in different ways. Mike Paki marvelled at the ingenuity involved in hiding the pink granules inside hand-crafted chocolates, mooncakes and lava lamps.

The woman would hide her ziplock bags under a dog kennel in her backyard until her son, or Jackie, called with the next set of instructions. They arranged for her to meet separately with two men, Morgan and Travis, on several occasions. Each time, Morgan or Travis paid her $10,000 for the pseudoephedrine. A month later, the woman was given meth to sell at street level a point – 0.1 gram – at a time, or sometimes two.

Once a week, or sometimes once a fortnight, the woman visited a money exchange on Queen Street to deposit large amounts of cash, $10,000 to $30,000 at a time, on behalf of Jackie. She'd call him inside Paremoremo, then pass the phone over to staff so they could complete the transaction. Money was also deposited in TAB accounts and canteen accounts (so prisoners can purchase treats and sweets), including the accounts of Wanzhe Gui and the woman's son.

The 50-year-old also told the court about dealing meth-amphetamine to a West Auckland woman she knew only as 'Kat'. This woman was also picked up on the wire talking to Rocky Pulete. Her full name was Kathleen Garrity, and her partner, Fraser Samuel Milham, was serving a 10-year sentence in Paremoremo for a prolonged sexual assault.

Milham would call Garrity incessantly at the behest of Rocky Pulete, who arranged for associates outside prison to give her cash, drugs and, on one sweet occasion, a car. In return, she ran errands for Rocky.

Garrity did a lot for Pulete. She ran drugs and cash for him. She banked his share of the profits. And she smuggled contraband into Paremoremo.

She would put drugs in plastic wrap, about the size of a Bic lighter, then wrap that in insulation tape and hide it in her bra. She would then leave the package in the women's toilets at Paremoremo.

In one bugged conversation, Pulete asked Garrity to meet a fellow King Cobra member, Matthew Vave Schwenke, to pick up drugs and deliver money. Police later found 66 grams of methamphetamine in Schwenke's Mount Wellington home, as well as $5000 in cash, plastic ziplock bags and 64 grams of pseudoephedrine.

Detective Sergeant Mike Paki could only laugh at how easy it had been for inmates in New Zealand's supposedly toughest prison to obtain drugs and mobile phones. If he hadn't laughed, he'd have cried.

He suspected the inmates, or their helpers on the outside, had corrupted at least one prison guard to either turn a blind eye or, worse, actually assist them.

There were genuine fears a bent screw might tip off the prisoners about the covert investigation. As such, Operation Web didn't seek the cooperation of Corrections Services, or even give prison management a heads-up, until the day before they swooped on Paremoremo in September 2008.

On 2 September, a squad of prison guards in riot gear inched towards Arthur William Taylor's cell, carrying Perspex shields to protect themselves in case inmates pelted them with projectiles.

Detectives were convinced Taylor was the mastermind of the syndicate, pulling all the strings behind the scenes. They turned his cell upside down, but didn't find a mobile phone, or any physical evidence to incriminate him. It was the same story in the other inmates' cells.

The climax of Operation Web fell a bit flat, and it would haunt Mike Paki and his team over the next three years as the prosecution slowly wound its way through the courts.

In 2010, the 50-year-old mother who turned Crown witness pleaded guilty to supplying and was sentenced to home detention.

The Crown cases against some of the accused were thrown out of court entirely for lack of evidence. Others, such as Fraser Milham and Matthew Schwenke, pleaded guilty early to get a discount on their sentences. In 2010 they got prison lags of five and two years respectively.

Rocky Pulete denied the charges against him, and endured weeks of sitting squashed in the dock at the High Court in 2011 listening to the evidence – only to plead guilty, with Kathleen Garrity, near the end of the trial. Pulete ended up with a total of seven and a half years in prison, which included the charge of conspiring with Taylor, while Garrity was sentenced to three years and 10 months.

Wanzhe 'Jackie' Gui was convicted of importing pseudoephedrine, but the trial jury couldn't decide whether he was guilty as a party to importing methamphetamine.

An extra two years were tacked onto the end of his 13-year kidnapping lag in Paremoremo.

A phalanx of high-profile defence lawyers got to their feet to make submissions on behalf of their clients at three High Court trials spread across 2011 and 2012, but none was as successful as Taylor, who represented himself during the proceedings. For years he had honed his bush-lawyer skills in Paremoremo, often helping other inmates prepare for their appeals or battles with prison authorities.

While self-represented litigants who think they know the law are often a disaster in court, Taylor was better prepared and more succinct in his questioning than most of the expensive lawyers alongside him. After being peppered by Taylor's confronting questions at a pre-trial hearing, Turbo Turner was left in no doubt that it was the best cross-examination he had experienced over his many years of answering questions in the witness box.

Taylor succeeded in having many of the drugs charges against him dismissed before trial. Then he persuaded a High Court jury to acquit him of three charges of offering to sell methamphetamine to three different associates: the most serious offences he was up against.

And it was his brilliance in court that forced prosecutors to concede that the Crown couldn't prove its case against Clarke, an inmate in Rimutaka Prison in 2007, and jointly charged with Taylor and Pulete for conspiracy to supply a Class A drug. Taylor pointed out to Clarke's lawyer that there was no evidence to prove that Wayne John Clarke, known as 'Wayniac', was *the* Wayne Clarke caught talking to Taylor on the phone. The charge against Clarke was duly dismissed.

But that victory was shortlived. Taylor was convicted of conspiracy to supply the Class A drug, together with his friend Rocky Pulete.

The evidence that underpinned the single conviction was those intercepted telephone conversations from way back in June 2007, when the Tauranga CIB was investigating the disappearance of Grant 'Granite' Adams. The case had come full circle.

In sentencing Taylor to seven years in prison, Justice Edwin Wylie said that the fact the offence had been committed while Taylor was in prison made a mockery of his previous jail terms.

'You have indicated absolutely no remorse. Rather, you demonstrate a total disregard for the criminal justice system,' Justice Wylie said. 'You are a recidivist offender who appears to revel in the minor celebrity status you enjoy within the prison system. In my view, you exhibit no insight into your offending at all.'

'No insight'? That was a strange way to describe the wily intelligence of Arthur William Taylor.

Not surprisingly, it was Taylor who had the last word. He appealed his conviction, representing himself again in the Court of Appeal, where he convinced the bench of three senior judges that Justice Wylie's judgment had been too harsh. He failed to get the conviction quashed, but his sentence was cut by 18 months to five and a half years.

Spurred on by his courtroom success, Taylor spent his extra years in prison battling for prisoners' rights to smoke and vote, with his lawsuits taken all the way to the Supreme Court. In 2017 he even launched a private prosecution against 'Witness C', later exposed as double murderer Roberto Conchie Harris, one of three prison informants who claimed David Tamihere had confessed in lurid detail to the 1989 murders of Swedish backpackers Heidi Paakkonen and Urban Höglin. Tamihere had been released on parole seven years earlier, but Taylor's dogged pursuit of Harris, 'to send a loud, clear message to jailhouse snitches', led to Harris's conviction for perjury. The verdict resulted in renewed calls for a retrial of Tamihere, convicted of one of New Zealand's most heinous crimes partly on the word of a liar.

Mike Paki could only shake his head and smile ruefully as Taylor's appeal brought Operation Web to a close. While the investigation had failed to yield the vast quantities of drugs that had been seized in earlier inquiries – notably Operation Major – it had exposed Paremoremo prison's bizarre role as a college of advanced criminal education. Even beyond the quite remarkable feat of organising an international drug-smuggling operation from behind bars, the inmates were running a business school for criminals. They called it Rock College.

For years, prison inmates had taught one another how to break into houses, steal cars, forge cheques and perform other fairly basic tricks of the trade, but Rock College was much more sophisticated. It provided an endless tutorial on sharing trade secrets, pooling knowledge, teaching one another the police traps that tripped them up, and forming far-reaching alliances.

And, as police knew only too well, a new class of Rock College students graduates every year.

4

BEND IT LIKE BECKHAM: VENGEANCE IN THE NORTHLAND UNDERWORLD

2008

MAX BECKHAM HAD EVERYTHING he'd ever wanted. He'd worked hard for it too.

Born and bred in Northland, Beckham had spent his whole life working the land and providing for his family through blood, sweat and tears. He'd been a dairy farmer, but had been quick to spot other opportunities, planting acres of olive orchards by hand as New Zealanders acquired a taste for the golden oil. Later on, Beckham subdivided sections of land to offer seaside views to potential buyers as property prices soared. He also purchased the ITM hardware store in Mangonui, as well as running a fleet of excavators and trucks through his civil contracting firm, and a commercial fishing vessel, *Unity*, which trawled the Northland waters every day. (He had a passion for the water, even receiving a bravery award for a sea rescue.)

As he neared retirement, the 60-year-old Beckham could comfort himself with the knowledge that his hard work had paid off. In addition to his business acquisitions, he'd bought two investment properties in Auckland, an inner-city apartment and a residential home in West Auckland, two lifestyle blocks, including his family home in Mangonui, and a few toys too, like his Ford Territory and two late-model Ford Falcons, one with the registration plate B4DBOY.

According to his accountant's estimate, Beckham's net assets were worth $5.9 million. By anyone's measure, he was wealthy. Even as the 2008 Global Financial Crisis sent the world's economy into recession, hitting deprived regions like Northland especially hard, Beckham never seemed too worried about the cash flow into his businesses.

Anyone who knew the truth would realise why Beckham had no reason to fret. He was secretly making millions from another business on the side.

His new venture had been born from deep-seated grief and guilt. Beckham had been planting trees on his Mangonui lifestyle block when his two-year-old son wandered off and fell into a pond, drowning in the shallow water.

He blamed himself for the tragic death, and suffered unending anguish – which he soon found was numbed only by the euphoria of methamphetamine. What started as a welcome escape from reality soon turned into heavy dependence, and then into enormous profits.

Beckham's addiction became an empire. He loved meth, but he had an equal passion for making money. With his keen intelligence and entrepreneurial savvy, and a sizeable streak of ruthlessness, Beckham would become one of the most powerful figures in the Northland underworld.

* * *

By 2006, he was regarded as a somewhat mythical figure. For years there had been rumours of drugs and violence surrounding him, such as stories that he'd smuggled exotic birds into New Zealand in the 1980s.

Local police never came close to laying charges. Beckham was seemingly untouchable long before his foray into the meth market.

In July 2006, the Northland Organised Crime Unit managed to convince a High Court judge to grant a warrant to intercept his private communications for 30 days. The warrant was granted on the basis of allegations by a criminal informant that Beckham was manufacturing meth. Nothing came of the investigation, coyly named Operation Bend in honour of the well-known film about his English football namesake.

Local detectives didn't bother trying to renew the warrant when it lapsed. Covert investigations are time-consuming and expensive, demanding weeks and sometimes months of surveillance, with no guarantee of a result at the end. District commanders usually prefer staff to spend their time solving cases with a strong likelihood of success, like getting the burglary stats down, rather than chasing shadows.

At the end of August, the Northland team decided to move on. But instead of closing the case outright, the detectives met with their AMCOS peers in Auckland to discuss their mutual problem.

At the time, AMCOS were stretched to capacity with Operation Ice Age and Operation Major. They simply didn't have the resources to launch an immediate investigation into the mysterious Beckham. But Bruce Good promised to take another look further down the track, and the following year, Detective Sergeant Lloyd Schmid was handed the baton.

Just like Beckham, Schmid was a son of the Far North, with deep family and iwi ties to the region. After Operation Manu ended in December 2006, Schmid and two of his more talented detectives, Stu Hunter and Josh McAllum, decided to stay at Harlech House when the rest of their team returned to Auckland City. All three enjoyed the thrill of the chase that came with covert policing, and knew they had to join AMCOS to get the time and resources needed to really make a dent in the meth trade. With a wink and a nod, Bruce Good advertised three vacancies and the trio of Schmid, Hunter and McAllum were offered the roles.

The intel team had received a CHIS (Covert Human Intelligence Source) report about a new business deal between three influential crime figures. According to the informant, Albert Wayne Hunter (known as Wayne), Gerrard Gordon Parkes and the now-notorious Max Beckham had each agreed to chip in $1 million to fund the ongoing importation of huge amounts of pseudoephedrine from China. Schmid would head up the investigation into these three men, entitled Operation Jivaro.

They made an odd trio. Hunter was short, not even 5 and a half foot, but ruled his underlings with an iron fist and a fiery temper: 'working for the Beast' was how his meth cooks described him. He even commanded the respect of Wayne Doyle, a convicted murderer and now president of the newly formed East Chapter of the Head Hunters gang.

In contrast to the diminutive Hunter, Gerrard Parkes was an *actual* beast. The heavily tattooed 'G' was 6 foot 6 and strong as an ox. He knew how to use his size to intimidate, violently bashing anyone who crossed him or defied his will.

Parkes hardly needed the protection of a gang patch to do business, but he was loosely aligned with the Mongrel Mob and, like Hunter, with the Head Hunters.

Police believed Beckham, Hunter and Parkes were planning to meet in downtown Auckland, but by the time Operation Jivaro was 'up on the wire' – with the necessary interception warrants in place – the deal was already done. Or perhaps it never happened. The trio never met while Jivaro detectives were watching them, and out of the thousands of phone calls police listened to over the next few months, just a few involved Hunter and Beckham.

There had been no falling out, as far as the police could tell; everyone had simply gone their separate ways. Gerrard Parkes drifted into the background – though he was later jailed for 11 years for supplying meth in a separate investigation – and Operation Jivaro split into two inquiries in August 2008, with different targets. Jivaro would continue following Beckham, while the operation investigating Hunter would be known as Helar.

* * *

When it came to Beckham, police enjoyed success sooner than they ever anticipated. Just halfway through Operation Jivaro, in August 2008, Beckham was arrested and charged – for offences that had nothing to do with meth. These offences also showed police what a dangerous criminal they were up against.

Earlier that same month, Beckham had hired a painting crew to redecorate his Mangonui home. Two big containers of high-quality cannabis head went missing; Beckham blamed the three painters.

He summoned the trio to his home to confront them about the theft, with his associates Frank Murray and Curtis Yates in tow. The painting crew were told, in no uncertain terms, to return the cannabis or pay the cash equivalent of around $25,000. A shotgun was sitting in plain sight, within arm's reach of Beckham, while Murray was armed with a taser and a pistol. The message was chillingly clear.

Unsurprisingly, the three painters didn't return to finish the job at Beckham's house. One was so scared he went into hiding in a remote part of the Far North, hoping to lie low until the whole saga blew over.

But Beckham was not one to forgive or forget. His suspicions and fury became focused on one of the painters in particular. He sent his right-hand man Mark Rogers to find the alleged cannabis thief, and Rogers tracked him to where he was living in fear with his partner and young children.

Around 4am on 18 August 2008, Rogers, Beckham and a third man who was never identified arrived at the property.

Rogers and the unknown man knocked on the door. The painter had never met either of them before. Their story was that their car battery was dead and they needed a hand.

Despite the hour, the painter agreed to help them, and walked outside into the winter air.

He'd only taken a few steps when Rogers smashed him in the face with a pistol.

Knocked to the ground by the force of the unexpected strike, the painter lay prone in the mud. A pillowcase was stuffed over his head, then taped up tight, before a taser painfully jolted his neck.

He was told exactly what he needed to do. Return the cannabis by lunchtime, or find $25,000 – or else. And he'd just been given a very clear message about what the 'or else' would look like.

The three men left the property. The painter was petrified. Police would come to believe he *had* taken the cannabis. But he had no way to repay Beckham. He dialled 111 and sang like a canary.

Max Beckham and Mark Rogers were arrested and charged with kidnapping and committing a crime with the use of a firearm. As for the painter, police put him and his family into the witness protection program.

Everyone who watches crime shows knows the drill about the witness protection program: police give secret witnesses a new name and a new life in an undisclosed town. In return, the witnesses give evidence in open court against someone who supposedly makes them fear for their life.

All of this unfolded shortly before the phone interception phase of Operation Jivaro went live. What happened next would never have come to light if not for the covert surveillance of Beckham's conversations by Lloyd Schmid and his team.

As soon as Beckham was released on bail for the kidnapping charges, he put the word out around the criminal underworld that it would be worth their while if his alleged victim were found.

The jungle drums reached the ears of Matthew Todd Woller, a 41-year-old with Black Power links and a criminal record stretching back to 1984. The most serious of his 34 convictions were for manufacturing and conspiring to supply methamphetamine, for which he had been sentenced to five years in prison.

When he bumped into the painter's younger brother in Auckland, Woller knew how he could boost his own criminal standing. The brother knew of Woller's reputation, and raised his brother's predicament out of concern for the safety of the wider family.

'I may be able to help you with your latest court case,' Woller texted Beckham on 18 October 2008: a message that was picked up by Operation Jivaro's surveillance.

Woller arranged for Beckham to meet the painter's brother at the Te Atatu Tavern in West Auckland. Police secretly filmed the rendezvous.

Beckham firmly told the man that it was in everyone's best interests for him to find out where his brother was hiding – then inform Beckham or Woller.

To protect the integrity of the covert meth investigation, Beckham and Woller were charged with conspiracy to pervert the course of justice only after Beckham was arrested on drug and money laundering charges in December 2008. If they'd arrested him straight away, Beckham might have realised that police could only have known about his dealings with Woller by listening to him covertly.

At his District Court trial in August 2011 for kidnapping, commiting a crime with a firearm, and attempting to pervert the course of justice, Beckham would concede that he confronted the painter at his home – because, he claimed, $25,000 worth of jewellery had gone missing, not cannabis. No weapons had been involved, he told the court.

The jury disagreed. He was convicted on all charges, and sentenced to seven and a half years in prison.

The next year though, the Court of Appeal would rule that a miscarriage of justice had occurred at the District Court trial. Intercepted conversations between Beckham and Rogers, not directly related to the alleged kidnapping but discussing other acts of violence and threats, as well as drugs, had been unfairly admitted into evidence. The trial judge was also criticised for unfairly questioning Beckham when he gave evidence, making sceptical comments that would have undermined his supposedly neutral role in the eyes of the jury.

The convictions for kidnapping and attempting to pervert the course of justice would be quashed. A retrial was ordered but never took place, for reasons unknown – as is the whereabouts of the painter in witness protection.

* * *

While the kidnapping drama was unfolding in August 2008, Operation Jivaro had been continuing its investigation into

Beckham's multi-million dollar drug empire.

Beckham's family lifestyle block was in Mangonui, at the bottom end of Doubtless Bay. Monday to Wednesday, he was at home with his wife and kids, keeping an eye on his legitimate businesses while his drug empire quietly ticked over in the background.

The Far North is covered in thousands of hectares of thick bush, where no one would ever stumble across a clandestine meth lab hidden in a ramshackle hut or shed. Beckham had an entire roster of meth cooks he could call on to manufacture the Class A drug, including Karl Hewitson, Curtis Yates and Frank Murray; Murray's fingerprints were later found on glassware in one abandoned lab.

The days he wasn't working on his lawful businesses, Beckham would arrange meetings in Auckland for his *other* business. He was careful to be discreet on the phone, but Lloyd Schmid and his team could tell he was discussing commercial-scale drug deals.

Every week, once the meetings were set up, Beckham drove down to Auckland often on a Thursday, and stayed at the apartment he'd purchased in the CBD. He'd conduct his meetings with buyers, then drive home on the Sunday.

The 60-year-old would break up the four-hour commute by stopping off at the homes of young women. It was pure barter: sex for methamphetamine.

While he was always cautious on the phone, Beckham let his guard down when driving his Ford Territory – which the police had also bugged.

He told a 19-year-old girl he was sleeping with that he planned to quit the drug game when he'd earned the magical but arbitrary figure of $10 million. In another bugged conversation, Beckham claimed he'd actually gone way past that figure, but said he couldn't stop: the money was too good.

He couldn't stop boasting. During a chat with a young Asian woman, Beckham talked about 23 'sets' of pseudoephedrine that were being smuggled into the country. (The police never identified Beckham's pseudo source – though travel records show he suspiciously travelled to China at the same time as a longtime Asian crook we'll soon meet.) Each set of pseudo consisted of 1000 capsules of ContacNT; 23 would be enough to manufacture 90 ounces of meth. The police recording device cleverly hidden inside the car captured these frank admissions, as well as the pair's excruciatingly graphic sexual talk.

One bugged conversation would prove especially damning. On 19 December 2008, three months into the electronic surveillance phase of Operation Jivaro, Mark Rogers was sitting with Beckham in his Ford Territory. Rogers was Beckham's loyal follower, trusted to exchange drugs and cash, and be the heavy muscle to enforce Beckham's will.

During a jumbled stretch of dialogue in which the pair constantly talked on top of one another, they picked over the bones of a transaction that had turned sour.

'I think I took five or six hundred thousand,' said Rogers, 'and I got two kilograms from them.'

Lloyd Schmid had his man dead to rights. The tape captured Rogers admitting to supplying a significant quantity of meth.

Three days later, Operation Jivaro swooped on Beckham's Mangonui lifestyle block. Police found a chicken coop that contained no hens but plenty of plastic containers of chemicals used to cook meth. They also discovered a ramshackle shed featuring the remnants of an abandoned clan lab, and meth residue in the walls. Around $300,000 and 4 ounces of meth were discovered inside Beckham's B4DBOY car, and another 9 ounces of drugs found buried near the driveway.

Everywhere detectives looked, they found more incriminating evidence. *Over here.* More than $500,000 in cash casually
thrown into a plastic bucket in the garage. *Over here.* Fish
bins on the front lawn full of cannabis seedlings. *Over here.*
A 'speedball' concoction of heroin, morphine and cocaine in
the master bedroom.

Beckham was charged with 57 counts of serious drug
and money-laundering offences. Police issued a press release
that proclaimed the arrest of a 'significant figure' in the
methamphetamine trade.

On top of a possible life sentence in prison, Beckham
faced losing his life's work. Police confiscated $875,720 in
cash, and obtained freezing orders over all of his assets: the
fishing trawler *Unity*, two lifestyle blocks together worth $1.1
million, shareholdings in his various companies, the $750,000
West Auckland home, the $630,000 apartment in downtown
Auckland, and his cars.

The empire of the once-untouchable 'B4DBOY' was
crumbling around him.

* * *

While Beckham had been conducting his double life between
Mangonui and Auckland, Wayne Hunter, the target of
Operation Helar, had been just as busy. He'd been distributing
methamphetamine from a concrete bunker underneath the
carpark of the Mount Albert Video Ezy store on New North
Road. It was accessible only by a side street parallel to the
railway line, with the entrance protected by a locked iron
gate and security cameras.

The police set up their own cameras on the other side of
the track, as well as intercepting phone conversations. They
gathered enough evidence between August and October 2008

to get some convictions beside Hunter's name – but it still only scratched the surface.

Hunter was renowned for his strong ties to the Asian organised crime syndicates that were valued by local criminals for their ability to smuggle in pseudoephedrine from China. He was convicted of conspiring to manufacture meth with Guozhi Li, as well as socialising regularly with Di Wu, both of whom had been locked up following Operation Manu, Lloyd Schmid's previous investigation into the drug syndicate run by the Four-Eyed Dragon from the VIP lounge of SkyCity.

According to the evidence gathered in Operation Helar, Hunter was involved in all aspects of the drug business. He sourced pseudoephedrine from Guozhi and King Cobra gang member Paul Golding, among others. He then had it delivered to his meth cooks, Kamal Jonathan Butt and Muckunda Horsfall. He ruled them like slaves, with Horsfall later claiming Hunter had an 'evil control' over him. Unfortunately, though, police surveillance gathered only enough evidence to prove Hunter had arranged the manufacture of 50 grams of meth on two separate occasions: just 100 grams altogether.

As well as sourcing pseudo and controlling manufacture, Hunter supplied the finished product to other drug dealers, and directly to addicts, from his gated bunker under the video store. He was heard on the phone talking about a 5-ounce deal, but he was never caught with his hands on the product. Hunter was arrested – along with Gouzhi, Butt, Horsfall, Golding and a street dealer named Rose Scott – in December 2008, although nothing incriminating was found when Operation Helar raided the underground den. 'The Beast' was too clever for that.

* * *

A few days later, Beckham was arrested too, refused bail and held at Ngawha Prison, a little over an hour's drive from his home in Mangonui. Understandably, he was angry, and desperate to stay out of prison. He tried playing the best form of defence: attack.

In August 2009, while he was still in custody, the police received an alarming report from a confidential informant.

According to the source, Beckham was planning a prison break and had also made threats against the life of Lloyd Schmid. At first it sounded laughable – but the police had seen first-hand what Beckham was capable of, when he'd pursued the painter who allegedly stole from him.

Besides, Beckham was wealthy enough to fund an escape plot, and had a vast array of criminal contacts in New Zealand and overseas who could offer him sanctuary. Given his deep-sea fishing experience on the commercial trawler *Unity*, it was even thought possible that he would try to head for open water on a boat.

The police weren't taking any chances. From that point on, the prison van carrying Beckham to court appearances in Auckland, or visits to hospital for a troublesome heart condition, was escorted by members of the Armed Offenders Squad on the road, and a police Eagle helicopter in the sky.

As it turned out, Beckham never attempted to escape. But the police kept investigating the alleged threats against Schmid. Detective Sergeant Jason Lunjevich, a member of the Special Investigations Group under the AMCOS umbrella, was put in charge of Operation Valley.

One piece of disturbing evidence intercepted by the prison authorities was a letter sent to Beckham that included the home addresses of Schmid, his team member Stu Hunter and, oddly, Detective Sergeant Bruce Howard, an AMCOS officer who had nothing to do with Operation Jivaro.

By the very nature of their work, where they are disrupting the lucrative business of some bad people, drug squad detectives are careful to cover the tracks of their personal lives. They keep their names off public records like electoral rolls, put power and other household bills in the names of their partners, and don't have social media accounts or other digital footprints to follow. Operation Valley came to the sinister conclusion that Hunter, Howard and Schmid had been tailed home from the office.

No one was ever charged over the alleged threats against Schmid. But the danger to his life didn't seem to faze him; his colleagues never saw any sign of fear or worry. If anything, the scare tactics steeled his resolve to see the case through to the end.

Beckham wasn't backing down either. If intimidation wouldn't work, he'd try to destroy Schmid's reputation. Given the strength of the evidence against him, undermining the integrity of the officer in charge of the case might be his only hope of an acquittal.

A series of front-page stories started appearing in a tabloid newspaper, accusing Schmid of unethical behaviour. There was an allegation that he'd asked a female informant to sleep with the target of an investigation, and an inference that he'd turned a blind eye to the theft of $6000 by one of his staff during a search. Schmid and his family were dragged through the mud by a third tawdry allegation of a very personal nature. But the whole thing was a hit job.

Behind it all was a reporter known as a close confidant of Gerrard Parkes and Wayne Hunter. He was donkey-deep in the meth world and although once a talented journalist, these stories were the worst form of journalism: a PR campaign on behalf of a dodgy client.

Police investigated each of the allegations and Schmid was cleared of any wrongdoing. But even though he'd beaten the false rap, the smear campaign allowed defence lawyers to attack his credibility in front of the jury during the trials of both Wayne Hunter and Max Beckham.

It didn't work.

On 31 August 2009, while Beckham was still languishing at Ngawha Prison, Hunter was convicted of manufacturing and supplying methamphetamine, as well as conspiracy to supply the Class A drug, and sentenced to six years in prison.

When Beckham's drug charges got to court in April 2011, not only did his defence team question Schmid's reputation, they also implied that police had planted drugs on Beckham's Mangonui property.

At the end of a hard-fought trial in the High Court at Auckland, the jury found Beckham guilty of the most serious charges, including two counts of manufacturing methamphetamine, and one count each of conspiracy to supply meth, cocaine and ecstasy. All told, Beckham was convicted of 24 offences, including the 2-kilo supply of methamphetamine he was caught talking about with Mark Rogers.

Rogers had already pleaded guilty to the same charge and was now serving 11 years. But he wasn't the only associate of Beckham's to be dragged down with the Northland businessman.

Sitting alongside Max in the dock was 60-year-old Yu Hung Szeto, better known as 'Uncle Paul', a legendary figure in the Asian underworld. Szeto ran a mah jong den in downtown Auckland, and also had links with Wayne Hunter. While still a free man, Hunter had often been seen socialising with Szeto, sharing either yum cha or a table at SkyCity.

Szeto had VIP status at the casino, until he was caught loan-sharking to other gamblers and banned for two years. A chain smoker, Szeto looked like a sick old man who was no threat to anyone. He never missed an opportunity to lift his shirt and display an ugly scar from a liver transplant.

Szeto's mind, though, worked like a steel trap.

At his seven-week trial with Beckham, the jury heard evidence that Szeto and his 28-year-old girlfriend Wei Na Shi, also known as 'Candy', had bought a 2005 Mercedes SLK convertible with $21,500 cash and two cheques totalling $50,000. They'd also purchased a 2003 Mercedes sedan with $17,000 cash and five cheques totalling $100,000. Likewise, a 2005 Porsche Cayenne was paid for with $66,785 cash.

The Crown alleged that the money was Beckham's drug profits. Szeto's defence was that it came from other sources, including gambling. He was acquitted of money laundering, even though the jury found Beckham – who had written out the cheques that paid for Szeto's luxury vehicles – guilty on the exact same charges. Szeto was also acquitted of conspiring to manufacture methamphetamine (as Beckham's suspected pseudoephedrine source) and supplying the finished product.

The jury was unaware of his colourful history. In May 1991, Szeto had been convicted of injuring with intent, causing grievous bodily harm and attempting to pervert the course of justice. He had ordered two men to beat up a Chinese restaurant owner in Hamilton who owed a business associate $5000. The victim's brother-in-law intervened with two meat cleavers, but was stabbed.

Police then bugged a telephone conversation with the victim's wife in which a man called 'Steven' told her to deny Szeto was involved in any way. At Szeto's sentencing hearing, in which he was sent to prison for four years, his lawyer Lorraine Smith revealed Szeto had been forced to leave the Hong Kong police force because of a criminal conviction, the nature of which was not revealed. On his release from prison,

Szeto returned to Auckland and cemented his position as one of the central figures in the Asian organised crime scene.

As a sickness beneficiary since his liver transplant nearly a decade earlier, Szeto had been given a Housing New Zealand property close to Narrow Neck Beach. Neighbours could scarcely believe their eyes when the pair of Mercedes-Benz and the Porsche showed up outside the two-bedroom house, taxpayer-funded accommodation meant for the most vulnerable members of the community.

But when drug detectives searched the place to arrest Szeto, they found it unoccupied. It contained nothing but empty cardboard boxes. Szeto had moved out to live in the upmarket suburb of Mission Bay, surrounded by homes worth in excess of $1 million, in a rental home with his girlfriend.

When he was arrested with Beckham in December 2008, the trio of cars – worth an estimated $250,000 – were seized under the *Proceeds of Crime Act* 1991. The outdated legislation required a conviction in order for the assets to be forfeited permanently, so on his acquittal, the valuable cars were supposed to be returned to Szeto.

However, shortly after Szeto's arrest but before his acquittal, the *Proceeds of Crime Act* was replaced by the new *Criminal Proceeds (Recovery) Act* 2009, which allowed police to freeze suspected criminal wealth without having to prove that an offence had occurred. It had been passed with the leaders of criminal organisations – who typically keep themselves at arm's length from criminal activity, but pull the strings nonetheless – in mind.

The new legislation relied on the 'balance of probabilities' evidentiary threshold used in civil cases, a lower standard than the 'beyond reasonable doubt' threshold of criminal prosecutions. It allowed police to confiscate Szeto's cars.

The case was one of the first in New Zealand in which police were able to strip a criminal of his assets without a conviction, and certainly the most significant such case in the early days of the new law, when police were still getting to grips with this powerful – some might say draconian – new tool.

His fleet of luxury cars might have been taken from him, yet Szeto still walked away with his freedom.

It was a bitter pill for detectives to swallow.

* * *

At least they had the consolation of knowing that Max Beckham faced spending the rest of his life in prison.

In sentencing Beckham on 12 August 2011, Justice Pamela Andrews described the scale of his offending between 2006 and 2008 as 'substantial'. She lifted the name-suppression order that had kept Beckham's identity secret for nearly three years.

Beckham's façade as a respectable businessman and loving husband and father was stripped away to reveal the ugly truth. He was a dangerous man, who had made millions from the misery of others.

'Every person who is involved in this court is very well aware of the social and financial cost to families and to the community that follows from the use of methamphetamine,' said Justice Andrews. 'It is destructive, it is devastating, and its effects are seen in New Zealand every single day.'

She had planned to hand down a prison sentence of 18 and a half years, putting Beckham in the top echelon of drug prisoners, but stopped short for one reason: he was already serving seven and a half years for kidnapping the painter along with Rogers, as well as attempting to pervert the course of justice along with Woller.

The mathematical gymnastics needed to balance the dual prison terms, in order to be fair to Beckham but also reflect the totality of his crimes, led Justice Andrews to impose a comparatively lenient sentence of 13 and a half years for the drug offending, to be served on top of the kidnapping term.

When the kidnapping charge was later quashed by the Court of Appeal, the victory for Beckham was pyrrhic. The panel of three senior judges reinstated Justice Andrews's original 18-and-a-half year sentence.

Max Beckham was no longer untouchable. He was now 63 years old, with a serious heart condition and cancer, and could very likely die in prison.

A ruthless drug baron had been taken off the streets. But he was hardly the only person with an eye for the vast profits to be made from meth, and with a pipeline to China to source cheap pseudoephedrine.

The tap had been turned on. The trickle was about to become a torrent.

5

A HEAD HUNTER IN A FERRARI: THE BALLAD OF LITTLE DAVE

2013

MICHAEL CAVANAGH WAS LIVING the dream.

Cavanagh was a drop-out, a drifter and an ex-con. He'd left prison three years previously with nothing to his name. He'd never finished college, never even held down a full-time job, and yet here he was in 2013, cruising around the streets of Auckland behind the wheel of his cherry-red Ferrari 360 Modena. It was a two-seater coupé that ran off a 3.6-litre V8. It accelerated from 0 to 100 kilometres in 4.9 seconds. Its licence plate was BGKHNA: 'Big Kahuna'. It had cost, quite obviously, a truckload.

Strangely, Cavanagh never parked it in the driveway of his Mount Wellington home for neighbours and passers-by to admire. It was one thing to drive around town explicitly displaying wealth and power, but it really wasn't in Cavanagh's best interests for anyone to know he owned such a desirable car. Instead, with the V8 purring, Cavanagh would inch the Ferrari into a lock-and-leave garage, then look anxiously around as he pulled the roller door down behind him.

The Ferrari was registered to a Paul Michael Alexander: the same name on the driver's licence Cavanagh had used to hire the garage. The ID was a forgery. As for the income that had paid for his big red coupé ... the police suspected he'd got rich from cooking meth.

Cavanagh had a talent for it, and he'd got in early.

* * *

Michael Cavanagh had been one of the first to learn the meticulous art of extracting pseudoephedrine from pharmacy cold and flu tablets, then chemically transforming it into methamphetamine. This was at the turn of the millennium, when pseudoephedrine was freely available in cold and flu medicine. And it was at the exact time when meth became the drug of choice for many New Zealanders, and gangs like the Head Hunters took control of the market.

They also took control of the meth cooks. Sometimes gang members kidnapped or 'taxed' them, forcing them to work in order to pay off a debt, perceived or real.

Under duress, one such indebted cook taught Cavanagh, who was hanging with the Heads, the tricks of the trade. Cavanagh learned fast. Meth had made him a millionaire before he turned 30.

Cavanagh's skill and notoriety as a cook were rivalled only by those of his good mate Brett 'Donut' Allison, of Operation Flower fame – and they soon brought him to the attention of the drug squads in Auckland District Services. But in 2001, when Cavanagh turned up in a flash Range Rover at a house linked to the Hells Angels, the police watching the house had no idea who he was.

By the end of the year, Cavanagh had become a principal target in Operation Illusion, led by Detective Sergeant Darryl Brazier (still years away from leaving Harlech House at this point). He'd already taken great pride in tackling members of the outlaw motorcycle gangs and their lucrative trade.

The investigation uncovered eight clandestine labs, one hidden inside a storage unit at East Tamaki, as well as other treasure troves dotted around town. When the detectives searched safety deposit boxes in Parnell they found jewellery, gold and silver bullion and $480,000 in cash. They also picked up five antique motorcycles. Another storage unit yielded a brand-new Harley Davison and $40,000 in gold bars and cash.

Inside Cavanagh's house they found $30,000. It later emerged that he had paid $330,000 in cash for the property. He would later claim his vast fortune had been earned legitimately, through trading in everything from mobile phones to jewellery, statues and even coal from the *Titanic*.

But for all Cavanagh's ill-gotten wealth, he was tripped up by pocket change. He and his fiancée Shannon Stevens had been on the run from Brazier and the Operation Illusion team for 10 months when the couple were caught in August 2002, shoplifting a $2.80 item from the PAK'nSAVE supermarket in Glen Innes.

It wasn't like they were skint. Cavanagh had $700 in his pocket.

On 4 April 2005 he was found guilty of the manufacture and supply of methamphetamine after a lengthy trial in the High Court in Auckland. There were 18 others convicted of methamphetamine offences in Operation Illusion, including Shannon Stevens, Cavanagh's previous long-term partner Debbie Henry (with whom he had a daughter) and a man called David Gerrard O'Carroll, better known as 'Little Dave'.

True to his name, Little Dave was a shortarse. But he was one of the most senior members of the East Chapter of the Head Hunters, based in the southeastern suburb of Ellerslie, along with gang president Wayne Doyle and Bird Hines.

Despite his diminutive stature, O'Carroll was a feared figure within the criminal underworld.

At the time, methamphetamine was only a Class B drug. Prison sentences were light compared with what was to come: two years for Debbie Henry, six for Shannon Stevens, and six and a half for Little Dave O'Carroll.

Cavanagh was given 12 years. But he only served about eight, once his three years in custody waiting for a trial date and early release on parole were taken into account. What hurt him more was forfeiting criminal profits of $1.9 million. That was as much as police could prove he had earned illegally; the real sum was almost certainly much, much higher.

* * *

By 2012, Cavanagh's mates in the Heads were back on the radar of the drug squad detectives in Harlech House. But by that time, the decorated AMCOS staff had been swallowed up by the Organised and Financial Crime Agency of New Zealand, or OFCANZ.

OFCANZ had been set up on 1 July 2008 as a new model based on an all-of-government approach to tackling organised crime. It was planned as a multi-agency group 'housed' within the New Zealand Police. Representatives from different government agencies would share intelligence and resources, enabling OFCANZ to go after the Mr Bigs of the underworld.

The theory was great. But in Auckland, AMCOS staff were forced to share Harlech House with the local branch of OFCANZ. It became a fight of the acronyms: OFCANZ in competition with AMCOS.

There had long been resentment within the police districts towards AMCOS, with its ring-fenced resources and staff.

AMCOS was still providing investigation support to the three Auckland police districts, but its drug squads in particular enjoyed a relative degree of autonomy free from interference from above. OFCANZ, on the other hand, reported directly to an assistant commissioner in Wellington, and enjoyed all the power and influence that came with having the ear of Police National Headquarters.

The arrival of the shiny new favourite child was trumpeted loudly in press releases from Wellington. But OFCANZ struggled to get early runs on the board. Its managers and staff were not as experienced in covert investigations, and more importantly, they didn't have a network of cultivated informants to give them the good oil.

In contrast, AMCOS were still knocking over big targets on a regular basis. But on at least one occasion, they were ordered to hand over control of a current investigation to OFCANZ.

One of the publicly stated goals of OFCANZ was to 'disrupt' organised crime in any way possible, making the lives of organised-crime figures difficult, even if their investigations didn't lead to criminal prosecutions. Many staff in AMCOS scorned the strategy, and made those feelings known.

When OFCANZ spent a year investigating the Hells Angels and laid only a handful of illegal deer-hunting charges against the gang, detectives entered the Harlech House kitchen to find a poster of a deer in the centre of a telescopic gunsight. Underneath were the mocking words 'OFCANZ: Officially Finding Criminals Around New Zealand'.

Office hijinks, maybe, but also a humiliating reminder of the growing divide between the two elite organised-crime forces and their different philosophies.

The established drug squads were proud of their record, and couldn't understand why the bosses in Wellington had stepped in to fix something that wasn't broken. Why not simply re-create new versions of AMCOS in other major centres such as Wellington and Christchurch, instead of reinventing the wheel?

Both groups were supposed to be working together. But with Wellington so directly involved, there was going to be only one winner.

In December 2011, AMCOS was disbanded 'as part of an administrative realignment'. All their staff were subsumed into the OFCANZ brand, which soon became further sullied by several high-profile bungles, such as the disastrous raid on the mansion of internet entrepreneur Kim Dotcom in January 2012.

Whether working for AMCOS or OFCANZ, seasoned pros like Mike Beal, Lloyd Schmid, Bruce Howard and John Sowter just wanted to get on with the job. A new set of top brass didn't matter, so long as Bruce Good's drug squads were free to go on with the same blend of camaraderie, black humour and serious work ethic that had proved so successful in the past.

It was in 2012, against this backdrop of political infighting, that Detective Sergeant John Sowter put his hand up for the first of many investigations that would target the Head Hunters over the next few years.

* * *

Under president Wayne Doyle, the East Chapter of the Heads had forged a fearsome reputation. Their numbers were relatively small – membership was about 30 or so core patched (fully initiated) members – but they dominated the Auckland scene.

Since their beginnings as a rag-tag bunch of teenage misfits in Glen Innes, Auckland, in 1967, the Head Hunters had grown in power and influence nationally with the explosion of the meth market. By 2012, police intelligence said that the older Head Hunters – wise to the ways of Darryl Brazier and his ilk, who had locked them up in the early days – had recruited an army of more than 200 young foot soldiers. They had spread across the country by muscling into rival gang territory in Northland and the Bay of Plenty, down to the Wairarapa and Wellington, and even as far south as Christchurch.

Sowter's aim in Operation Magnet was to slow that growth. His plan of attack was innovative to say the least; defence lawyers and civil libertarians might have called it an affront to human rights.

Instead of charging individual Head Hunters if and when they committed specific criminal offences, Operation Magnet set out to prove that simply *being* a Head Hunter made you a criminal. The goal was to charge the Head Hunters with participating in an organised criminal group.

The investigation drew up a list of the gang's top patched members and compiled a 400-page dossier of their lengthy criminal histories. Drug dealing, aggravated robbery, murder ... To Sowter's way of thinking, the entire point of putting on a patch was to further the criminal ends of this feared fraternity.

If Operation Magnet had led to arrests and prosecutions, they would undoubtedly have been appealed all the way to the Supreme Court. If the Crown had won, the Head Hunters would officially have been declared an organised criminal group, making membership illegal.

As it happened, Operation Magnet tripped over at the first hurdle. In a preliminary meeting with the police and Crown prosecutors, a High Court judge indicated he was unlikely to approve an interception warrant for such an operation.

So much for the innovative approach. But Sowter refused to give up.

* * *

The following year, 2013, stories of the Ferrari Modena with the licence plate BGKHNA made their way along the criminal grapevine to what was now OFCANZ. By this point, just three years after his early release on parole, Cavanagh was a patched member of the Head Hunters.

'Sowts' felt he had been given a second chance. Here was an opportunity to prise open the gang's defences the *old-fashioned* way: months of slogging away with surveillance.

Operation Genoa was launched in May 2013. It soon became clear that Cavanagh had got the old band back together. Although he'd married another woman, Victoria, Cavanagh had rekindled a working relationship with his ex-fiancée Shannon Stevens. To Sowter's team, it seemed clear that the former couple were using a nearly identical modus operandi to their earlier Bonnie-and-Clyde routine, foiled by Operation Illusion.

Shortly after her release from prison in January 2008, Stevens – like Cavanagh – managed to get her hands on a false driver's licence. She immediately used it to hire storage units and safety deposit boxes under the false name. So did Victoria Cavanagh.

Despite having no declared income or employment, the Cavanaghs had amassed more than $3 million in cash and assets. There was the Ferrari 360 Modena. There was a Maserati Gransport. A Porsche Boxster. An Audi A3. Millions of dollars tucked away in safety deposit boxes. Four properties, including their Mount Wellington home. And none of these assets were in their real names. Some of the cars were registered to Lisa Ryan, Victoria Cavanagh's mother. Cavanagh secretly photographed the details of her driver's licence to put the luxury vehicles cars in her unwitting mother's name, as well as yet another storage lockup. Lisa Ryan thought she was just signing the insurance papers.

To confuse matters even more, Shannon Stevens was in a new relationship with Peter Shaw – Victoria Cavanagh's brother. And the family links didn't end there: Michael Cavanagh also persuaded his *other* former partner Debbie Henry – the mother of his first child – to open a safety deposit box under a false name. She put $300,000 cash inside.

Through painstaking physical surveillance, Operation Genoa tracked down more than a dozen storage units and safety deposit boxes. Each one was opened covertly, with the approval of a High Court warrant.

No methamphetamine was ever found. But to John Sowter and his team, it seemed very obvious that Cavanagh and Stevens were back in business.

This time around, though, there was one very significant difference. Stevens and Cavanagh had learned a thing or two from spending years in prison. To the frustration of Genoa detectives, they picked up nothing 'on the wire'. They listened to Cavanagh and Stevens for months, but the pair never said anything that explicitly linked them to the manufacture of methamphetamine.

One of the few incriminating conversations caught on tape happened by total fluke. It led Operation Genoa down a very different path – and towards a very familiar name.

* * *

In the first few months of 2014, Shannon Stevens and Michael Cavanagh had a bitter falling out and ceased all contact with each other. Stevens, an astute meth cook in her own right, moved on to form a partnership with another senior Head Hunter from her Operation Illusion days: David Gerrard O'Carroll, aka Little Dave.

He'd walked free from prison in 2008 and stayed in the thick of the methamphetamine scene ever since, according to police sources. But information from fizzes and solid evidence are two different things. By now, Operation Genoa was listening to his phone calls, to no avail. Little Dave was too disciplined ever to give anything away on the phone, even in code.

And then something unexpected happened.

O'Carroll and Stevens met for dinner at SkyCity casino in March 2014. Another man, Nigel Bowker, was supposed to join them. He was running late. O'Carroll called to see where he was. Bowker didn't pick up. When the phone went to voicemail, Little Dave failed to properly hang up. He placed his phone back down on the table, and snippets of his unguarded dinner conversation with Stevens were recorded on Bowker's voicemail, to the joy of the Operation Genoa detectives listening live on the wire.

O'Carroll was overheard saying, 'Either way … I feel sometimes it's like too wet.' And then, 'Let it dry.' There was a 'kilo still left'. It would be 'fine when it's dry'.

The fragments were clear references to steps in meth manufacture. It's common for meth cooks to use an electric fan to help evaporate the unfinished substance. If that step isn't completed, the result is very damp methamphetamine hydrochloride.

Every investigation needs a little bit of luck. Sowter's bit of luck was hearing Little Dave, one of the most senior Head Hunters in the country, accidentally caught on the wire talking about how to dry out meth.

Over the next few months, O'Carroll was frequently in touch with Stevens, who in turn was getting Nigel Bowker and her partner Peter Shaw – Cavanagh's brother-in-law – to run errands. While the tone of their conversations was suspicious, they said nothing to prove outright that the group was moving methamphetamine.

But the intercepted phone calls were still useful to police. They were able to work out when and where to secretly watch their four suspects. This surveillance led Operation Genoa to numerous storage units around Auckland that Shannon Stevens had hired under false identities.

Over three months, from February to May 2014, her locked garage at Storage King in Botany was opened 10 times. Nearly every time it was Nigel Bowker driving through the gates in his Holden Commodore SS ute. Twice he left with a covered trailer in tow.

From searching the garage previously, police knew that beneath the fibreglass canopy of the trailer were Parr bombs – chemical pressure-cookers – as well as stainless-steel vessels, funnels, plastic tubing, reaction vessels, jugs, hotplates, gloves and 25 kilos of caustic soda. It was a meth lab on wheels.

Police believed that Bowker took the mobile laboratory to remote rural locations on the instructions of O'Carroll, cooked a batch of methamphetamine, then brought the trailer back.

On 11 March 2014, video footage showed Bowker leaving Storage King with the trailer. The following day, the Genoa team watched as Shannon Stevens drove towards O'Carroll's lifestyle property near the village of Miranda, on the Firth of Thames.

The detectives couldn't tail Stevens without blowing their cover. The 8-hectare property was located in a remote piece of country at the end of a winding gravel road, where any vehicles could be seen, and heard, from miles away.

But later that day, Stevens met up with Peter Shaw at another storage unit in East Tamaki, where they dropped off a large chilly bin.

To find out what was inside, the police applied for yet another covert warrant. (Years later, Sowter couldn't remember another job where he'd needed so many.)

So far, only guns, cash and the 'mobile meth lab' had been uncovered in the dozen or so storage units secretly searched by police. This time, when the police officers lifted the lid on the chilly bin they found a damp, white sludge.

It was photographed in situ and just a pinch taken as a sample, to 'prove product', as detectives say. The few granules they removed tested positive for methamphetamine. Weighing 830 grams, the fresh batch of meth was still wet: the problem O'Carroll had complained about at the SkyCity dinner.

If sold by the ounce, the stash would probably be worth close to $500,000.

It was an important breakthrough. Unlike the first phase of Operation Genoa, in which Cavanagh had been the focus, the detectives could now link manufacture of a Class A drug directly to Shannon Stevens.

Every covert investigation includes at least one moment when a tough decision must be made. Police could seize the meth, but it would destroy any chance of catching Little Dave. The hard evidence against him so far simply didn't stack up.

Or they could leave the drugs – enough to feed the addictions and prolong the misery of hundreds of people – and keep building their case.

Sowter decided the chance to catch a big fish like O'Carroll was worth the risk to other lives.

The problem was that O'Carroll would need to be caught more or less red-handed. He was too cautious ever to slip up over the phone, and covert surveillance on his rural property was difficult, bordering on impossible.

What did that leave? Sowter had been around the block. He knew the answer: another bit of luck.

* * *

On 9 May 2014, two months after the cops made their secret discovery in the chilly bin, Nigel Bowker once again visited Storage King Botany. Once again he hooked up the trailer to his Holden ute.

He had no idea that police had hidden a tracking device in his mobile meth lab. It plotted GPS coordinates as Bowker made his way to 189 Rataroa Road, Miranda: Dave O'Carroll's address.

It didn't matter that the property was listed in someone else's name. What the police were about to discover was cast-iron proof directly tying O'Carroll to the manufacture of methamphetamine.

There were three buildings on the property, which was surrounded by thick bush. They included a recently built two-bedroom house, and a large shed where the cooking was most likely to be taking place.

Police moved in after dark. They arranged for the Armed Offenders Squad to execute the property search.

Dressed head-to-toe in black, the AOS normally travel at high speed inside powerful four-wheel drive vehicles, lights and sirens flashing. It's not exactly an inconspicuous mode of arrival when the element of surprise is necessary. But this time, the heavily armed AOS were hiding in the back of a horse float, hitched to an old ute. To O'Carroll, or anyone else who saw the headlights and heard the tyres on the gravel road, it would look like a farmer or track rider getting home late.

Once the ute got close enough to the property, the AOS burst through the wooden gates. Hearing the commotion, O'Carroll and Bowker – who were in the middle of the cooking process – did a runner towards the bush.

Members of the Special Tactics Group, the elite armed unit of the New Zealand Police, came out of the shadows, also dressed in black. They train alongside the Special Air Service, and like their military peers, the STG are adept at living off the land and melding into the local terrain to conduct surveillance. They'd put those skills to use earlier in Operation Genoa, when they'd concealed cameras in the bush around O'Carroll's property. On the night of the bust, they'd crept through the bush for several kilometres, and were in position, spread out around the treeline, when the AOS broke down the front gates on the other side of the house.

Bowker ran one way – straight into the STG. O'Carroll hived off in the other direction. He ran down a paddock, and into the bush.

Sowter couldn't believe O'Carroll's arrogance in cooking meth on his own property. But now he saw his chances of a serious conviction slipping away. If police failed to arrest O'Carroll that night, the Head Hunter would be able to claim he'd never been at the property that evening, that the silhouette seen running away into the night had been someone else.

The police Eagle helicopter was hovering above, looking for body-heat signatures, while police dogs and their handlers were trying to find a scent. There was also a literal trail of clues: O'Carroll had grabbed a bag of meth as he headed out the door, which he'd scattered as he ran in a bid to discard the evidence.

In the dark, Sowter picked up 200 grams of meth granules strewn across the paddock O'Carroll had run through, even scraping some off fresh cow dung. It was a trail of meth crumbs. But there was no sign of O'Carroll himself.

Finally, an hour and a half later, O'Carroll was found lying in a nearby stream with only his face above water, his body submerged and hidden under toetoe grass.

Again, he tried to run. His second escape bid ended in dog bites and a broken wrist, which meant the manufacturing charges were laid against the 49-year-old at his bedside at Middlemore Hospital, not at the Manukau District Court.

* * *

At a press conference at Harlech House the following day, the impressive results of the Operation Genoa raids on five properties including O'Carroll's were laid out on tables for media organisations to film. Pistols, semi-automatic firearms, ammunition, and cash, lots of cash.

There were thick bundles of $20, $50 and $100 notes wrapped in rubber bands and tape, stacked inside five safety deposit boxes. More than $2 million had been seized, not to mention five Auckland properties, a 30-foot launch, gold bullion and silver ingots, as well as the expensive cars belonging to Michael Cavanagh: the Audi A3, the Porsche Boxster, the Maserati Gransport, and of course, that gleaming, cherry-red Ferrari 360 Modena, the car that had set off the entire investigation.

In his typical understated fashion, Detective Inspector Bruce Good fronted the media and rattled out the basic facts of the case. He was careful not to say too much. The arrests of two senior Head Hunters were deeply satisfying, but convictions are earned inside a courtroom.

Despite the success, Good had an air of resignation about him. He'd been in charge of the Auckland drug squad, with its various names and acronyms, for 14 years. His staff had been responsible for some of the most complex and difficult investigations in New Zealand history, had locked up countless underworld figures, and had seized ever-increasing amounts of methamphetamine.

Yet nothing had changed. The street prices of meth remained high, and the drug was as easy to get hold of as ever.

'Let's not kid ourselves. These aren't the only people manufacturing. *That* concerns me. The size of the market is large. *That* concerns me,' Good told the gathered media.

'The stress and strain meth puts on our health system, our mental health system, and everything else that flows from that. *That* concerns me.'

Still, there was one discovery that gave police a much-needed laugh. Among the items seized at the storage units was a manuscript titled 'The Devil's Dandruff'.

It was Cavanagh's memoirs. He'd written them while serving his prison sentence following Operation Illusion, putting his meth adventures on paper in colourful detail.

One particular passage about Darryl Brazier made Sowter grin. Cavanagh described the physical appearance of his original police nemesis in extremely unflattering terms.

Sowter sent a copy to his old mate DB in Tauranga, who roared with laughter on reading it.

* * *

The Crown tried to use 'The Devil's Dandruff', as well as Cavanagh's criminal history, as propensity evidence, to show that he typically acted in a certain way.

They pointed out his similar behaviour before his 2002 arrest in Operation Illusion: the same unexplained wealth, the same use of storage lockers, the same personal relationships.

The inference was obvious, the Crown argued: Cavanagh was cooking meth again.

At first, the legal argument tempted Justice Christian Whata, who agreed there were 'unusual points of coincidence' in this case. But then he changed his mind.

'It fills the yawning gap in the Crown's case … there is a two-fold risk that the jury will not appreciate the significance of this deficiency and then simplistically reason from the narrative … it must have occurred again.'

Translation? The judge thought Cavanagh wouldn't receive a fair trial if the jury were allowed to know about his past. He wasn't having a bar of it.

This led the meth manufacturing charge against Cavanagh to be dropped. Instead, he only pleaded guilty to money laundering, possession of a pistol and supplying 1.8 kilograms of ephedrine, a Class B drug. In October 2015, he was sentenced to just five years and 10 months in prison. A mere slap on the wrist – although for the second time, all his ill-gotten gains were taken away.

His wife Victoria pleaded guilty to using a false passport, money laundering and possession of ephedrine for supply. She was sentenced to three years and four months in prison.

Her brother Peter Shaw pleaded guilty to manufacturing and supplying meth, supplying ephedrine, forgery and unlawful possession of a firearm. He got 11 years and five months.

Shannon Stevens, Cavanagh's former fiancée, pleaded guilty to manufacturing and supplying methamphetamine, possession of ephedrine, unlawful possession of firearms, and using a fake identification document to hire the storage. She was sentenced to 15 years and five months in prison, later cut to 13 and a half years on appeal.

Nigel Bowker also admitted to manufacturing methamphetamine and was sent to prison for 12 years.

Little Dave O'Carroll didn't admit to anything. He pleaded not guilty to all charges and, to the chagrin of Sowter, was granted bail ahead of the High Court trial despite his lengthy criminal history.

It wasn't long before O'Carroll's name was whispered around the traps. He was back in business.

And so was Sowter.

Just a few months after Operation Genoa ended, Operation Gakarta set out to prove the Head Hunter was offending while on bail.

O'Carroll was now living at another Miranda property, just 2 kilometres from the Rataroa Road address where police had found him submerged in the stream. Just before Christmas 2014, the police raided the bail address. A Customs cash-sniffer dog was especially excited by a waterbed: police found $900,000 in cash carefully concealed inside the wooden frame. There was another $100,000 casually stashed in a cupboard. Little Dave had amassed $1 million in just a few months.

Operation Gakarta made an even more startling discovery at O'Carroll's other home in Rataroa Road. The floor of the kitchen was lined with large ceramic tiles, about 600 millimetres square, and covered by a rug. Nothing seemed amiss. But one of the tiles was in fact the entrance to a secret concrete bunker.

Sowter had heard rumours of O'Carroll's 'hidey hole', where the Head Hunters supposedly kept a cache of firearms, but the police had missed it the first time round. It wasn't hard to see why. Either the rubber grouting was replaced every time the tile was moved, or the tile was lifted out with suction cups. Either method meant that the concealment was nigh on perfect.

The gap was just big enough for a person to squeeze through, before lowering themselves into a cavity around

1 metre high and wide, and 3 metres long. Inside the tiny bunker were 14 firearms and thousands of rounds of ammunition. They had been stolen in a burglary of a gun collector in Bucklands Beach a few months earlier.

This time, O'Carroll was refused bail. He maintained his innocence at another trial in the Auckland High Court in September 2015. He claimed Nigel Bowker had been in control of the Rataroa Road property where the cooking took place.

It didn't wash with the jury. O'Carroll was convicted of manufacturing more than 2 kilograms of methamphetamine. The firearms charges were eventually thrown out, though, as the Crown couldn't prove O'Carroll knew about them.

The jury were not made aware, however, that the short, shaven-headed man in the dock was actually one of the most senior members of the Head Hunters. This irked Sowter. It was, of course, the reputation of the gang that had bolstered O'Carroll's standing in the criminal underworld, and Sowter felt the jury ought to know.

In sentencing O'Carroll to 16 years and five months in prison, Justice Mary Peters said she had no doubt he was intelligent, industrious and his own man. 'I cannot imagine you are subservient to anyone,' the High Court judge told him, reinforcing the jury's verdict that O'Carroll – not Nigel Bowker – was in charge.

Little Dave was a big scalp for the police to put in their trophy cabinet. But the war on the Head Hunters was just getting started.

6

TIGER TESTICLES, SHARK FINS AND P: INSIDE THE ASIAN DRUG EMPIRE

2013

FELIX LIM WAS VERY good at talking the talk. If there was a buck to make, a deal to broker or a hand to shake, Lim was the middle man for the job.

Born in Malaysia, the 57-year-old had immigrated to Auckland in the early 1990s and quickly put his fingers into different pies.

Officially, Lim ran a decorating crew that painted and plastered walls across the city. When the Mainzeal construction company went under in 2013, Lim complained long and loud, like so many other contractors around town who lost money.

He also ran some interesting businesses on the side.

He sold New Zealand wine and infant milk powder. There was boastful talk of buying expensive European cars cheap from a bankrupt business in Malaysia, but the deal fell over at the last minute. He imported Chinese sexual performance pills made from ginseng and tiger testicles. He also had friends in the restaurant business who'd ask him to find sea cucumbers and shark fins, sought-after Chinese aphrodisiacs often used in soups.

But that's exactly where his big mouth landed him: in the soup. In 2012, he was buying and selling black-market paua. Not the crime of the century, but Lim also boasted of how he could wrangle other deals. For the right buyer, he could get his hands on 'white' and 'pink': criminal parlance for methamphetamine and pseudoephedrine.

Felix Lim – real name Poh Guan Lim – was already a person of interest to the drug squad detectives in Harlech House. They knew him as someone who mixed in criminal circles, according to informants, and now a golden opportunity to gather intelligence on Auckland's Asian organised crime scene had fallen into their lap.

When Bruce Good and Detective Senior Sergeant Chris Cahill, later the Police Association president, heard the intelligence briefings on Lim wheeling and dealing in drugs, they knew not to let such a chance slip between their fingers.

A plan was hatched in May 2012 for a 'special duties constable', or undercover agent, to pose as a drug dealer from out of town. With any luck, it would give drug detectives enough evidence to lock up Lim – and who knew where else it would lead?

Lim was a loose thread. Pull on it hard enough, and almost anything might unravel.

The true identity of the undercover agent remains secret, but during the operation he went by the name of Joe Arama. Under this assumed identity, he immersed himself in the Auckland underworld. Like Felix Lim, he could talk the talk. He quickly established his criminal credentials and gained Lim's trust.

They liked to meet at Denny's, the 24-hour diner on Hobson Street, just across the road from the SkyCity casino. Sitting in one of the American-style booths, Lim would slip samples of pseudoephedrine and methamphetamine across the table in full view of any restaurant staff or customers who happened to be looking.

There was nothing suspicious about one guy who passed another guy a tin of Eclipse Mints. But hidden inside was that great pink elixir, pseudo.

* * *

When Helen Clark's Labour government had reclassified pseudoephedrine as a Class C drug 10 years earlier, it had inspired a range of ingenious methods of smuggling pink ContacNT granules from China into New Zealand. One of the most creative was to disguise them as the icing in biscuits.

In 2009, an investigation by the *New Zealand Herald* exposed the extent of the black market in methamphetamine, and the misery it caused. Prime Minister John Key, who had been in power for less than 12 months, took action.

The change that captured the most headlines was a complete ban on over-the-counter sales of pseudoephedrine-based cold remedies. Pseudoephedrine – and ephedrine, another meth precursor drug with a similar chemical structure – were now Class B controlled drugs, and carried a maximum 14-year prison sentence. Anyone with a cold has been cursing druggies ever since.

On the surface of things, the changes worked. From a record of 1.2 tonnes of pseudoephedrine seized in 2009, just 300 kilograms were stopped at the border four years later, in 2013. A press release from Customs Minister Maurice Williamson crowed about the success as a 'direct result of border activity'. The message was clear: Customs was finding less pseudoephedrine, because there was less to find.

But the data was interpreted differently in a 2013 report to the Prime Minister, who set up a cross-agency team within his office to tackle the methamphetamine crisis. Key's officials had a stark warning: 'The ongoing decline in the quantity of precursors seized is likely to be a reflection of a change of modus operandi by the syndicates involved, rather than an indication of reduced quantities entering New Zealand.'

Just as that troubling report landed on Key's desk in the Beehive, Joe Arama discovered the hard truth with his own eyes.

* * *

Auckland was awash with pink. This wasn't a few packets of ContacNT coming through the mail centre at Auckland International Airport, sent to the home addresses of expendable pawns. Pseudoephedrine had far outstripped methamphetamine as the number-one drug being smuggled into New Zealand.

This noticeable sea change in criminal trends was driven by strategy. For the Asian importers, the risk was lower: the potential prison time for pseudo was far less than the life sentences on offer for importing meth. And the financial rewards were just as good. The distribution of pink was now clearly being carried out on a commercial scale, even greater than the glory days of Operation Major, and no one knew how such large shipments were slipping through the border unnoticed. Behind it all was a cabal of Asian organised-crime figures who loved nothing more than to gamble mind-blowing sums at SkyCity's high-roller lounge.

Lim was a member of the VIP lounge, and enjoyed gambling on the baccarat tables, sometimes borrowing heavily if he was short of cash. He frequently invited his new friend Arama to join him in the lounge as a guest.

When he could risk it, Arama wore a concealed wire to record his conversations with Lim and others he met. Wineglass in hand, or puffing a cigarette on the lounge deck with its views of the Waitemata Harbour, Lim pointed out who was smuggling white, and who was selling pink.

'She's the biggest one here,' Lim said quietly one day in April 2013, identifying a Chinese woman who had parked her white Porsche Cayenne underneath the casino. 'Biggest gambler and also the largest … She's the boss. No one know, no one know it.'

The woman lived in a two-storey McMansion in east Auckland. She often gambled with a younger woman, an unassuming mother-of-three who was another 'boss', according to Lim.

Around the room he went, pointing out this person and that: literally a round-table of criminal figures drinking and smoking together, rubbing shoulders and making deals, all while betting tens of thousands of dollars at a time.

But it was Arama who had hit the jackpot. He had uncovered a treasure trove of intelligence that offered many targets for investigation. Almost too many, for the limited resources at Bruce Good's disposal.

It must have been tempting to score an easy win, and engineer a sting operation in which Lim arranged a deal between Arama and a big dealer. The evidence would be rock-solid, the case open-and-shut.

But instead of getting a quick run on the board, Good decided to take a risk. They'd target not just one dealer, but all of them – as far as they could go, for as long as possible.

Joe Arama had opened the door, just a crack, to a network of high-ranking crooks. For years most of them had been known to the drug squads in Harlech House only as shadowy characters. In many cases the cop didn't even know these figures existed. Or if they did, it was often only by their unusual nickname like the 'Four-Eyed Dragon', who was eventually unmasked in Operation Manu. The opportunity that Arama's undercover work presented was too good for the detectives to play it safe. Who knew how long the opportunity would last? Anything could go wrong and then the door would once more be shut tight.

In May 2013, Taskforce Ghost was split among the teams of Detective Sergeants Colin Parmenter, John Sowter and Mike Beal, with Detective Inspector Bruce Good keeping abreast of the different strands of the case. The plan was to use Joe Arama's relationship with Lim to climb up the ladder, one rung at a time.

First things first. Arama had to keep Lim close, and build more of a rapport with him and the others he was mixing and mingling with in the VIP room.

Sometimes the topic of conversation came very close to the bone. Lim once talked about the investigative techniques of the police in New Zealand, who were not easily corrupted like overseas.

Without missing a beat, Arama told him that New Zealand was a small place. Lim should be cautious, Arama warned: *anyone* could be an undercover officer.

Ironically, Lim and his friend 'Baldy Mark' – real name Hoo See Meng – advised Arama to be 'suspicious of Asians', alluding to police informants who snitched on one another. Arama soon saw that Baldy Mark was the next rung on the ladder.

On 8 May 2013, Arama phoned Lim to ask about 'pink stuff'. He only wanted five sets, which sold for between $8000 and $10,000 each on the black market. But Lim's contact normally supplied no fewer than 10 sets at a time to strangers.

Why ask for less? Quite simply because the cops couldn't afford to pay drug dealers nearly $100,000. Their budget only stretched so far. Even handing over close to $50,000 of taxpayers' dollars was enough to create angst among the risk-averse executives at Police National Headquarters, whose approval was needed to sign off the deal.

After hanging up on Arama, Lim got straight on the phone to Baldy Mark. He said someone wanted 'half a dozen red wine'. A painter living in Ellerslie, and blissfully unaware the police were now listening to his phone calls, Hoo – Baldy Mark – rang someone else. Lim and Hoo were the first of about 40 individuals whose phone conversations were intercepted in the sprawling Taskforce Ghost investigation. 'Felix is taking five friends to yum cha,' Hoo said to Van Thanh 'Peter' Tran, who gave his blessing to the deal.

A refugee who'd left Vietnam for New Zealand in the early 1990s, Tran was a tiler by trade but had been receiving unemployment benefits for nearly 20 years. Not that anyone in SkyCity's VIP lounge would have guessed. Known as 'Ah Ching', a Chinese term for brother, Tran was a prolific gambler and loan shark, lending up to $300,000 at a time to others down on their luck. With hefty interest rates, of course.

He spent $15 million in just 16 months at the casino, between April 2012 and July 2013, as well as banking $2.5 million in gaming chips, cheques and cash in his VIP account. His gambling churn – the total of wins and losses combined – added up to $67 million. He once lost $800,000 in a single week. It was clear to the Taskforce Ghost team that the 47-year-old unemployed tiler from Botany was sitting near the top rung of the Asian organised crime ladder.

A deal was struck. Arama agreed to pay $46,500 for five sets of ContacNT. Lim drove him to Baldy Mark's home in Ellerslie, where the cash and drugs were exchanged.

The police started listening to Tran's phones and watching him, learning more and more about his drug-dealing empire. He sold in bulk to wholesalers with their own distribution networks. They included Chuck Lou Tarm, who owned a fish and chip shop in Howick, and 'Alex' Zhi Tong Li, a chubby student with a floppy haircut.

Peter Tran himself kept his hands clean. Lieutenants like the Ma brothers, Ziyang and Zigeng, were at his beck and call. It was they who visited the safehouses dotted around Auckland and delivered packages to buyers.

Baldy Mark believed there was a 500-kilo stockpile of pseudoephedrine hidden somewhere, according to one bugged conversation. It was a staggering amount that dwarfed anything the drug squad veterans had ever seen, or even imagined to be possible. If such a cache did exist, though, it was never found.

Over a few short months, intercepted phone calls and physical surveillance helped police piece together a picture of Tran's network. There was evidence to show Tran had supplied 213 sets of ContacNT, plus a bulk stash of 6 kilograms to one buyer. It added up to nearly 55 kilograms, for which he would have received around $2 million in cash.

Even if the operation had ended with the arrest of Tran and those buying from him, Taskforce Ghost would have been a huge success. But detectives still hadn't worked out how such huge shipments of pseudoephedrine were slipping through the border.

They'd seen this story play out before. Tran and everyone who worked for him could be locked up, but within weeks of Tran's arrest, someone else would step up to take his place.

They needed more time to find the puppet master pulling the strings.

And their patience would pay off.

* * *

Tran used 10 different burner phones to conduct his activities. It was meant to keep him one step ahead of detection, but somehow police managed to listen in to every conversation. Each time Tran changed phones, the new number would flash up on the phones of other targets under surveillance, resulting in a mad dash for another interception warrant for Tran.

One day they eavesdropped on a new name: 'Tall Man'. Instead of dishing out orders, Peter Tran was now taking them. Tall Man ran Tran.

Tall Man instructed Tran to meet him at the basketball courts on Chapel Road in Botany as soon as possible. Tran was to bring 'the key', as well as a vehicle for Tall Man.

A team of surveillance officers tailed Tran to the meeting place, where he waited alone in a blue Toyota van.

When Tall Man showed up, police were soon able to identify him as Shao Da Wen. Words were exchanged between Shao and Tran, then Shao drove off in the Toyota. He headed towards Auckland International Airport. Surveillance officers continued to follow him as he stopped outside the Countdown supermarket near the domestic terminal.

A black Audi Q7 SUV pulled up alongside Shao's van. The driver was a woman in dark sunglasses: Yixin 'Lonna' Gan, the younger of the two female 'bosses' Lim had pointed out to Joe Arama in the casino. Police knew only that Gan ran a legitimate business, shipping food from China to a supermarket in Tonga, with a short stop in New Zealand.

She spoke with Tall Man for a few minutes, then drove her Audi to the McDonald's restaurant around the corner. She was covertly photographed inside with Mosese Uele, a Tongan man who ran a freight-forwarding company, Ezi World Cargo.

At the end of the meeting, Gan drove back to the Countdown carpark to pick up Shao. They departed together in her Audi SUV. Uele strolled into view a short while later, then drove Shao's Toyota van straight into his Ezi World Cargo warehouse a few hundred metres away. This was the opportunity Mike Beal, who was running this phase of Taskforce Ghost, had been waiting for.

Expecting the van to be full of pseudoephedrine, police were granted a covert warrant to break into the warehouse in the middle of the night, and whisked the van away to a nearby Customs compound. Inside it they found 20 boxes, all sealed up with tape. Each was X-rayed and four of them were opened.

The X-rays revealed 50 silver packets marked as 'Cornstarch' inside each. A Narcotics Identification Kit test, an instantaneous drug test, showed that the supposed cornstarch was in fact ... cornstarch.

Disappointed, deflated and not a little puzzled, Beal's team carefully repacked the boxes into the van and transported it back to Ezi World Cargo.

The puzzle was solved over the next 48 hours, as the detectives listened to Gan bark orders to Uele over the phone.

The pair had conceived a sleight of hand as effective as any magic trick. They had exposed a loophole in New Zealand's border control that was big enough to drive a shipping container through.

On 4 October 2013, Gan's consignment of 270 cartons, weighing 2539 kilograms, had arrived on the *Cap Campbell*, which had docked in the Ports of Auckland. But because the shipment was 'goods in transit' destined for Tonga – and therefore technically not coming through the New Zealand border – the cartons were not inspected by Customs.

Instead, the goods were taken by truck to Ezi Cargo World, inside the secure Customs-controlled area at Auckland International Airport.

Mosese Uele was Gan's inside man. Under cover of darkness, Uele swapped the Toyota van's dummy consignment of genuine cornstarch with the 'goods in transit' boxes of cornstarch, which actually held smuggled pseudoephedrine. The legitimate boxes of cornstarch were the same weight as the dummy boxes, so nothing appeared to be amiss. Meanwhile, hundreds of kilograms of pseudoephedrine were trundled into Auckland in the back of a van with no one the wiser.

Once Uele confirmed that the swap was complete, Gan gave the final orders to move. Uele abandoned the Toyota in a carpark in Onehunga, from where Tran – on the orders of Shao – drove it to a residential home on Medvale Street in Flat Bush. He reversed it into the garage and closed the door.

Over the next 48 hours, there was a flurry of phone calls, car swapping and face-to-face meetings in open spaces such as the Botany basketball courts. Beal's surveillance team were run off their feet trying to keep up. They watched as Shao backed his black Toyota Prado into the garage beside the blue van, then drove the Prado to another residential home in Addison Street, Blockhouse Bay.

Not for the first time since Taskforce Ghost had begun, Bruce Good had a tough decision to make. His teams weren't ready. Terminating a job of this size requires days, if not weeks, of planning. And they were still listening to the phones of around 40 people.

Move too quickly and months of work could be jeopardised. Move too slowly, and boxes and boxes of pseudoephedrine would be used to manufacture a drug that was wreaking havoc on New Zealand society. Vast amounts of meth would end up on the street.

In the end, Good and his team spent two weeks furiously planning before they moved on the safehouses. Inside the Medvale Street garage and a wardrobe in Addison Street were more than 250 kilograms of ContacNT: by far the biggest single amount ever seized in New Zealand.

It was an eye-opener for detectives. They knew there was plenty of pink around, but this was on another level. They were looking at $10 million worth of pseudoephedrine stacked in a garage and a wardrobe in suburban Auckland (if it had sold at the usual price of $8500 a set).

But to keep up the appearance that the raids had been the result of a random tipoff, the police arrested just the two men linked to the safehouses, the sole occupants of each address. The high-level targets – Gan, Tran and Shao – were left to roam free in order for Taskforce Ghost to gather more evidence. Shao and Gan were even allowed to leave the country.

The decision to let them fly out was risky, but also carefully considered. Their trips were obviously planned in advance, rather than some kind of hasty flight. Arresting them at the departure lounge at Auckland International Airport could jeopardise the rest of the investigation.

Besides, even if they failed to return, police were confident of tracking them down. Bruce Good had built a strong relationship with the senior New Zealand Police liaison officer in Beijing, Superintendent Hamish McCardle, a fluent Mandarin speaker who had forged close ties with Chinese law enforcement.

In fact, China was exactly where Lonna Gan and Shao Da Wen were when Good decided on 4 December 2013 that time was up on Taskforce Ghost.

No one could remember a bigger termination in the history of Harlech House. About 250 police officers waved search warrants across dozens of addresses right across Auckland.

Close to 40 people ended up in handcuffs, although none of them were really talking – except for Mosese Uele.

In a recorded interview at Harlech House, Uele denied knowing what was truly inside the boxes of cornstarch. 'It wasn't my business. My role was to swap boxes and get money. That was my only concern,' Uele said. The money 'was too great ... [I was] too greedy'.

The price to wilfully turn a blind eye? $60,000 in a brown envelope.

Shao returned from China 'voluntarily'. Technically he was an illegal immigrant in the country of his birth, as he had relinquished his Chinese passport when he became a New Zealand citizen. When contacted by New Zealand Police, the Chinese authorities deported him.

Yixin Gan didn't have to return to New Zealand to face the music. She came back for her three children – and had an arrogant belief she would beat the serious charges.

Confronted with the overwhelming evidence, Uele would throw himself on the mercy of the High Court, as would Shao and Tran, when the trio pleaded guilty to their part in the record 250-kilo importation.

In July 2015, Tran would be sentenced to 13 years and eight months in prison, after receiving a generous discount for the early guilty plea. He even tried to blame his dealing on his gambling addiction in a bid to get an even lighter sentence.

Justice Geoffrey Venning described methamphetamine as a 'blight on our community' and said Tran supplied millions of dollars' worth of the key ingredient needed to cook it. 'You took a business risk that you might be caught. And you have been.'

On 14 October 2016, three years to the day after the 250-kilogram shipment of ContacNT slipped into New

Zealand, the 'puppet master' of the smuggling loophole would be sent to jail.

Justice Mathew Downs left the court in no doubt as to who he thought was sitting at the very top of the ladder. 'Intelligent, worldly, even shrewd' was the way he described Gan. Those adjectives weren't compliments. The judge said Gan had received the 'super profits' while leaving the dirty work of distribution to the likes of Tran.

'The Crown contended to the jury this was "a near-perfect scam". There was no overstatement in that language; you were caught only by chance,' Justice Downs told Gan. 'I am sure, which is shorthand for satisfied beyond reasonable doubt, you were the primary architect – at least in New Zealand – of the October 2013 importation.'

With those words, Gan was sentenced to 14 years in prison. She was found guilty of two counts of importing a Class B drug, although acquitted on a third.

She also forfeited assets worth $3 million to the Crown, including the late-model Audi she was driving when police surveillance first spotted her. She had put $15 million across SkyCity's tables in a 15-month period, with a gambling turnover of $67 million during that time, as well as depositing millions of dollars into her casino account. There were also $7 million worth of cash deposits into multiple bank accounts that Gan could not explain to the satisfaction of the High Court jury.

* * *

While all this was unfolding, Felix Lim was leading a second drug squad in a completely different direction: lunch.

Lim was bugged by police booking a table at a popular Chinese restaurant in downtown Auckland (which cannot be identified because of a permanent suppression order). He was friends with the owner, Zhang Hui, another familiar face in the SkyCity VIP lounge.

Detective Sergeant Colin Parmenter, a genial Englishman who had joined the police after emigrating to New Zealand in 1997, was in charge of this phase of Taskforce Ghost. Known as Operation Gem, it led to the back door of Zhang Hui's popular yum cha destination. As well as monitoring telephone calls to the restaurant, detectives placed a hidden camera across the street to capture drug deals taking place in the carpark.

One day they gathered surveillance photographs of Lulu Zhang, Zhang Hui's girlfriend, passing a bag containing newspaper-wrapped parcels through the window of a silver Lexus sedan. The driver was Chen Guo Pei, or 'Ah Pei', a loan shark at the casino until he was exposed by a Television New Zealand investigation.

Banned from the casino, Ah Pei had moved on to become a mid-level pseudoephedrine supplier. He was one of Zhang Hui's best customers. Police often heard him calling the restaurant to book a table for lunch or dinner.

There was a rudimentary code. If Chen asked to reserve a table for 12 people at the restaurant, he was actually asking for 12 sets of pseudoephedrine. Lulu Zhang would then ask the restaurant's 'delivery man', Ma Ziyang, for $1200 – another code for 12 sets. This was the same Ma Ziyang who ran drugs for Peter Tran, along with his brother Zigeng. Clearly there was plenty of business to go round.

Ma Ziyang would collect the pseudo from a safehouse in Botany Downs, and deliver it to the restaurant. Lulu Zhang would then hand the pseudoephedrine parcel, disguised as a takeaway meal wrapped in newspaper, to Chen Guo Pei or another customer in the carpark at the rear of the yum cha diner.

As if the covert photographs and bugged telephone conversations of the operation weren't damning enough, Parmenter's team also convinced Zhang Hui's ex-girlfriend to give evidence against him.

Why did she agree to become a snitch? Everyone is familiar with the timeless truth of English playwright William Congreve's 1697 verse: 'Heav'n has no Rage, like Love to Hatred turn'd, Nor Hell a Fury, like a Woman scorn'd.'

Let's start with the scorn. Zhang's ex – let's call her Penny; her real name is suppressed by a court order – first met Zhang Hui at the casino shortly before he went into the restaurant business in 2012. She helped get the legitimate business up and running. The pair also began a romance. Zhang was a kind and gentle partner, and good to Penny's two boys from her previous relationship.

Just two weeks into their relationship, Zhang asked if Penny knew the true nature of his business.

When he confided that he was actually selling ContacNT, his girlfriend was confused. 'I thought he might have been selling Contact Energy shares or something,' Penny later told detectives.

Zhang went on to explain that he was a friend of Zhi Wei Yang, whom Penny vaguely knew from the casino. Zhi's nickname was 'Pull Uncle', an apparent reference to how he played baccarat. Pull Uncle was one of the biggest pseudoephedrine dealers in town.

Zhang had the idea that Penny and Pull Uncle were good friends; as such, he reasoned that she'd be aware of his reputation, and would accept his secret life. In actual fact, she was hopelessly naïve.

It wasn't long before Penny noticed Zhang would frequently take phone calls at the restaurant, then disappear for an hour or so without explanation. Slowly, he started to confide in her about the ContacNT business. Deals were done in the restaurant office, to which she simply turned a blind eye. Over time, she would count cash for Zhang – bundles of $50,000 to $100,000 – or hand over newspaper-wrapped parcels to customers when he was away.

The most reliable customer was 'Uncle' Paul, a thin man in his early 60s with hard eyes.

Real name: Paul Szeto, none other than our old friend from Chapter 4, who just a few years earlier had escaped convictions on money-laundering and methamphetamine charges while standing beside Max Beckham in the dock.

Every night, Zhang Hui would go to Szeto's place on Wellesley Street in the Auckland CBD and stay there until the small hours of the morning. The older man was the only customer Zhang trusted enough not to ask for cash upfront for pink. The pair would play mahjong and smoke cigarettes until Szeto's couriers returned with cash from his own deals.

Mahjong bored Penny. On the few occasions she joined them in 'the office', as Zhang and Szeto called Szeto's place, she felt sick from the thick cigarette smoke hanging in the air.

Once, when Penny quizzed her partner about whether ContacNT was legal, Zhang started to justify his criminal behaviour by saying he had been working three jobs before he started dealing, and still had no money. With an ex-wife and children to support, elderly parents in China to take care of, as well as business expenses, Zhang had been drowning in debt.

It was Paul Szeto who had shown him 'another way' in 2010, with pseudoephedrine. Zhang promised Penny he would stop once the restaurant was profitable. But he didn't stop, even when the mahjong 'office' closed down in 2012 as Szeto's health deteriorated. There were plenty of other customers, such as Felix Lim, who were quick to call the restaurant for business.

The pressure got to Penny. She was running the genuine yum cha business, as well as dealing with the pink customers. Stressed out, she also suspected Zhang of cheating on her.

Penny's hunch was right. Her role in Zhang's life – lover, restaurant manager and drug-deal pawn – was being taken over by Lulu Zhang. She was the one later caught on the Operation Gem camera in the alley behind the restaurant.

Penny was caught too, arrested alongside her lover Zhang Hui and his mistress in December 2013. The 43-year-old Penny eventually admitted one charge of supplying pseudoephedrine and was sentenced to two years seven months in prison, a lenient lag given she passed on 115 'sets', or 25 kilograms of ContacNT, over six months. Her prison time was cut by 50 per cent because of her early guilty plea and 'assistance' given to the police. The opportunity to twist the knife in the back of Zhang Hui *and* spend less time in prison was too good a deal to pass up.

Penny signed her 61-page statement to police in June 2014, just a few weeks after Paul Szeto passed away in Auckland Hospital aged 62. One of the godfathers of the Asian underworld was no more.

Penny's insider account of Zhang Hui's drug business was important evidence for the Operation Gem prosecution case, independently corroborating what Colin Parmenter's team had gleaned from the covert surveillance.

A trail of breadcrumbs, however, was literally the clue that solved the puzzle of how Zhang had smuggled pseudoephedrine into the country undetected for so long.

When Taskforce Ghost terminated, bringing the two intertwined pseudoephedrine empires to an end on the same day, police raided Zhang Hui's safehouse on Aviemore Drive,

Botany Downs. Inside a locked metal box, haphazardly dumped in a hallway cupboard, were 47 sets of ContacNT – worth around $400,000 – wrapped in newspaper. Scattered among the drugs were opened plastic packets of Chinese 'chicken breader', or breadcrumbs used to coat fried chicken.

After combing through shipping documents, detectives concluded that 153 kilograms of chicken breader bags delivered to Zhang's restaurant a few months earlier, in May, had in fact included bags filled with pseudoephedrine.

Then, with a growing sense of excitement, Colin Parmenter realised Zhang's next shipment was already on the water heading to New Zealand. On 28 November 2013, a container listed as holding 'seasoner' and cooking utensils had been loaded onto the *MOL Delight* at the port of Guangzhou, China.

The address for delivery? Zhang Hui's restaurant in the heart of Auckland.

A little more than a week after the 4 December 2013 raids on the safehouse, the *MOL Delight* docked at the Ports of Auckland. Investigators from Customs and Taskforce Ghost were waiting. They singled out a certain container for inspection and unpacked all the cardboard boxes. Inside 10 of them were 160 packets of Chinese chicken breadcrumbs, identical to those discovered at the Aviemore Drive safehouse.

Well, the bags were *labelled* as breadcrumbs. But when the plastic wrappers were cut open, 150 packets held the very familiar sight of pink ContactNT granules. The remaining 10 parcels held a whitish powder, which testing revealed to be ephedrine. This ingredient removed one step in the meth manufacturing process, as cooks didn't need to chemically extract the ephedrine from the pseudoephedrine.

All told, police had found another 250 kilograms of critical meth ingredients linked to Zhang Hui. Just like with

Lonna Gan, the inquiry team had traced Zhang's network from Felix Lim backwards, all the way to the importation.

* * *

'[It was] a massive seabound shipment that Zhang needed to breathe life into his business,' Crown prosecutor Bruce Northwood would tell the jury in the resulting trial, held in the Auckland High Court between June and August 2015.

The evidence was overwhelming. Zhang, 44, was convicted of importing an epic 403 kilograms of ContactNT in two shipments: a record amount, and enough to cook an estimated $116 million of methamphetamine. He also pleaded guilty to 33 counts of supplying pseudo. He received a jail sentence of 20 years, the longest ever for Class B drug offences.

While the maximum penalty for a single Class B drug importation is 14 years, Justice Kit Toogood believed Zhang's offending was so serious it was worthy of a longer prison term. He ruled that Zhang's sentence for the ongoing supply of pseudoephedrine should be served *on top* of the 14 years, instead of *concurrently*, which often happens in less serious cases.

'That is a long sentence for pseudoephedrine dealing; it is at a level which exceeds many sentences for dealing in methamphetamine for which the maximum penalty is life imprisonment,' said Justice Toogood. 'But the massive scale of your offending has no precedent.'

* * *

As well as taking out the key players behind the pseudoephedrine trade, Taskforce Ghost went after any of their assets funded with dirty money. Again, SkyCity's VIP lounge was front and centre of the investigation.

At least a dozen of the most prolific pink dealers in town were either members of the exclusive high-roller club, or frequent guests there. While they weren't physically dealing drugs from the casino, like those arrested seven years earlier in Operations Manu and Ice Age, their illegal trade was obviously funding their gambling. Eye-watering sums in the tens of millions of dollars passed back and forth over the tables, just between individuals.

If someone managed to slip the net and avoid arrest, or there was not enough evidence to press charges, the police had a powerful new tool to hold people to account: the *Criminal Proceeds (Recovery) Act* 2009. It enabled them to target the assets of nearly everyone charged in Taskforce Ghost.

And in one case, someone who was not even in the country.

Pull Uncle, or Zhi Wei Yang, had flown out of New Zealand before the police raids in December 2013. He had gambled $14 million at SkyCity in less than two years. Over the same period, he had declared just $4217 of income to the Inland Revenue Department. Together with his partner, who was receiving unemployment benefits, Yang owned three mortgage-free homes in Auckland and had nearly $700,000 in the bank.

They lost the lot – nearly $4.5 million of assets – after Justice Edwin Wylie determined that Pull Uncle was a 'substantial wholesaler' of pseudoephedrine and that the assets were criminal profits.

All told, Taskforce Ghost pulled in a $20 million haul of cash, property, expensive cars, jewellery and bank funds. By any calculations this was a pretty good return for Joe Arama's $46,500 drug money investment.

* * *

William 'Bird' Hines, a senior member of the Head Hunters motorcycle gang, at his High Court trial on methamphetamine charges in 2002. *Glenn Jeffrey/New Zealand Herald*

Detective Inspector Bruce Good with the 95 kilograms of methamphetamine, plus firearms and ammunition seized in Operation Major in 2006. It was the largest haul of the Class A drug at the time. *Paul Estcourt/New Zealand Herald*

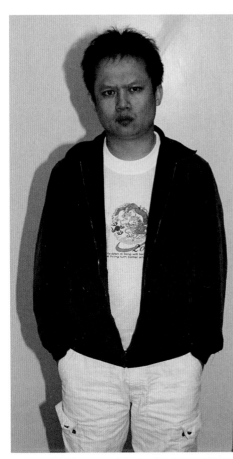

Left: Zhou Ri Tong, known as the Four Eyed Dragon, was the primary target of Operation Manu as a large-scale methamphetamine dealer. *New Zealand Police*

Below: Zhou Ri Tong (seated at pokie machine) and Tac Kin Voong (wearing jacket, walking towards camera) headed rival drug dealing syndicates from inside the VIP lounge at SkyCity Casino. *New Zealand Police*

Above: Arthur Taylor defended himself at the High Court trial on methamphetamine charges laid in Operation Web. *Paul Estcourt / New Zealand Herald*

Left: Ulaiasi 'Rocky' Pulete, a senior member of the King Cobras, was one of the inmates at Paremoremo Prison charged in Operation Web. *Dean Purcell / New Zealand Herald*

Detective Senior Sergeant Greg Turner speaks at a press conference about the disappearance of Grant Trevor Adams, known as 'Granite'. *Alan Gibson/New Zealand Herald*

Paul Szeto, a sickness beneficiary, lived in a state home with two Mercedes-Benz and a Porsche parked outside. He was acquitted of money laundering charges in Operation Jivaro. *Greg Bowker/New Zealand Herald*

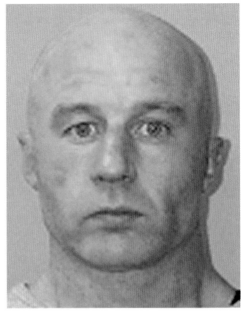

Max Beckham outside the High Court in Auckland during his trial on drugs and money laundering charges in 2011.
Brett Phibbs/New Zealand Herald

Police mugshot of David Gerrard O'Carroll, senior Head Hunter gang member.
New Zealand Police

Talented methamphetamine cook and patched Head Hunter Michael Cavanagh. *New Zealand Police*

The secret entrance to an underground bunker in David O'Carroll's home where police found a cache of firearms. *New Zealand Police*

The Ferrari 360 Modena owned by Michael Cavanagh which drew police attention in Operation Genoa. *New Zealand Police*

Millions of dollars and firearms found by detectives in Operation Genoa. *Richard Robinson/ New Zealand Herald*

The mobile methamphetamine lab hidden inside a trailer seized by detectives in Operation Genoa. *New Zealand Police*

Felix Lim was the initial target of an undercover police agent which led police to uncover a sprawling pseudoephedrine distribution network in Taskforce Ghost. *New Zealand Police*

Hundreds of kilograms of ContacNT seized in Taskforce Ghost laid out at a police press conference at Harlech House in December 2013. *Richard Robinson/New Zealand Herald*

A meeting at a McDonald's restaurant between Yixin Gan, left, and Mosese Uele caught on camera by a surveillance team in Taskforce Ghost. *New Zealand Police*

Hui Zhang was importing hundreds of kilograms of pseudoephedrine to his restaurant in downtown Auckland. The drugs were disguised as takeaway meals and exchanged in the carpark out the back. *New Zealand Police*

Van Thanh Tran, left, and Shao Da Wen caught by surveillance teams in Taskforce Ghost. *New Zealand Police*

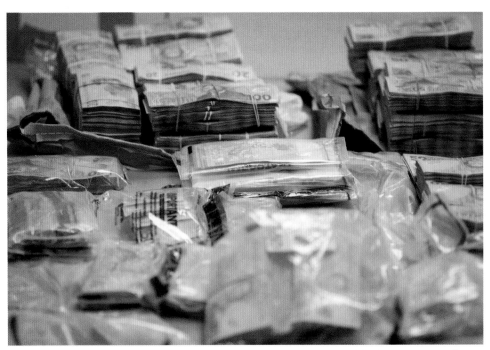

Some of the $3.5 million seized in cash in Taskforce Ghost. Many of the key targets in the covert investigation also gambled millions of dollars at SkyCity casino. *Richard Robinson/ New Zealand Herald*

The Head Hunters are one of the more influential motorcycle gangs in New Zealand, with a reputation for violence. *Alan Gibson/New Zealand Herald*

William 'Bird' Hines, left, meeting with pseudoephedrine supplier Jia Sun at a Nandos restaurant. *New Zealand Police*

The three bedroom house in Waiotira kept under surveillance in Operation Easter. High Court Justice Simon Moore later described the property as a methamphetamine factory. *New Zealand Police*

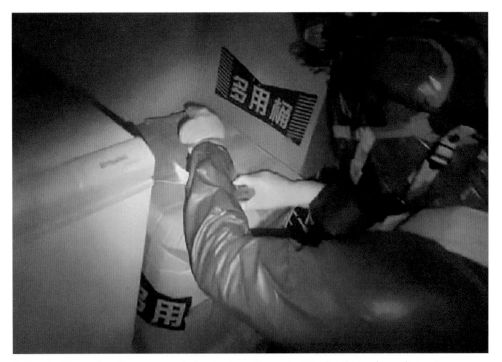

Police in Operation Easter secretly broke into Brownie Harding's methamphetamine laboratory to film evidence and hide a recording device to covertly listen in to the meth cooks' conversations. *New Zealand Police*

Head Hunters president Wayne Doyle (in grey t-shirt) talking to police officers. No charges were laid but $6 million worth of assets linked to Doyle were restrained under the Criminal Proceeds Recovery Act. *New Zealand Herald*

The abandoned boat on 90 Mile Beach that led to the record-breaking methamphetamine haul of 501 kilograms in June 2016. *Northland Age/New Zealand Herald*

Above: The record-breaking 501 kilograms of methamphetamine pulled out of a campervan. An off-duty police officer just happened to see the wanted vehicle while driving home. *New Zealand Police*

Left: Selaima Fakaosilea at the High Court at Whangarei. She was sentenced to a total of 27 years for methamphetamine offences uncovered in Operation Virunga. *Mike Scott / New Zealand Herald*

The Comanchero patch found in the home of Viliami Taani. He was convicted of the murder of Abraham Tu'uheava and sentenced to life imprisonment. *New Zealand Police*

A torch shines from the stern of the *Maersk Antares*, a 337 metre container ship docked at the Port of Tauranga. The light was a signal to collect 46 kilograms of cocaine hidden aboard the vessel. *New Zealand Police*

Former soldier Mario Habulin, a Croatian national, received a 27 years and 6 months sentence for importing at least 76 kilograms of cocaine into New Zealand. The sentence was the longest ever for cocaine offences. *Andrew Warner/Bay of Plenty Times*

Patched Tribesmen MC member Akustino Tae at his first appearance in the Manukau District Court after shooting Josh Masters, the Killer Beez president, in April 2019. *Doug Sherring/New Zealand Herald*

Josh Masters at his first appearance in the Manukau District Court on methamphetamine and money laundering charges laid in May 2008. He was later sentenced to 10 years and 5 months' imprisonment. *Greg Bowker/New Zealand Herald*

Comanchero MC vice president Tyson Daniels, left, and treasurer Jarome Fonua were among the senior members of the gang hierarchy arrested in Operation Nova. *New Zealand Police*

Senior Waikato Mongrel Mob members Dwight Fatu, left, and his son Sonny Fatu Jnr seen here with Comanchero president Pasilika Naufahu, centre, 'patched over' to the Australian gang. *New Zealand Police*

One of two gold-plated Harley Davidson motorcycles seized from the Comancheros in April 2020. *New Zealand Police*

Tyson Daniels, wearing a Versace top in Comanchero colours of black and gold, and Auckland lawyer Andrew Simpson (right) in the High Court at Auckland in February 2020. The pair pleaded guilty to money laundering. *Michael Craig/New Zealand Herald*

But here was one loose end. Whatever happened to Felix Lim? He was the guy who started it all; he was the thread whom Joe Arama pulled, eventually unravelling a multi-million-dollar drug empire run out of the casino and a yum cha restaurant.

His name would crop up regularly in each trial, but the irony is that Lim would never stand in the dock with the others.

He left the country three months before the termination of Ghost in December 2013 and never came back.

And he says he'll never return. I heard this from the horse's mouth.

Following my investigative feature on Taskforce Ghost in the *New Zealand Herald*, Lim phoned me from Malaysia. He adamantly denied being a willing, or paid, police informant. This claim was corroborated by court records.

It was a coincidence that he was overseas when his friends and gambling buddies were arrested, he said. 'It was my first holiday in twenty years.' He had had no idea that Joe Arama was a police officer, and claimed to have no involvement in drugs.

'I wasn't directly involved, I just introduced people. Someone called to say "Felix, the guy you introduced was an undercover" ... I was so bloody angry, I didn't know what to do.'

Given that more than 30 people arrested by Taskforce Ghost have gone to jail for a long time, Lim has sworn never to return to New Zealand out of fear for his life. 'Everyone blames me,' he said.

Well, not everyone. The police will always be grateful for his unwitting assistance.

7

OUT WITH THE OLD: THE TWILIGHT OF THE HEAD HUNTERS

2014

NO ONE LIVED IN the house, but the lawn was mowed once a week. The only person on the property was the caretaker. Passers-by would see him pottering around outside, keeping the grounds tidy.

Monday to Friday, loud cars would come and go from the three-bedroom house in Waiotira, a tiny community about 30 kilometres southwest of Whangarei. No one ever visited on the weekends.

It was an unremarkable brick-and-tile bungalow like any other in small-town New Zealand, nothing that would catch the eye of anyone who saw it. Only those who knew what they were looking at, like Detective Sergeant Andy Dunhill, would have noticed that the thick liquid the caretaker was pouring on the garden was the chemical waste left behind from cooking meth. The highly toxic sludge is a terrific weed killer.

If anyone had cared to stop and peer through the windows, perhaps via a crack in the curtains, they wouldn't have seen a stick of furniture inside. The entire house was stripped bare, right down to the wooden floorboards, so it could house the chemicals and lab equipment needed to manufacture massive amounts of methamphetamine, every single week.

For years, there had been rumours of a mythical clan lab somewhere in Northland, controlled by the East Chapter of the Head Hunters. Its senior members kept a safe distance hundreds of kilometres away, in the gang pad at 232 Marua Road, Ellerslie.

P had begun its life in New Zealand as a drug of choice for the white middle and upper classes. It was cool, its white lines a faster, more powerful form of speed.

But over the years since, meth had become a dirty word. The insane rage of P-freak Antonie Dixon, who chopped off the left hand of one of his two partners and partially severed both arms of the second when he was on a meth high in 2003, made him the poster boy for everything that was wrong with the drug. It messed you up, turned you into a monster.

But Dixon was an extreme case. For the most part, P was more of a private living hell for addicts. Impoverished urban areas and provincial townships, with high unemployment rates and social deprivation, were hit hardest, and none more so than Northland. There was so much meth swirling around Whangarei the locals would often say it was 'snowing'.

With members of the Head Hunters aggressively expanding and controlling the market, there was now an urgent need to find the rumoured Northland clan lab. Operation Easter started in July 2014, with Dunhill in charge, soon after the end of Operation Genoa, the previous operation targeting the Heads.

A former member of John Sowter's squad at Harlech House, Dunhill had spent years dealing with the Head Hunters and their ilk. Now leading his own team, Dunhill was keen to show that anything his old boss could do, he could do better.

The intelligence-gathering phase of Operation Easter led to the identification of Brownie Joseph Harding as the principal target. Swarthy and stocky, the 37-year-old had joined the Head Hunters' East Chapter 12 years earlier, and now had a crew of other patched members who answered to him. Browning had a sister who lived with her husband in Australia, but owned a brick bungalow on Taipuha Road in Waiotira, population 500 and counting. It was their father, Joseph Harding, who was later seen tipping out the toxic waste.

Everyone knows everyone in Waiotira, so surveillance of the property posed its own unique challenges. The detectives were careful in how they moved around in the community, as well as who they approached for help.

When the surveillance phase started in September 2014, a single motion-activated video camera was installed to scan part of Taipuha Road and the northern side of the house. But it was too far away to properly capture the faces of those coming and going. So a second camera, also motion-activated, was covertly placed much closer to the action. It covered the front driveway and the eastern face of the dwelling.

It recorded a strict routine. Nearly every day over the next three months, Head Hunter gang members and their hangers-on would arrive by car and enter the house around 7am. Then, around lunchtime, they'd emerge for short break, and go back inside until 6pm. It was one of the most professional meth clan labs Dunhill and other experienced drug detectives had ever seen.

As well as watching, the police were listening. While monitoring bugged phone conversations is standard practice in a covert investigation, Operation Easter was the first in New Zealand history in which an audio device was planted inside an active meth lab. The audacious feat was achieved by members of the Special Tactics Group, who broke into the house on the night of 17 October 2014 when no one was home. They took photos of the materials and equipment they found, as well as swabs in the kitchen that revealed high contamination readings consistent with manufacture.

Planting the audio bug inside the meth lab gave Dunhill and his team a crucial advantage: they were able to make calculations about how much of the drug was being cooked at any one time. A rough total became immediately apparent: a lot.

When the surveillance started in September, it was only Harding and one other who would cook. By the time the listening device was hidden inside the house the following month, at least four cooks were working at the same time on different stages of the extraction and distillation process, like a factory production line.

As for the working conditions, the worst of it was that everyone had to answer to a despot.

* * *

Head Hunter members cooking at Taipuha Road called Brownie Harding 'the Boss', according to the intercepted conversations. They were apologetic at times, and at others submissive, compliant, perhaps even scared.

The most telling example of Harding's total domination of his cooks emerged during the fifth manufacture observed by police, on 28 October 2014. Elijah Rogers and Jaydean Hura, two patched Head Hunters, arrived at the address shortly after 7am. By the evening, it was obvious they had experienced technical difficulties. The product was leaking from the lab apparatus.

The hapless pair called Harding at 9.30pm. He drove straight to the property. Incandescent with rage, he harangued them for their ineptitude and made it clear they would have to explain the loss 'down in Auckland'.

'You fullas have got no choice. I don't know what went wrong … but it's somewhere … You find it. It's somewhere,' Harding was recorded as saying.

His rave continued: 'I don't give a fuck if it's on the floor. Mop that shit up. Everything goes in there. I don't give a fuck if you have to fucken pull this floor up. You chuck it in there.'

At no point did either Hura or Rogers – hardened gangsters in their own right – attempt to contradict or challenge him. He was the Boss. Brownie Harding was in complete control of every step of production: sourcing pseudoephedrine; arranging the premises; finding the chemical reagents and equipment; organising the shifts of cooks, giving them instructions and advice on their techniques, as well as transport to and from the address; and delivery of the methamphetamine to Auckland.

Even when Harding was sentenced to home detention for an assault on his partner part-way through Operation Easter, he maintained an iron grip. He relied on his youngest son Evanda, just 17 at the time, to pass on orders while he was stuck at home in Whangarei with an electronically monitored ankle bracelet.

The teenager acted as his father's eyes and ears for a while. Later, he was promoted to right-hand man. When pseudoephedrine supplies were running low, dad dispatched son to Auckland to pick up 50 sets of ContacNT hidden in a bucket and courier them back to Northland.

Evanda was right in the thick of the family business now. Bad move. When Operation Easter terminated, Evanda would be caught with a massive haul of meth. Heading south in their father's Mercedes-Benz saloon, Evanda and his brother Tyson – each named after an American heavyweight boxing champion – were on their way to the gang's headquarters in Marua Road.

Tailing the brothers on State Highway 1, an unmarked police car put on its lights and sirens so the Mercedes-Benz would pull over, just north of the Auckland Harbour Bridge.

Sitting in the rear footwell on the passenger side was a black sports bag. Inside were 80 self-sealable bags of methamphetamine, each weighing an ounce. If sold for the going rate of $12,000 an ounce, the total of 2.2 kilograms would be worth nearly $1 million. The discovery meant Dunhill could prove 'beyond reasonable doubt' that the group was manufacturing methamphetamine.

After Evanda's arrest, Brownie Harding's crew hastily tried to clean up the meth lab at Taipuha Road and destroy all the evidence. But it was far too late for that. A month later, in December 2014, Harding and four other patched Head Hunters were arrested, along with six other gang associates. The raids came just a few weeks after $900,000 was discovered in senior member Dave O'Carroll's waterbed (as detailed in Chapter 5): a double whammy for the East Chapter of the Head Hunters.

Eventually, in a steady trickle of court appearances, everyone pleaded guilty to the serious charges. In the final sentencing hearing, Justice Simon Moore said that Brownie Harding had escaped the maximum of life imprisonment only by a 'fine margin'. The High Court judge was sure Harding had been in charge, and responsible for manufacturing 'at least' 6.5 kilograms of the Class A drug.

'To put it in perspective, it is the largest single case of manufacturing to have come before the Courts in New Zealand, and that is by a very substantial margin indeed,' said Justice Moore. 'Neither counsel nor I have found any other cases of methamphetamine manufacture which are even comparable in terms of quantity. That puts you in an unenviable league all of your own.'

Harding was sentenced to 28 and a half years, and would be required to serve at least 10 before being eligible for parole.

Having served as Auckland Crown Solicitor before his appointment to the judicial bench in 2014, Simon Moore had first-hand knowledge of the destruction wreaked on people's lives when meth first emerged in the city. 'To describe it as a scourge is an understatement. It captures those who use it, even if only for a short period, and inevitably leads them down a path of personal ruin,' Justice Moore told Harding at the April 2017 hearing.

'Otherwise decent people are robbed of their dignity and, eventually, their self-control. The frequent consequence is that those addicted resort to crime and violence to feed their ever-growing habits. Not only are they left dreadfully physically and psychologically damaged, but their cohort of family and friends are caught up in the maelstrom of their misery. The unadorned truth is that no part of our community is left untouched by the effects of this awful substance.'

The charges against Tyson Harding were dropped, although Evanda Harding received a nine-and-a-half-year sentence for obeying his father. Justice Moore noted that Harding senior was more concerned about himself than the fact he had put his own children in a terrible predicament. He was the undisputed ringleader of the 'factory', as Justice Moore deliberately called the laboratory.

The judge did acknowledge, though, that there was evidence Harding answered to someone above him in the Head Hunters hierarchy. There was no hint in the High Court as to who that might be. But there was a clue in the transcripts of calls intercepted by police.

* * *

On learning the police had arrested his sons, and seized 80 ounces of meth bound for 232 Marua Road, Harding had made a phone call. He dialled the gang pad's landline and asked to speak to Bird. He was told Bird happened to be out.

Everyone in the underworld knew William 'Bird' Hines. He sat at the very top of the Head Hunters hierarchy, alongside Wayne Doyle, the East Chapter president. He was revered by gang members as a godfather figure and, despite being in his 60s and riddled with health problems, was still feared in the criminal fraternity.

Bird was a hard man with a ruthless streak. He had a crew of young troops keen to prove their loyalty and obey his orders. No one in their right mind would cross Hines.

Since being targeted along with Waha Saifiti and Brett Allison in Operation Flower, then sentenced in 2003 to seven years in prison for his lead role in 'the Methamphetamine Makers Co Ltd', Hines had kept out of trouble. Like any senior criminal figure, he was often the source of rumours or pieces of intelligence from police informants, but these were never enough to prompt police to start an investigation. Bird was always just out of reach.

By the start of 2015, a few months after Operation Easter terminated, the intelligence unit at Harlech House had worked up a new profile on William Hines.

John Sowter put his hand up for the job. Sowts was well known among his drug squad peers for avoiding any investigation in which intercepted conversations needed to be translated from a foreign language. He'd leave those to Mike Beal. Sowter preferred to go after local gang members, and there weren't many bigger than Bird Hines.

Targeting the leaders of bikie gangs, or other criminal groups, is difficult. They're generally very savvy and aware of police investigative techniques, often because they, or their peers, have been caught before. To the dismay of most drug squad detectives, every time an investigation ends and the case goes to court, the *Criminal Disclosure Act* says they have to hand over the entire case file to the defendant's legal team. It's done to ensure a fair trial, so the accused knows exactly what evidence underpins the allegations against them.

But it also means that if the police have successfully tried a new and innovative tactic, every criminal worth his salt soon knows about it. Word travels fast in remand prisons.

Criminal figures of the ilk of Hines become disciplined in their tradecraft. They give orders to their underlings in person, not by phone. Members of the Head Hunters always met at their Marua Road headquarters, but bugging the pad, as police had bugged Brownie Harding's meth factory, was out of the question. Patched members, or prospects (gang apprentices who want to become full members), are rostered on guard duty; the pad is watched seven days a week, 24 hours a day. The Special Tactics Group are ninjas, but they're not ghosts; there's no way they're getting in there to plant a listening device.

Generally speaking, covert investigations will start from the bottom and work their way up. Discipline tends to slide down each level of the criminal syndicate. A minion might be sworn to secrecy, but they'll often let something slip. It's human nature.

Operation Sylvester sought to identify the group of individuals in Hines's orbit, then target the weakest link.

One step down from Hines was Te Here Maaka, 36, while beneath *him* in the pecking order was 37-year-old Travis Sadler. Both were patched Head Hunters. Also circling around Hines was Sadler's father, Thomas Edwardson. He was a prospect, not a patched member yet; it meant that Edwardson took orders from his son.

Surveillance teams were constantly following Bird as he left the Marua Road pad. On 10 April 2015, they tailed the 62-year-old to his favourite fast-food restaurant, Nando's, in nearby Panmure. With him were his pair of burly gangsters, Maaka and Sadler.

At Nando's the three met up with an unidentified Chinese man. Their 1.30pm lunch date provided Sowter with invaluable intelligence. There was likely to be only one reason why an old gangster like Hines was meeting face to face with a young man of Asian ethnicity: pseudoephedrine.

As we've seen in previous chapters, a Chinese pharmaceutical company produced ContacNT, a cold and flu remedy rich in pseudoephedrine, which is the active ingredient in meth. The unidentified man was Sun Jia, who had previous convictions for supplying the Class B controlled drug.

Having met Sun, Bird Hines sat back and let everyone else do the dirty work. He took no further part in the manufacturing process, but Operation Sylvester had found a weak link to exploit: Sun Jia.

Later, temporarily forgetting to use the criminals' code, Sun told Sadler over the phone he could get him '20 sets', the equivalent of 20,000 tablets of ContacNT: enough to cook around 1 kilo of methamphetamine. But Sun needed the money upfront. The price was $200,000.

Just a few hours later, in the late afternoon, CCTV footage captured Sadler meeting Sun in Newmarket and handing over a bag, presumably filled with cash. It wasn't long before Sadler wanted what he'd paid for.

Somewhat naïvely, Jia said he might not be able to provide same-day service. That wasn't good enough: Sadler reminded Sun who he was working for. 'It's for the missus, it's not for me,' he said, referring to Hines in code.

The message was clear. Finally, at 11.45pm, Sun gave Sadler the 20 sets of ContacNT: a total of 4.4 kilograms of the pink granules.

Over the next few days, cryptic and guarded conversations between Hines, Sadler, Maaka and Edwardson hinted at growing anticipation of a pending significant event. There had been unexpected delays too.

'He's still working on it,' Sadler assured Hines, who demanded a progress report. His patience was wearing thin.

'Fuck me. Days, man,' Hines told Sadler. 'Yeah how long? Another whole night and a whole day?'

Police were in the dark. But eight days after the pseudo-ephedrine sale, Operation Sylvester got the sort of lucky break that makes the difference between knowing someone is cooking drugs, and proving it. It also made the difference between success and failure.

* * *

With a wire tap on Te Here Maaka's phone, the police listened in as a call was made to a man called John Vijn. He was at an address in Glen Eden, which police suspected was a clan lab. It wasn't Maaka on the other end of the line, but a very familiar figure: Peter Francis Atkinson, or 'Pete the Terrorist'. Like Hines, Atkinson was a legendary figure in the underworld, who retired from robbing banks to become one of the first meth cooks in the country in the late 1990s.

Jailed for 10 years in 2000 for manufacturing with the leaders of rival gangs Highway 61 and the Filthy Few, Atkinson was now well past retirement age, at 72. But he showed no signs of slowing down, and was still regarded as a skilful cook.

On this occasion he had been hired by the Head Hunters, and Maaka was supervising the manufacturing. But something had gone wrong. Atkinson, using Maaka's phone, asked his friend Vijn to bring him 20 litres of the precursor ingredient toluene.

Vijn could get his hands on only 10 litres of 'tolly' on such short notice. Atkinson handed the phone back to a frustrated Maaka, who left him in no doubt that was unacceptable.

There was a flurry of phone calls back and forth, late into the evening. By now, Te Here Maaka had been joined at the Glen Eden address by his younger brother, the equally imposing Falco, who was also a patched Head Hunter.

You don't keep the Maaka brothers waiting. In the early hours of the following day, Vijn arrived with the equipment. Falco Maaka told him to snap his phone in half, but it was too late. Desperation to finish the cooking process meant their discipline was failing. Over the course of six hours or so, Operation Sylvester recorded as many incriminating conversations as they had over the past three months.

On the very same day, an attractive young woman hired a storage unit in Panmure. Two hours later, to the surprise of the manager who'd leased it to her, 'two scruffy Maori men' drove a black Toyota Hiace van inside and locked the garage door.

The woman, who worked for a real-estate firm, was friends with Travis Sadler and, to a lesser degree, Te Here Maaka. 'You don't want to know,' was the answer when she asked Maaka over the phone what was inside the van. When she pressed him, Maaka joked, 'A dead body', before reassuring her it was 'nothing dodgy'.

When Sowter's team broke into the van – which had extra locks on the doors and an internal cage for added security – they found 136 grams of meth packaged for sale in ounce bags and surrounded by rice to keep it dry. There were also 9 kilograms of iodine and 33 litres of hypophosphorous acid, both commonly used in the meth manufacturing process.

But wait, there's more. Police also found a large amount of ammunition and five high-powered firearms: a M1A Springfield semi-automatic rifle, a pair of Heckler and Koch military-style rifles, a Lapua tactical rifle, and a Smith and Wesson pistol wrapped in a blue bandanna – with traces of Bird Hines's DNA on the fabric.

It was enough firepower to start a war.

In Operation Genoa the previous year, Sowter had made a calculated gamble and decided against grabbing 800 grams of Shannon Stevens's meth, hoping to catch Dave O'Carroll. Not this time. The risk was too great.

The young real-estate agent was charged with possession of the drugs and guns. Her arrest prompted a flurry of guarded phone calls between Hines, Maaka, Sadler and Edwardson. Hines advised them to 'wait and see what happens'. Sowter was content to let them stew for a few weeks more.

In the meantime, Sadler had been sent to Mount Eden Prison on unrelated charges. He and his father comforted each other by saying there was no 'hard evidence' and any criminal charges 'won't stick'. In another intercepted conversation, Edwardson remarked how 'everything's been quiet', but raised concerns that their phones were being monitored. He said he could hear a clicking sound when his son picked up the phone. Sadler reassured his father he was clicking his pen in the background.

A week later, in July 2015, Operation Sylvester terminated with a raid on the Head Hunters' pad in Ellerslie and on a nearby panel-beating shop. Allister Vousden, the owner of Ellerslie Collision Repairs, was a friend of Hines's. A fleet of cars, as well as a $420,000 house in Papakura paid for in cash in September 2014, had been purchased in Vousden's name to disguise their true ownership.

In several bugged conversations captured a few months before the raids, Vousden had called Hines to ask permission to drive one of the classic vehicles home from work, where the cars were kept.

A Ford Thunderbird, a Ford Galaxie and a Dodge Challenger were among the 20 cars and motorcycles taken away on the back of a truck, confiscated along with Hines's Papakura house under the *Criminal Proceeds (Recovery) Act*. At the 2017 trial, Vousden was found not guilty of all the money-laundering charges he faced, but agreed to forfeit the tainted property taken under the criminal proceeds law. It was a concession, of sorts, that Vousden might not win the case on the lower civil standard of proof.

He was the only one to escape conviction. While John Vijn and Thomas Edwardson were found guilty on slightly less serious charges, everyone else – Te Here and Falco Maaka, Peter Atkinson and William Hines – was convicted of manufacturing at least 1 kilo of methamphetamine.

At the sentencing hearing in April 2017, Justice Mathew Downs made special mention of the 'sinister nature' of the firearms and drugs found inside the storage unit hired on the same day as Sowter's lucky break. 'This careful packaging, the nature and collection of articles, and the rental of the unit on the same day as the manufacture of the methamphetamine imply this was the work of an organised criminal enterprise.

'You led that enterprise,' Justice Downs said to Hines. 'And although you were careful to act from behind the scenes, I am sure you directed this offending … You sat atop an organisation which made a very large amount of methamphetamine and intended to make more.'

Standing in the dock, the feared and revered Hines, now 64, was a proud but broken-down old man. He was sentenced to 18 and a half years in prison. It's likely to be a life sentence: Hines suffers from Type 2 diabetes, heart disease, and end-stage renal failure, which requires dialysis every second day.

The police had now taken out two of the most senior members of the gang, with 'Little Dave' O'Carroll already serving a long prison sentence alongside Bird Hines. Only Wayne Doyle was above them in the hierarchy.

* * *

The president of the East Chapter of the Head Hunters has a business card that simply reads: 'You have just met Wayne.' He needs no further introduction. If someone convened a round-table meeting of New Zealand gang leaders, Doyle would be chairman.

He was one of the earliest members of the Heads, which started as a street gang in Glen Innes in 1967. It's fair to describe him as the epitome of staunch. In 1985, Doyle and another Head Hunter, Graham 'Choc' Te Awa, were charged with the murder of Siaso Evalu, a member of the rival King Cobra gang. He was beaten to death in a street brawl in Ponsonby, the heart of 'KC' territory.

Doyle was adamant he had never laid a finger on the victim. But police could place him at the scene of the crime, and he knew he might go down for murder anyway. He refused to rat out his fellow Heads, despite the best efforts of detectives to squeeze him for more information by questioning the prospects of his wife and children while he languished in prison.

Doyle chose the gang over his family. He and Te Awa were convicted of murder and sentenced to 10 years in prison.

In the mid-1980s, there was effectively only one chapter of the Head Hunters, based at 12a View Road in Henderson. Dave 'Smitty' Smith was president. Following his release from prison, Doyle forged his own path, and in 2001 he started a second chapter at 232 Marua Road, Ellerslie. Doyle was 'East', Smith was 'West'. By this stage, the Head

Hunters Motorcycle Club Inc. was officially on the Register of Incorporated Societies, filing accounts and reporting some of its income.

Doyle also registered a charitable trust called the That Was Then, This Is Now Trust. According to its deed, the trust aims to act as a bridge between prisoners and the community, helping former inmates 'through their own efforts … choose to have a better future'.

Apparently born from a conversation in a prison gym, with a goal 'to develop physical motivation and health', the trust offers a large gym at the gang's Marua Road headquarters, daily group walks or runs up nearby Mount Wellington, boxing, kickboxing, weightlifting and other personal training, and an annual children's Christmas party. Marua Road also hosts Fight Club 88 evenings, to showcase 'up and coming talent' in the mixed martial arts scene.

Police are sceptical of the health-and-wellbeing philosophy. They regard it as a public-relations exercise to soften the gang's image.

Doyle himself is an active member, fit, lean and disciplined. Photographs from various fitness events show him in the middle of the action, surrounded by hundreds of people – many in the red and white regalia of the Head Hunters – revelling in the family atmosphere. There is a clear camaraderie, reminiscent of the loyalty that bound the original Head Hunters together.

It is ironic, then, that those tight bonds were the very reason the Charities Registration Board revoked the charitable status of That Was Then, This Is Now in 2015. According to a statement on the registration board's website, instead of reintegrating prisoners, That Was Then, This Is Now was set up solely to 'provide benefits to the Head Hunters Motorcycle Club, its members, associates and their families'.

'To be registered as a charity,' the website continued, 'a trust must have exclusively charitable purposes, and be available to a sufficient section of the public. It is not charitable to provide private benefits to individuals or a closed or tightly-defined group.'

The gig was up, the charade was over – or so the Charities Registration Board thought. Just two years later, though, the Head Hunters won a legal reprieve and were granted the right to appeal to the High Court. The High Court was told that the charity had been denied natural justice, had never been given the opportunity to respond to the allegations before being shut down and, crucially, had never been given any details about the police notification that led to the revocation.

Seeing the writing on the wall, the Charities Registration Board decided to reverse its decision before the High Court made a ruling, and pledged to review the evidence with a fresh pair of eyes.

A few months later, though, the reason why police's opposition to the charity had never been disclosed to the Head Hunters became crystal clear.

* * *

On 25 September 2017, police raided the Head Hunters' pad in conjunction with the Serious Fraud Office, the Ministry of Social Development and the Department of Inland Revenue. In a press release, the police said the search followed an extensive investigation into 'alleged accumulation of criminally derived wealth by a senior member of the Head Hunters gang'.

The man, described as a '62-year-old beneficiary', was not named in the press release, and no criminal charges were laid against him. But property records showed that

Wayne Doyle was the target of Operation Coin. Five properties linked to him, including the gang's Marua Road pad, were restrained (frozen) by the High Court following a police application under the *Criminal Proceeds (Recovery) Act* 2009. Their total value was estimated to be in excess of $6 million.

'A significant amount of work has gone into Operation Coin by a dedicated group of detectives and investigators from partner government agencies,' Detective Superintendent Iain Chapman, head of the police's Financial Crime Group, was quoted as saying in the press release. 'Police are committed to ensuring that people cannot accrue wealth and assets as a result of criminal behaviour, at the expense of the safety of our community.'

As detectives swarmed through the Heads' gang pad and gym, then carried out computers and boxes of paperwork, Doyle stood outside speaking to senior police officers. Dressed in a grey sweatshirt emblazoned with the Head Hunters' insignia, the shaven-headed Doyle looked stressed. He was not arrested, or facing any charges, but the police had him in a bind. And he knew it.

His personal assets – and those of the gang he led – would be tied up in the courts for years to come.

Doyle's old Head Hunter mate Peter 'Pedro' Cleven was indirectly to blame for his current predicament. Cleven had been accused of making a fortune from dealing cannabis and methamphetamine between 1996 and 1999. He had a palatial Titirangi home, a Harley-Davidson motorbike, a Mercedes-Benz convertible and a speedboat. All of his assets were seized following Operation Mexico in 1999, led by Detective Sergeant Darryl Brazier, in which Cleven was caught talking in bugged conversations about making a million dollars a year from methamphetamine.

Cleven was acquitted in 2002 after two controversial trials. The jury in the first trial was unable to reach a verdict, while the second jury was sequestered in a secret location for nearly three weeks. The reason why is still suppressed. But the jurors found him not guilty this time.

Cleven's defence against the charges was that he had been making empty boasts to impress a woman, and that his wealthy lifestyle was in fact funded by the innovative methods of angora-goat farming and 'taxing' other criminals.

Admitting to taxing was essentially confessing to a crime. It was a calculated risk on his behalf. He knew that criminals will almost never make an official complaint to police about being ripped off. Without a conviction, in spite of the ludicrous explanation for where they came from, Cleven's assets had to be returned.

Never again, swore the police, who finally convinced politicians that the only way to battle organised crime was by following the money and passing the *Criminal Proceeds (Recovery) Act* 2009.

No conviction was needed with the 'Cleven clause' – and the police now had new powers to go after the untouchable.

While they went on to seize hundreds of millions of dollars' worth of assets – houses, lifestyle blocks, farms, cars, boats, motorcycles, diggers, investment portfolios, art collections, cash, bank accounts, even cryptocurrency – the attempt to take Doyle's property was the most ambitious.

Doyle had not set foot in a courtroom dock for nearly 20 years following his prison lag for murder. Peers like Dave O'Carroll, Brownie Harding and Bird Hines were all serving lengthy prison sentences for methamphetamine manufacturing. Yet there was never any direct evidence that Doyle, their leader, had profited from the Head Hunters' crimes, as the gang president of the fictional Sons of Anarchy gang did in the TV show of the same name.

But that's exactly what Operation Coin alleges. The evidence is yet to be tested in court, but to gain orders to freeze Doyle's assets, the police had to convince a High Court judge there were 'reasonable grounds' – a relatively low bar in legal terms – to believe someone had profited from 'significant criminal activity'.

Seven affidavits were attached to their application, including one sworn by Detective Sergeant Andy Dunhill, who ran Operation Easter; one from Ashna Achari, a forensic accountant with the Serious Fraud Office; and three from staff at the Ministry of Social Development.

Justice Geoffrey Venning, the chief High Court judge, granted the restraining orders 'without notice'. It meant Doyle had no warning before the police turned up at the door of 232 Marua Road in September 2017.

The judgment of Justice Venning revealed that six different companies and trusts had been established by Doyle, or on his behalf, including the That Was Then, This Is Now charity, which owned the five properties confiscated by police. Doyle was a signatory to the bank account for each entity and able to withdraw or deposit funds. An investigation by the Ministry of Social Development alleged that Doyle failed to declare substantial income and assets, enabling him to fraudulently claim social welfare payments of $380,992.80 between 5 May 1994 and 16 July 2017.

But benefit fraud is one matter, money laundering another.

According to analysis by the Serious Fraud Office, a staggering $19.9 million – half of it cash – was deposited into the bank accounts of the six entities associated with Doyle between 2002 and 2016. Of that amount, $9.2 million was deposited into the That Was Then, This Is Now charitable trust.

Justice Venning said there also seemed to be a discrepancy of \$2.4 million between the trust's declared income and funds deposited into the bank account. 'Further, there is evidence from two recent drug investigations conducted by the police that payments were made to the Head Hunters East Chapter, to senior patched members of that chapter, and in the case of one to Mr Doyle directly and/or the other interests associated with him,' Justice Venning said, obliquely referring to the Operation Easter and Operation Sylvester investigations.

This led to a possible inference that the trusts were involved in money laundering, said Justice Venning. On the basis of the so-far-uncontested evidence, the chief High Court judge was satisfied there were reasonable grounds to believe the properties linked to Doyle were acquired by fraud, criminal dishonesty, money laundering and other significant criminal activity.

All of his assets were frozen. It's now up to Doyle to prove he paid for them legitimately.

Three years on from the September 2017 raids, Doyle remains in limbo, still waiting for his day in court.

Even if the Operation Coin allegations are ultimately unsuccessful, the attempt to take on the once-untouchable Doyle is viewed as the pinnacle of the police war against the Head Hunters. This sustained targeting over a three-year period has stopped the growth of the gang in its tracks.

By late 2017, with Little Dave, Bird, Brownie and their loyal troopers inside, and Doyle's status under suspicion for the first time, the Head Hunters faced a vacuum of leadership at the most inopportune moment. For so long, they had dominated the New Zealand underworld, but now they were wounded, their position under threat. And not just because of the vice-like pressure applied by the police.

There was a new challenger to the Head Hunters' crown, with a brash Aussie twang and an arrogance to match, rolling into Auckland on gold-plated Harley-Davidsons.

In the words of a quote from classic film *The Godfather*, once written on a wall in the Head Hunters' pad: 'Real power can't be given. It must be taken.'

8

COMEDY AT SEA:
THE AUSTRALIANS ARRIVE

2016

CONSTABLE THOMAS NANKIVELL HAD a very long and very strange day at work on Sunday, 12 June 2016. He worked out of the police station in Kaitaia. They don't call it the Far North for nothing: the sandy tip of the North Island is one of the most remote regions of New Zealand.

Nankivell was on the morning shift. A worried phone call came in as soon as he arrived. A storm had whipped up the seas off 90 Mile Beach, on the Far North's western coast, and locals were scouring the shoreline for washed-up shellfish at first light.

They found more than scallops and oysters. On the slick wet sand, stranded high and dry, was a brand-new, 9-metre rigid-hull inflatable boat (RHIB).

Everyone knows everyone up in the Far North, especially the boaties. But no one recognised *this* inflatable. It was a distinctive vessel, perfect for navigating the notorious swell and unforgiving currents of the North Island's west coast.

Such a useful boat was valuable too. By the time Nankivell arrived at the site, near Hukatere, about 45 kilometres from Kaitaia, bystanders were arguing about salvage rights.

At first glance, Nankivell thought he might be dealing with a Search and Rescue mission. His initial instinct was to get a helicopter or plane up into the air. Survivors might be bobbing off the coast, running out of time. Or, in a worst-case scenario, there might be bodies to recover.

Something didn't quite fit that narrative, though. The boat wasn't lolling around in the shallows, lying parallel to the shore and buffeted incessantly by the waves, as you'd expect if it'd drifted aimlessly without crew.

Instead, the RHIB looked like it had been driven hard, straight onto the beach, and left stranded as the tide went out. Whoever was behind the wheel hadn't bothered to raise the outboard motor out of the water. The propeller blades bit deep into the sand.

And those on board hadn't stuck around to ask for help. They'd just up and left, completely vanished.

It wasn't long before people started phoning the Kaitaia Police Station with their suspicions. One of those was Leo Lloyd, a mechanic by trade, who had helped a party of seven strangers launch a RHIB shortly after dark the night before.

Lloyd lived in Ahipara, at the southern end of 90 Mile Beach, about 60 kilometres from Hukatere. Sergeant Kevin Anderson returned Lloyd's call, and later he and Nankivell drove down the coast to meet with Lloyd at his Ahipara home. Lloyd had kindly towed the RHIB there for them.

The three men stood around outside as Lloyd told his story. He described four of the men he had helped as Polynesian but with thick Australian accents. Another two had been Chinese and one, Stevie – with whom Leo had dealt the most – had been Maori. They'd driven a maroon Toyota Prado.

As good fortune would have it – make that *extraordinarily* good fortune – a maroon Toyota Prado rolled past just as the two police officers were about to take their leave.

'There they go!' yelled Lloyd's wife Yvette. 'They're driving past!'

Nankivell and Anderson didn't waste any time. They jumped into their patrol car and followed the Prado down Kaka Street towards the Ahipara golf course. It's a no-exit road; there was no escape route for the Prado or its occupants.

The two officers drove slowly, scanning properties as they went past, just in case the SUV had ducked into a driveway in the hope of a miraculous U-turn getaway. The Prado had in fact pulled into the golf-course carpark, which was nearly full: a tournament for club members was in full swing.

There were two young men inside the vehicle. Nankivell spoke to the driver first. He hopped out of the car and handed over a Tongan driver's licence in the name of Ulakai Fakaosilea. Nankivell searched him and found $1605 in cash.

The passenger, Amoki Fonua, was also patted down. A small amount of cannabis was discovered in his pocket.

The pair were arrested and taken back to the Kaitaia Police Station. It seemed highly suspicious: two strangers in town on a strange morning when an abandoned boat had been found on the shore. Still, there was no hint of the scarcely believable crime the police would soon uncover.

At 4.05pm, nearing the end of his shift, Nankivell visited the Northerner Hotel in Kaitaia, where the men were staying in Rooms 61 and 63 respectively. The constable rifled through the rubbish bins in their rooms, but found nothing of note. He also took away video footage from the hotel's security cameras.

But there was something missing from the hotel: a staff member at reception told Nankivell that the group of men had left a white campervan with the registration plate EWS19 in the hotel carpark. Now it was nowhere to be seen.

Twelve long hours after he was called out to the abandoned vessel at Hukatere, Nankivell finished his shift. Off duty and heading home for the day, Nankivell noticed a few cars travelling below the speed limit, perhaps 60 or 70 kilometres an hour, along State Highway 10.

He was starting to make a right turn off the main road when he experienced his second slice of extraordinary good fortune for the day. He got his first good look at the vehicle that was holding up the traffic. A white campervan. With the registration plate EWS19.

Nankivell spun his marked car around to pull back in behind the campervan. He called for backup, and tailed the vehicle for about 40 minutes until his police colleagues arrived.

As soon as Nankivell flashed his red and blue lights, near Taipa, the campervan pulled over to the side of the road. It was 8.40pm. When Nankivell walked over to the motor home, the 18-year-old driver was slumped behind the wheel. He knew it was all over.

Behind his seat, strewn across the floor and slung over bunks and tables, were at least a dozen bags. Most were made of cheap nylon canvas with blue, white and red checks. The sort of bag a family might use to carry a picnic lunch and blankets to sit on, but no one worries about if it gets ripped or lost.

There were so many of these bags in the back of the campervan that Constable Kelly Bates could barely get inside when she opened the side door. Her colleague Constable Brett Walford, wearing gloves, slid open the zip of the nearest bag. It was full of smaller plastic ziplock bags containing white crystals: methamphetamine.

There was no need to open the remaining bags. Given how many there were in the back of the campervan, the Kaitaia police knew they had stumbled over a snowy mountain of P.

* * *

News of the bust was relayed that night to Detective Senior Sergeant Lloyd Schmid at Harlech House. He'd been promoted since we last heard about him in Chapter 4. The agency he was working for also had a new name: police had quietly retired the OFCANZ badge in early 2016 after the series of debacles that had plagued it. The National Organised Crime Group (NOCG) was born.

With his decades of experience, Schmid knew that time was of the essence. The first thought that flew through his head was that he had to get out of Auckland so he could be on the ground in Northland, fast.

He started moving the machinery on an investigation with high stakes. Most inquiries by NOCG are *proactive* jobs: using intelligence reports and covert surveillance to piece together the puzzle, then planning coordinated raids to arrest all the targets and hopefully gather more incriminating evidence. But this investigation, Operation Frontia, was a *reactive* job.

A large stockpile of methamphetamine had been chanced upon. Three young men were locked up in a prison cell, with an unknown number of co-offenders – at least four others, going by Leo Lloyd's statement – in the wind.

As Schmid put his plans in place, Constable Justin Fleet was driving the campervan back to the Kaitaia Police Station, about an hour away, with marked police cars in front and behind as an escort. The convoy stopped only once: with the fuel light glowing orange, the campervan pulled over to the side of the road and police radioed for someone to bring them a jerry can of diesel. Diesel engines can be difficult to restart once the tank runs dry, and the police didn't want to be stranded with a campervan full of meth.

Once safely back at the station, five or six police officers lined up in a chain gang to pull the nylon bags out. There were 20 of them. All of them were carefully unpacked, and up to 30 smaller plastic ziplock bags of meth were found inside each one.

A GPS device found in the console of the Toyota Prado led another team of officers back to 90 Mile Beach, where two more bags were found buried in the sand dunes. They were added to the pile locked away in the cells at the Kaitaia station, kept under guard overnight by the Armed Offenders Squad, who were carrying M4 Bushmaster semi-automatic rifles.

The final tally was an incredible 501 kilograms of meth.

By this point – early Monday morning – Lloyd Schmid was already in the Whangarei headquarters of the Northland Police District. He'd been involved in all the big drug squad investigations over the years, including Operation Major in 2006. For 10 years, the 96 kilograms of meth hidden in the bottom of green paint tins had been easily the largest amount of P ever seized in New Zealand. But the 501-kilo haul was next-level. It was half a tonne of the most expensive, most sought-after, most damaging drug in existence.

And there it was, stored in the cell of a rural police station. People would kill for it. That's not a tabloid exaggeration; that's an accurate assessment of the risk. Schmid's first decision was to call in the heavily armed Special Tactics Group to transport the cache to a more secure location in Auckland.

With Schmid running the show on the ground in Northland – authorising the use of resources, sorting out warrants, signing off on anything that carried risk – it was left to his long-time colleague in Auckland, Detective Sergeant Mike Beal, to do the practical work of tracking down the unidentified suspects on the run.

Like Schmid, Beal was a long-serving veteran of the drug squads. He'd played a key role in many of the secretive group's most successful investigations, including Operation Major. Fair to say he'd been around the block.

But without the benefit of intercepted communications or informant information, Beal's team were starting from scratch. They had descriptions of the suspects but no names to chase down. They were acutely aware of the magnitude of the seizure – and that the other crooks involved in the audacious smuggling attempt would try to flee the country.

The clock was ticking.

* * *

It didn't take long for a star witness to come forward.

Within hours of his arrest on Sunday night, the young driver of the campervan 'flipped' and decided to come clean to police. His true identity is protected by a permanent suppression order. But he was given the codename 'Louie' by the other members of the drug syndicate, so we'll call him that.

Louie was born in Auckland, of Polynesian heritage, and raised in Australia. In 2015, he was 18, with a pregnant girlfriend, no job and no real prospects. At a friend's birthday party in Brisbane, a chance meeting led to an opportunity to make some easy money.

The teenager had been chatting to a man he referred to as 'Big T'. The man later contacted Louie on Facebook with an offer he couldn't refuse.

Big T arrived on his doorstep with another man in tow, Mack, a second-generation Australian with Tongan parents. The pair handed him tickets to Bangkok and proceeded to pack his suitcase with vacuum-sealed stacks of cash. Louie couldn't remember how many cash bundles were in there, only that the number 90,000 was scrawled across each one with a permanent marker.

Louie flew to Bangkok and waited in his hotel room for an entire week before someone knocked on his door to collect the cash. Then he came home.

His partner gave birth to their baby, a little girl. He was still unemployed. As his daughter's first birthday approached, Louie became desperate. He sent Big T a Facebook message asking if there were any 'jobs going'. There were.

In February 2016, Louie was dispatched from Brisbane to New Zealand. Waiting for him at Auckland International Airport were Big T and Mack, as well as a Tongan-Australian man introduced as 'Thugga'. He was handed a Blackberry with end-to-end messaging encryption, solely to communicate within the group. The trio sent him to Bangkok on another money run, while they booked their own flights to Hong Kong.

Now living in Auckland, where most of the group's activity was taking place, Louie soon became an unquestioning foot soldier. As well as Thugga and Mack, there was a tall, attractive Polynesian woman Louie only knew as 'Blaze'; she seemed to be in charge whenever Big T was out of town.

They called him Louie. He never asked their real names, and they never offered them.

Tasks needed completing, orders were given, and Louie did as he was told. The kid was in deep with hardened criminals before he even knew it. Weighing and packing meth into ziplock ounce bags, or driving across the country in the middle of the night to pick up buckets of cash, Louie was simply a pawn in the game.

Pawns are always the first to be sacrificed. If anything went wrong, *his* fingerprints would be all over the money and drugs, while his bosses would keep their hands clean.

Swapping a heavy bag of meth with strangers for bundles of cash carries its own special kind of danger in the underworld.

Louie explained to the Operation Frontia detectives how a deal would be given the green light.

Thugga would text him a serial number from a $5 or $10 note. If the purported buyers handed over the correct note, Louie would give them the drugs in exchange.

One night, Louie was asked to count a pile of $20 and $50 notes, then bind the cash into bundles with rubber bands. The total was $850,000: more money than most people will ever see with their own eyes. But to Louie's dismay, Thugga accused him of being $100,000 short. Panicking, Louie retraced his steps and looked high and low for the small fortune that had apparently vanished.

It might not have even been his fault. It didn't matter. Louie now owed a substantial debt to the gang. In fact, he was in over his head, although he didn't realise it yet.

In May 2016, a few months after Louie had moved to New Zealand, Thugga texted him to say there was a 'job going', and that the 19-year-old would earn $200,000. Enough to pay back his debt twice over.

He was asked to rent a campervan, then buy 10 large toolboxes, approximately a metre wide, and some shovels. Louie drove the campervan to Mangere to meet Mack, who then got behind the wheel and declared that they were heading to Northland.

The pair drove up State Highway 1. To the anxious teenager, the ride seemed like it went on forever. They drove past Kaitaia, finally stopping at the township of Pukenui on the eastern coast of the Far North.

That was where Louie was introduced to two other men, nicknamed 'Marvel' and 'Gravel'. Gravel was another Tongan-Australian, while Marvel was Maori.

Mack had a private conversation with the pair, which Louie overheard. He later told the cops, 'He was talking about a big boat waiting out at sea. He spoke about how a smaller boat would be bringing 500 kilograms of methamphetamine to the spot.

'They started talking about the swells … it was rough … we would be waiting on the beach for the arrival of the gear.'

The plan was for the Chinese crew on board the mothership – which had chugged 6000 nautical miles from Hong Kong – to bring the drugs to shore in a smaller boat.

Once they landed on the beach, the 500-kilo haul would be split in two, with half buried in the sand dunes, and the other half immediately transported south to Auckland. That way, if the first half was discovered by the police, or stolen by other crims, there would still be 250 kilograms tucked safely away.

On hearing about the job, and the incredible amounts of P involved, Louie became even more anxious. Yet he felt he had no choice but to go through with it. When the cops asked why he stayed, he replied: 'Fear.' Mack had told him about the kind of people they were working with. As Louie said to police, 'I didn't have the courage to say no.'

The shore party – Louie, Mack, Marvel and Gravel – went shopping for supplies for the mothership. They also kept busy by testing walkie-talkies on the beach and practising marking GPS coordinates.

They waited and waited. Two weekends went by and the shipment still hadn't landed.

'This was when things started to go pear-shaped,' said Louie. 'The smaller boat [on the mothership] was not working and it couldn't come in. Mack was saying that we needed to find a way to – well, to get the stuff.'

There was talk of hiring a skipper to take them out to sea. The idea was dismissed; it was too much of a risk. Well, they reasoned, the best thing was to buy a boat and figure out a way to take it out to sea themselves. They couldn't find one for sale in the Far North, so Mack and Gravel drove all the way back to Auckland, where they purchased a new Bayliner motorboat. They paid $49,000 in cash for the 7-metre vessel, which had a V8 inboard engine.

Only one problem: they had no one to skipper it.

Calls were made. Their partners in crime, based in Hong Kong, sent three men to help. Two had sailing experience. The third was a management figure within the criminal organisation.

When the trio arrived, the plan started to unravel, fast.

* * *

The original decision was to set out from 90 Mile Beach and navigate the notoriously treacherous waters of the west coast of the Far North. This would have been difficult for any craft, but the Bayliner was a heavy fibreglass boat, usually launched from a marina or a ramp into the calm harbour waters of the east coast – not backed into wild surf off a sandy beach.

To make matters worse, the two Chinese sailors were denied entry at Auckland International Airport. Arriving on flight CX197 from Hong Kong, Wong Kam Hung, 56, and Cheung Fuk Shun, 53, spoke no English and claimed they were visiting New Zealand to discuss deals with a seafood business, despite only booking their tickets on short notice. Customs officers didn't buy their cover story. They were promptly sent back to Hong Kong.

But the third man, Tsai Chiang, *was* let in. He was met in the arrivals lounge by Wan Ka Yip, a short, bookish student from Hong Kong who had done a bunk from a tour-group holiday to New Zealand earlier in the year. His job was to translate for Tsai, who spoke very little English.

Together, Wan and Tsai waited hours for the sailors. They held up a welcome sign to identify themselves to Wong and Cheung. It was all in vain; they didn't know the pair had been sent packing.

The two eventually left the airport and were picked up by someone imaginatively called 'Tall Guy', also of Tongan descent. Tall Guy was a tall guy. He had been deported from Australia just a few days earlier.

Tall Guy drove the two men straight to Kaitaia so they could join the shore party, then came back to Auckland. Tsai and Wan really weren't much use: neither of them had the skills and experience to skipper a boat.

Mack ordered Louie and Marvel to make inquiries about launching the boat off the west coast. Nearly everyone told them to forget it. But they *were* given the name of one local who might help.

* * *

Leo Lloyd had lived in the Far North for 23 years. His home in Ahipara was about 15 minutes' drive west of Kaitaia. A commercial fisherman in a previous life, Lloyd now works as a mechanic, fixing forestry and farm machinery, as well as boats. He loves to fish along the west coast, either off the rocks or in the deep water, where he chases marlin. 'They're like pigs, they travel back to the same spot,' Lloyd says.

On 8 June 2016, Lloyd got a phone call from someone called Stevie, asking if he could help launch their boat. He drove to the Northerner Hotel to meet Stevie and his five friends and check out the vessel.

Bayliners weren't typically launched off the west coast, but with his years of local knowledge Lloyd told them he could handle it. 'I wouldn't like to see a new chum do it without someone with experience,' he told them. 'On the west coast, you've got to know what you're doing … I know the consequences and all the problems you run into.'

Stevie wanted to launch at 5.30pm that afternoon. Lloyd refused. The tide was wrong, the swell was up; it would be too dark and dangerous.

They agreed to meet in Ahipara the following day at 11am. Stevie and his five friends didn't turn up until 12.30pm; by then, the tide was wrong again, and the swell had grown to 3 metres. Lloyd decided it would be safer to launch from nearby Shipwreck Bay. Its beach was more sheltered.

What happened next was a comedy of errors.

They tried to start the engine, to do a test run, but the carburettor seized up.

Lloyd tinkered around for 40 minutes. He managed to fix the problem, but when he announced he was ready to back the trailer into the water, Stevie asked for more time. He had an urn in his hands and explained they were going to spread some ashes at sea.

Stevie was 'holding it, cradling it in his arms and the second person was kissing it and tears started rolling down his eyes, which I was quite surprised to see,' said Lloyd.

He asked Stevie whether he had been granted permission from local kaumatua to spread the ashes. He was assured that was the case. Lloyd became suspicious. Stevie was Maori, but his three friends were Polynesian; it was their brother, or close friend, in the urn. And yet it was the two Chinese men (later identified as Tsai and Wan) who clambered into the boat, ostensibly to spread the ashes at sea, while the others stayed on shore. Stevie tried to convince Lloyd that this was because Tsai was the one with the boating experience.

As for the launch attempt, that was a complete disaster – making it clear that Tsai had no boating experience whatsoever. On the first go, he was unable to get the stern leg, which powers the boat from the inboard engine, into the water. They had to winch the boat back in and replace a blown fuse.

On the second attempt, the stern leg finally seemed to be working. But Tsai still couldn't get his act together. 'He would start the boat, then he'd rev it up and he'd put it in gear and the stern leg would be too deep – hitting the sand,' Lloyd said. 'The motor stalls and everything turns to custard.'

Again, Lloyd winched the boat up and had stern words to Tsai and Wan. He was annoyed that Wan was talking on a satellite phone, instead of translating his instructions for Tsai. This was their last shot, he warned.

'We put the boat back into the water. I got out deeper, so when I drove out of the water, he can just start it up and turn around,' said Lloyd. 'But he just started it up and drove it straight back onto the shore, onto the beach. That's when I'd had enough.'

Four hours had flown by. The brand-new Bayliner had suffered serious damage. In another touch of farce, a tyre on the boat trailer had gone flat, and had to be replaced. Eventually, Lloyd towed the Bayliner back home to repair.

The next day, Friday 10 June 2016, Stevie and the others visited Lloyd to ask how long it would be before the boat was seaworthy. Three to four days, Lloyd advised. Stevie told him to go ahead with the job.

Later, while rummaging around on the boat, Lloyd switched on the navigation system. Curiously, he noticed GPS coordinates for a spot about 30 nautical miles out to sea.

Despite telling Leo Lloyd to fix the Bayliner, the shore crew were panicking. They couldn't actually wait three or four days. The crew on the mothership were running low on fuel, water and food. Not to mention the fact that they were suspiciously sloshing around off the Far North coast with 500 kilos of methamphetamine on board.

Tsai and Wan's bosses in Hong Kong were getting nervous. The decision was made for the shore party to purchase another boat.

By this time, Thugga had sent Tall Guy back to the Far North with new mobile phones for the two Chinese men. Thugga had stayed out of Northland to put some distance between himself and the drugs.

Once again, they couldn't find one in the Far North; once again, Mack and Gravel drove back to Auckland.

The following day, Louie got a text from Mack. They'd purchased a new rigid-hull inflatable boat (RHIB) – which was much more suitable for launching off the west coast – for $98,000. They'd paid cash from a bundle kept in a shoebox. They were coming straight back to Ahipara, and would arrive around 6pm – and wanted to launch immediately, come hell or high water.

At 5pm, Leo Lloyd had just arrived home from coaching rugby when the phone rang. Stevie told him they had bought a RHIB with a powerful outboard engine, and they wanted his help to launch it in an hour's time.

While Lloyd waited, he had another nosy around in the stricken Bayliner, which was still parked at his house. There was enough food to 'feed a marae' for a week, he later told police, as well as 20 or so containers of fuel.

Stevie and the shore party – which now numbered seven with the addition of Tall Guy – pulled up outside. It was dark now, but they were desperate to go.

They urgently moved the food and fuel into the RHIB as Lloyd prepared for launch. Once again, the two Chinese men were the only men on board the vessel, with the older man, Tsai, acting as 'skipper'.

Lloyd thought it was odd that the group were wearing gloves to load supplies onto the boat, but he got on with the job, and this time the launch was successful. Somehow.

Lloyd: 'The skipper had the outboard up in the air and the motor was screaming and then he had it in the water, or too deep and it hit the sand.'

He watched as the RHIB started by heading parallel to the beach, perilously close to being tipped over by the surf, before eventually heading out to sea.

It slowly disappeared into the winter gloom and out of sight.

* * *

Lloyd took the boat trailer back to his house, followed by the shore crew. Stevie put $500 into his hand. As soon as Stevie and his mates left, Lloyd got on the phone. He figured it was high time he called the police.

He told them: 'I know this is turning to something more than just a trip out on a boat to spread ashes ... I'm a local and it just doesn't add up.'

Meanwhile, the remaining members of the shore party – Louie, Mack, Marvel, Tall Guy and Gravel – went back to the Northerner Hotel to regroup. Years later, at their trial, Louie would tell the jury, 'Mack was saying it'll take the Chinamen a few hours to get to the big boat and return to the spot. He said that we needed to be ready at the spot before they came back.'

The spot was Hukatere, about 60 kilometres north of Ahipara.

This time, their unlikely cover story was that they were tourists having a barbecue on the beach. In fact, their fire would act as a beacon to help guide the RHIB. Marvel would then drive Tsai and Wan back to Auckland. The others would unload the methamphetamine and bury half of it on the beach as per the original plan.

While they waited, Thugga sent a message instructing Louie and Tall Guy to dig a hole in the sand dunes, locking the GPS coordinates into a hand-held device.

Hours passed, and it was now early on Sunday, 12 June 2016.

Finally, the group spotted the faint green and red lights of the RHIB out at sea. They started flashing the headlights of the campervan and the Toyota Prado SUV.

'So the boat came straight on the sand, you know, like beached,' Louie would say at their trial.

'The two Chinamen went straight into the car. They left straight away. Gravel ran, jumped inside the boat and started unloading bags for myself, Mack and the Tall Guy.'

Marvel drove Tsai and Wan to Auckland in a silver Toyota RAV4, the third vehicle the group had rented.

The rest of the shore party lugged the chequered nylon bags, which weighed about 30 kilograms each, two at a time to the campervan, parked about 40 metres away. Some of the bags had split open, and the smaller plastic bags of methamphetamine were washing around in the waves. Louie and Tall Guy madly scrabbled around in the surf to pick them up.

While the original plan had been to split the 500-kilo load and bury half in the sand dunes, the shore crew buried only two bags in the moonlight. They were nervous about getting caught. This change in plan was not relayed to their bosses.

They drove the campervan to the nearby Houhora camping ground, safe for now. But there was a new problem. The RHIB was stranded on the beach and the sun would rise in just a few hours. And they had a campervan with around 450 kilos of Class A drugs in the back.

Tall Guy and Gravel drove to Leo Lloyd's in the maroon-coloured Toyota SUV, hoping he could help them tow the boat off the beach. But it was far too late for that. The local police sergeant, Kevin Anderson, had finally returned Leo Lloyd's phone call and told him about the boat beached at Hukatere. Not long afterwards, Gravel and Tall Guy turned up on his doorstep.

Lloyd told them, 'You'd better get up the beach because there are people trying to claim the boat … The police are involved.'

He told police later, 'That's when I saw his body language change. [Gravel] was nervous and shaking, shaking all over. I never saw him again.'

Lloyd drove to Hukatere and towed the RHIB – unconnected with any crime at that point – back to his house for the police. Within a few hours, Sergeant Anderson and Constable Nankivell were interviewing Lloyd about his dealings with the group.

When Nankivell's first stroke of good luck led to the sighting of the maroon Toyota Prado and the arrests at the Ahipara golf course, Louie was behind the wheel of the campervan, with the huge haul of methamphetamine in the back. He started to panic. He'd messaged Gravel but hadn't heard back for several hours, then messaged Mack to say police cars had been seen around. He started to suspect the worst.

Mack told him to calm down. Their boss, Thugga, had been pulling the strings from Auckland, sending orders by Blackberry to Mack and the others. With the plan falling apart at the seams, Thugga was trying to arrange a rendezvous point where Louie could meet Mack, his second in charge. Thugga asked if Louie knew how to get to Taipa Bay, about 30 minutes away on the eastern coast.

Louie would tell the jury, 'I just wanted to get out of there because I had the feeling that Gravel and Tall Guy had been picked up by police … I just said yes because I wanted to get out of there, I didn't really know exactly where it was.

'I wasn't sure where I was, whether I was close to Taipa or whether I was driving past it, but during the drive I noticed that a police car was not far behind me … It was all over from there.'

* * *

Louie sang like a canary. But even his enthusiastic cooperation with Operation Frontia investigators gave Mike Beal and his long-time colleague Detective Jane Scott only the slimmest of leads to chase.

They had Gravel – Amoki Fonua – and Tall Guy – Ulakai Fakaosilea – in custody after arresting them in the Ahipara golf course parking lot, but they still didn't have names for most other members of the group. Louie had spent weeks with these men and only knew them by nickname. Except for Marvel: Louie had accidentally seen his real name on a prescription medicine label. Stevie Cullen.

Beal and his team started searching for Cullen, but there was something else Louie mentioned that they quickly jumped on.

Back in February 2016, when Louie first arrived in Auckland at the behest of Big T, he was ordered to stump up the cash for three flights to Bangkok. Big T, Thugga and Mack were going to Thailand to seal the 500-kilogram deal – and their tickets had to be booked under their real names.

A warrant to search the records of Flight Centre in Manukau gave the investigation team a big break: the true identities of Thugga, Mack and Big T, the bosses dishing out orders.

Big T left the country; police were unable to gather enough evidence to extradite him back to New Zealand and his identity has never been revealed. Thugga was Jeremiah Iusitini; Mack was Malachi Tuilotolava. Both were second-generation Australians of Tongan heritage, with criminal records across the Tasman.

It was now Tuesday, 14 June 2016. Two days had passed since the astonishing discovery in the back of the campervan. Beal hadn't had a moment's rest since coming into Harlech House on Monday morning, but he couldn't stop now.

Iusitini and Tuilotolava were no longer in New Zealand. Both were in the air on different flights, trying to escape the long arm of the law: Tuilotolava was heading towards Guangzhou, China, with a stopover in Cambodia, and Iusitini was en route to Bangkok.

If the pair managed to slip through the airport when they reached their destinations, the chances of ever catching them were slim to nonexistent. Even if they were found, with the assistance of local law enforcement, the extradition process is fraught with difficulties. It can take years. The best bet was to have Iusitini and Tuilotolava stopped on arrival, then sent back to New Zealand on the next available flight.

Beal worked through the night – pulling a 36-hour shift – to prepare the evidence for New Zealand Customs and police liaison officers in Thailand and China to persuade the local officials to deny the pair entry. He got what he wanted.

Waiting for Iusitini at Bangkok International Airport was a New Zealand Customs officer. He then sat beside him on the 11-hour flight all the way back to Auckland.

Tuilotolava nearly got away. Detective Sergeant Bruce Howard, another original drug squad member, was now the police liaison officer based in Guangzhou. Howard was ready and waiting when word came through that Tuilotolava was actually on a flight to the Philippines. He'd purchased a new ticket while in transit in Cambodia, very nearly giving police the slip.

Howard scrambled to catch a flight to Manila and managed to arrive just before the wheels on Tuilotolava's flight touched down. Another 30 minutes or so and Tuilotolava would have got away scot-free.

Instead, he landed back in Auckland International Airport with Howard at 3.45pm on Friday 17 June 2016, just five hours after Iusitini.

In the meantime, Operation Frontia had rounded up two more from the shore party. Marvel, whom Leo Lloyd knew as Stevie, meekly handed himself in after the police called his sister. After the botched landing on 90 Mile Beach, Cullen had driven Wan and Tsai straight to SkyCity in downtown Auckland. Security camera footage showed them entering their rooms, booked under their real names. Jane Scott arrested Wan Ka Yip in the departure lounge at Auckland International Airport.

Within just five days of the mammoth meth haul, seven members of the shore party – Louie, Gravel, Tall Guy, Mack, Thugga, Marvel and Wan – had been arrested.

Tsai, the management figure from Hong Kong, had booked an earlier flight out than Wan Ka Yip and was the only one to escape. But he might well have wished he had been caught in New Zealand. He was last seen by the outside world in handcuffs on a boat floating on Taiwanese waters, with 693 kilograms of heroin stowed under the deck.

On every level, Operation Frontia was a public success. The police had stopped a massive amount of methamphetamine from ending up on the streets, and caught nearly everyone involved.

Inevitably, and certainly very entertainingly, the media played the story for laughs. The smuggling ring were portrayed as a bumbling bunch of idiots and the doomed launching of the Bayliner at Shipwreck Bay was narrated as pure farce.

The crooks *were* bumbling idiots and the launch *was* a LOL, but the comical scenes masked a deeper, more serious truth: that a clever bunch of criminals with international contacts were able to arrange for 500 kilograms of methamphetamine to be brought to New Zealand by sea.

Sure, they made mistakes. Their most obvious blunder was the original decision for the mothership to wait off the west coast. If they'd chosen the gentler waters of the east coast, the shore party would have been less likely run into trouble with the Bayliner and RHIB, and the unwanted attention of nosy locals that followed.

But they did a lot of things very, very well. They had deep pockets, deep enough that they could afford to lose nearly $150,000 in cash buying the two boats.

They also demonstrated sophisticated criminal tradecraft. Members of the group only ever referred to each other by codename, and used encrypted devices and satellite phones to thwart any attempts by police to covertly listen in.

And despite everything that went wrong, including the fact that the two sailors were turned away at Auckland International Airport, the group managed to successfully land half a tonne of Class A drugs without anyone knowing.

If it hadn't been for the quick thinking of Constable Thomas Nankivell, the well-founded suspicions of Leo Lloyd and some good luck, there's a good chance the meth-laden campervan would have trundled down to its Auckland destination with no one the wiser.

Cause, then, for police to celebrate. But the back-slapping bothered Beal. While the Northland police had done a good job in the first 24 hours, and his team had moved quickly to make arrests, the hard-nosed detective knew Operation Frontia had only picked the low-hanging fruit.

They'd banged up a handful of foot soldiers, and a couple of middle-management figures in Tuilotolava and Iusitini. But there had to be countless others higher up the pecking order, like Big T in Australia. Besides, Louie told the police they hadn't caught them all.

Beal's experience from Operations Major and Ice Age, 10 years earlier, told him that any well-organised importation syndicate would have a wider distribution network and infrastructure in place. New Zealand's biggest drug bust had a distinctly Australian flavour. This group of expats might be behind bars, but others would surely follow.

Beal was convinced that, despite losing their precious half-tonne of meth, the network would soon be back up and running with impunity. The P trade only knows one rule: the drugs must get through.

* * *

In September 2016, Beal was put in charge of a second investigation, Operation Virunga, and soon discovered that the network was indeed still in business. What had happened in Northland had been a setback, nothing more.

One of the first breakthroughs in Beal's new investigation was identifying the woman Louie knew as Blaze. Her real name was Selaima Fakaosilea. She was the sister of Ulakai Fakaosilea, or Tall Guy, recently deported back to New Zealand from Australia after a stint in the detention centre on Christmas Island. They were cousins of Jonah Lomu, the late great All Black wing.

Tall Guy was born in New Zealand, but moved to Australia with his family in his early teens. He'd lived half his life in Australia. Even so, he was among the first wave of 501s – a nickname derived from the new section of Australia's *Migration Act* that allows people to be deported on character grounds.

Australia was getting rid of its bad rubbish – dumping it in New Zealand.

Ulakai's sister, whom he affectionately called 'Tongan Barbie', also returned to New Zealand. They were later joined by their younger brother. As mentioned in Chapter 12, Seiana Fakaosilea would later come to the attention of law enforcement in Auckland as a member of the New Zealand chapter of the Comancheros, one of Australia's most feared outlaw motorcycle gangs.

There were other connections to Australia. Selaima Fakaosilea was in a relationship with Callan Hughes, or 'CJ', another Australian deportee, whose right-hand man, Kane McArley, was also a 501 deportee. CJ had been in close contact with Thugga and Tall Guy in Auckland leading up to the 500-kilo import, and his name had been on the periphery of Operation Frontia. It was now becoming clear to Beal that Callan Hughes was much higher up the pecking order than first thought.

Within a few weeks, Virunga's covert surveillance had paid a handsome dividend. Police listened in as Selaima Fakaosilea arranged a meeting on 29 September 2016 with Adrian Le'Ca, a patched member of the Thailand chapter of the Bandidos motorcycle gang.

Neither Fakaosilea nor Le'Ca personally handled the product. They sent lieutenants to do their dirty work instead, Fred Uputaua for Le'Ca and Henry Robati for Selaima.

Detectives watched as a sports bag was handed through a car window, Robati to Uputaua, while Le'Ca supervised the handover from another vehicle. Fifteen minutes later, Fakaosilea called Hughes, who seemed to be calling the shots, to confirm the deal was done. Police pulled over Uputaua and discovered 14.9 kilograms of methamphetamine and 1.9 kilograms of cocaine inside his vehicle.

This proved something very important. The drug syndicate had lost half a tonne of meth just a few months earlier. But they were back in business, and quick-smart. Clearly they had another supply pipeline, or potentially another hidden stockpile.

Operation Virunga had caught them red-handed, but police kept going to see what else might unravel if they continued tugging the thread. On 8 November 2016, Callan Hughes arranged to meet his girlfriend for 'dinner' on Auckland's Dominion Road. This was not a romantic date. Hughes parked his car, texted Fakaosilea the number on the registration plate, left the keys on the dashboard and walked away.

It was left to Fakaosilea to watch the car from a distance as an unknown individual removed 9 kilograms of methamphetamine from the boot and left hundreds of thousands of dollars as payment.

There was so much money to be made. In a three-week period over October and November 2016, Fakaosilea – a 29-year-old mother of two – was seen on four occasions handing over suitcases of cash to be laundered overseas – a total of $3.5 million. She was arrested a month later, along with Callan Hughes, Kane McArley and a number of other dealers living across the country, as far south as Christchurch.

* * *

The evidence gathered by Operations Frontia and Virunga was overwhelming. Louie was the first to plead guilty to importing methamphetamine, agreeing to give evidence for the Crown, for which he received a hefty discount when he appeared for sentencing in the Whangarei High Court in December 2016. He was sent to prison for 12 years. Most of the others followed suit in admitting guilt.

Jeremiah 'Thugga' Iusitini got 25 years and seven months, with Malachi 'Mack' Tuilotolava not far behind on 24 years. They were the ones passing on orders, in New Zealand at least, with Iusitini in contact with bosses like Big T overseas. Wan Ka Yip, who was in touch with the Hong Kong end of the operation, got 23 years, while grunts Amoki 'Gravel' Fonua and Ulakai 'Tall Guy' Fakaosilea got 22 years and 22 years seven months respectively.

Callan 'CJ' Hughes and Kane McArley, who were not charged in connection with the 500-kilogram import, pleaded guilty to distributing large amounts of meth in New Zealand. Hughes got 15 years, with McArley receiving 9 years.

Only Selaima Fakaosilea and Stevie Cullen refused to plead guilty and went to trial over importation charges.

Fakaosilea admitted her role in laundering money and the distribution of meth, but denied any role in smuggling the 500 kilograms into the country. She claimed to have been oblivious to what was happening in Northland, playing up to her 'Tongan Barbie' reputation.

The jury didn't buy the bimbo act. After a five-week trial in the High Court at Whangarei, both she and Cullen were convicted of importing a Class A drug and participating in an organised criminal group.

In August 2019, Cullen and Fakaosilea returned to the same courtroom to be sentenced in front of Justice Christine Gordon. Wearing a low-cut jacket and pants suit, Fakaosilea put on a brave face for the television cameras and her family present in the courtroom. There was no generous discount on offer as there had been for those who had pleaded guilty. She and Cullen were sentenced to 27 years in prison; Cullen will serve at least nine years before being considered for release by the Parole Board, and Fakaosilea will serve at least seven.

In her closing remarks, Justice Gordon said the discovery of 501 kilograms of methamphetamine – worth somewhere between $130 and $150 million – was a 'momentous event' in New Zealand criminal history.

The hearing brought the curtain down on the country's largest-ever drug-smuggling case. Operations Frontia and Virunga were over.

But police had confirmed that the evolution of the P trade in New Zealand had taken a new turn. Meth was no longer just the domain of local gangs like the Head Hunters who had affiliations with Asian crime syndicates.

There was a new power in town: Australia.

9

AN EXECUTION AT MIDNIGHT: THE CONDOR EMPIRE RUFFLES FEATHERS

2018

EVERYONE KNEW YOLANDA TU'UHEAVA as 'Mele', and Mele's affectionate name for her husband Abraham Tu'uheava was 'Fatty'. Fatty really *was* enormous.

On the night of 1 May 2018, the couple parked their silver Toyota Camry on Greenwood Road, a quiet side-street in Mangere flanked by commercial sites and the local wastewater treatment plant. Not a very romantic spot. It was more of a business appointment. Mele just wasn't quite sure what 'business' Fatty had got them into.

A black BMW pulled in behind them soon afterwards, at 11.15pm. Abraham got out, walked to the other car and talked to someone inside.

Mele stayed in the Camry. The headlights of the other car shone brightly in the Camry's rear-vision mirror. Mele couldn't hear what Fatty and the other man were talking about, but every now and then she'd recognise her husband's distinctive laugh.

Fatty had never outright told her what the meeting was about, but Mele knew it was dodgy. She suspected he was dealing drugs. Fatty worked part-time as a truck driver, but in the boot of the car was a suitcase holding $48,000, and on the back seat was a backpack with $15,000 stuffed inside.

Fatty told Mele his goal was to earn $50,000 every week. He didn't actually explain, though, how he hoped to do that. He *did* say that he was excited about the late-night rendezvous, that he felt he'd finally 'made it'.

So she sat and waited. Their conversation was dragging on. She finally lost patience with the brick-puzzle game on her iPhone. She turned the phone off, then held up the blank screen in front of her face, squinting at the reflective surface so she could see what was happening behind her. She could make out Fatty – his shape illuminated by the orange glow of the streetlights – still talking to the person in the car. She went back to her puzzle game.

Suddenly she heard screaming: 'Mele, Mele, Mele!'

Fatty pulled open the driver's door, then looked back at the men he was running away from. The Tongan giant started begging: 'Please, please, please don't. My wife, she has nothing to do with it.'

Mele looked back to see someone pointing a gun at Fatty.

The man calmly asked Fatty to shut the driver's door. 'Please,' the man said.

Confused, startled, downright terrified, Mele jumped out of the car and tried to lock eyes with a second man standing on her side of the Camry, who also had a gun in his hands.

'Please don't, I'm pregnant,' she lied, hoping to tug at the heartstrings of the armed strangers.

The men told Mele and Fatty to move towards a fence. They motioned with their guns to indicate that the couple should hurry up.

Abraham and Yolanda Tu'uheava reached out and grabbed each other. It was all they could do. They stumbled to the ground, and kneeled on the side of the road. Then they clambered back to their feet.

With the guns pointing straight at them, Abraham made a final plea for mercy. The 28-year-old told the gunmen to take the $63,000 in the car, and swore he would never tell a soul.

The leader just smirked. 'Nah,' he kept on saying. 'Nah. Nah.'

Still gripping each other tightly, Mele and Fatty kept walking backwards, walking backwards, to keep some sort of distance between themselves and the barrels of the guns.

'Run!' Fatty suddenly yelled. They turned, and he gave Mele a push to propel her away from danger. They sprinted across the grass beside the road, Mele barefoot in the autumn night, but they didn't get very far before they ran out of steam.

Ducking for cover behind a tree, Mele could see Fatty's eyes anxiously follow something down the road. It was a car, perhaps a Good Samaritan who could whisk them to safety, or at least frighten the armed men.

But it was the black BMW, driven by the smirking leader with the gun, with two other men inside. The driver got out. He told Fatty and Mele to move away from the tree and pointed towards a stand of flax. Mele knew that if they went in there, they would die.

Her husband was crying, holding on to her, trying to hide behind her. She angrily shoved him off: if anything, her giant husband should be protecting *her*.

Refusing to walk towards the flax, where any bodies would be less likely to be discovered, Mele and Fatty were marched at gunpoint towards a grass verge and forced onto their knees.

Mele had the presence of mind to position herself side on to the shooters. This would make her body a smaller target – ever so slightly.

She heard a bang and felt her arm go limp. There was a second bang. She felt the blood pour out. Still on her knees, she turned to the right and saw someone aiming at her husband. The shooter turned around to finish her off, so she threw herself onto the ground, and screamed out a prayer: 'Jesus shield me!'

Click. Click. Click. The trigger was pulled three times without firing. It'd run out of ammunition.

Fatty was on his knees. He looked at Mele, looked at the men trying to kill them, and ran towards the Camry.

It was the last time Mele saw him alive. She heard a gun fire three times and watched her husband topple forward.

Then Mele heard a different sound, more of a ding, and she knew she had been shot in the head.

There was another ding. Swaying back and forth, looking up at the sky, then down at the ground, Mele was struggling to remember how to breathe and told herself to fall. 'Idiot – fall. If you don't fall, they're going to keep shooting at you.'

She fell backwards. She lay still, playing dead. The men jumped back into the car, did a U-turn and drove away.

Mele thought her husband was playing dead too. She waited until she thought it was safe, then called out: 'Fatty!'

He didn't reply.

* * *

Abraham Tu'uheava had died at the scene. He had been shot seven times: twice in the arm, three times in the head and twice in the back.

Mele had been shot four times, and there were two bullets lodged in her skull. Incredibly, she survived.

She doesn't know how long she lay on the road, but remembers the sickly fragrance of blood flowing from the wounds in her head, and the crunching footsteps of her rescuer. She'd dragged herself out of the long grass and closer to the road, to make it easier for any passing motorists to see them and raise the alarm. She lay very still, slowly singing Tongan hymns and reciting the Lord's Prayer:

> Our Father, which art in heaven, hallowed be Thy
> name. Thy kingdom come, thy will be done, on earth
> as it is in heaven. Give us this day our daily bread.
> And forgive us our trespasses, as we forgive them that
> trespass against us. And lead us not into temptation, but
> deliver us from evil.

* * *

The execution-style shooting shocked the local community and veteran homicide detectives alike.

Officers who worked in the Counties Manukau Police District – the busiest in the country – were no strangers to violence. Most suspicious deaths revolved around family assaults: women and children beaten to death in the supposed safety of their home. There were also alcohol-fuelled fights in bars or at parties, where one punch was enough to kill an unsuspecting victim.

Even deaths involving gang members were more likely to be wanton violence, stupid acts of bravado. Most drug debts were settled with beatings, or by 'taxing' the debtor of their valuables, rather than by assassination.

But the shooting of Fatty and Mele was different.

This was the callous attempted murder of a married couple who were apparently lured unsuspecting to an isolated street in the middle of the night. They were unarmed and defenceless. They were both shot in the head. Only a miracle –

the divine intervention Mele cried out for? – had stopped her from dying alongside her husband.

Who could have done this? Who had this kind of MO?

The Auckland rumour-mill went into overdrive. Soon, the name on everyone's lips was that of a newcomer to New Zealand's criminal underworld: the Comancheros.

* * *

The Comanchero Motorcycle Club – named after the 1961 John Wayne movie – was founded in Sydney in 1968 by William 'Jock' Ross. A breakaway group of Comancheros led by Anthony 'Snoddy' Spencer formed a second chapter in late 1982. After meeting in Texas with representatives of American motorcycle club the Bandidos, Spencer and his followers 'patched over', or shifted allegiances, to become the first Bandidos chapter in Australia. They incinerated their Comanchero colours – depicting a black and gold condor – in a ceremonial bonfire and put on the 'Fat Mexican' patch of the Bandidos.

The acrimonious split added fuel to the already bitter gang rivalry. An escalating turf war put the Comancheros and Bandidos on a collision course, which came to a head in an infamous date in Australian history: 2 September 1984.

A trap was laid at a bike show at the Viking Tavern, in the Sydney suburb of Milperra. The press would dub it 'the Milperra Massacre'.

Armed with firearms and walkie-talkies, 19 Comancheros spread themselves across the tavern carpark to lie in wait for the Bandidos, who were expected to turn up at the bike show. Jock Ross waited in the middle. He wanted to give the appearance that he was alone, in the hope of drawing the Bandidos into a pincer trap. An ex-soldier, he had been inspired by a similar tactic used during the Boer Wars.

But the Bandidos were late. Thinking their rivals weren't coming, Ross and the Comancheros went inside the Viking Tavern to drink.

About 20 minutes later, 34 Bandidos – also heavily armed – caught the Comancheros off guard. The confrontation was verbal at first, and members of each side challenged each other to settle the dispute 'like men', without firearms, brandishing hand-held weapons such as lead pipes, chains and baseball bats. The standoff erupted into chaos when someone discharged a shotgun into the air, triggering a mêlée that lasted for at least 10 minutes before the first of 200 police officers arrived.

When the fighting finally came to a halt, the carpark looked like a casualty ward. Seven people were dead and 20 needed hospital treatment. There was little public sympathy for the four Comancheros and two Bandidos killed by shotgun and rifle fire, but the seventh victim was an innocent bystander, 14-year-old Leanne Walters, struck in the face by a stray round from a .357 rifle.

Jock Ross also took a gunshot to the head but survived. He suffered a permanent brain injury that impaired his vision and left him unable to read or write.

Ross was convicted of murder in 1987, on the ground that he instigated the Milperra Massacre. The 'Supreme Commander' of the Comancheros was sent to prison, but released just five years later, in 1992, when the murder conviction was downgraded to manslaughter on appeal. His iron grip on the gang would last another 10 years, before a new leader – one of a new breed of Australian outlaw bikies – stepped forward to wrest power from his grasp.

For decades, members of motorcycle gangs like the Comancheros had often looked comically stereotypical:

sporting scruffy beards and dated leather, and almost exclusively white in ethnicity. Things had begun to change in the late 1990s. The Comancheros, and other gangs such as the Nomads, had started to recruit heavily from the Middle Eastern and Pacific Island communities emigrating to Australia. These young men wore designer clothes and jewellery, spent hours in the gym honing their physiques, and had attractive girlfriends hanging off their muscular and heavily tattooed arms.

The emergence of the so-called 'Nike Bikie' generation was about more than just a difference in fashion taste. New South Wales detectives would come to believe the new blood marked the evolution of the Comancheros from a small-time Sydney motorcycle club to an organised criminal group with international connections.

Mahmoud 'Mick' Hawi was a member of this new generation. Born in Beirut, Lebanon, Hawi emigrated to Australia with his parents and siblings in 1984, the year after the Milperra Massacre. He joined the Comancheros as an 18-year-old and ousted Jock Ross as president, reportedly by force, in 2002. By then, Ross was 60. Hawi was barely 21.

Under his leadership, the Comancheros continued recruiting young Mediterranean and Middle Eastern men, as well as Serbian ex-soldiers who'd fought in the Yugoslav Wars of the 1990s, and Pacific Islanders, who were valued for their impressive size and strength. The aggressive expansion, in numbers and also into the lucrative drug trade, rubbed their rivals – such as the Hells Angels, Nomads, Bandidos and Finks – up the wrong way. Bashings, drive-by shootings and firebombings of gang-controlled tattoo parlours were common tactics in the Sydney gang turf wars.

A chance meeting on a flight from Melbourne to Sydney was the spark that ignited a powderkeg on Sunday, 22 March

2009, setting off the worst public display of gang violence since the Milperra Massacre.

Seated on Qantas flight 430 were Mick Hawi and five other Comancheros, as well as Derek Wainohu, the president of the Sydney chapter of the Hells Angels. The accidental encounter triggered a flurry of text messages by both sides, calling for reinforcements to meet them at Sydney Airport in case of reprisal.

On disembarking from the plane, Hawi walked up to Wainohu and punched him, and said: 'You're dead, do you hear me? You're fucking dead.'

The two gangs went at it in Domestic Terminal 3. A dozen Comancheros and five Hells Angels members and associates wildly punched and kicked each other in front of hundreds of terrified passengers waiting at the airport.

One of those who responded to Wainohu's call for help was Anthony Zervas. He picked up a pair of scissors and tried to stab Hawi in the left temple. The Comancheros' leader partially deflected the blow with his hand. Zervas was punched to the ground in the mêlée, as members of the Comancheros and the Hells Angels picked up metal bollards, used to rope off passenger queues, to swing as weapons.

As he lay defenceless and vulnerable on the ground, Zervas's head was violently bludgeoned by one of these 17-kilo, blunt-force instruments. His torso was punctured with scissors and knives. He died as the wild brawl dispersed, and bloodied gang members scarpered from the airport in taxis.

The brutal world of bikies, in which violence is suffered in silence and given back in harsh retribution, had spilled into the public arena. Hundreds of passengers had witnessed the horrific death of Zervas, but so too did anyone watching television or reading a newspaper: security cameras inside the airport had captured the sickening violence in slow motion.

The Australian public was disgusted. This time, the gangs had gone a step too far.

The chaotic violence of the airport brawl led to public calls for the New South Wales Police to crack down on bikies. Strike Force Raptor was born.

Police had been investigating bikie crime for decades, but Raptor was different. It took a proactive approach. That is to say, members of the elite police unit went out of their way to look for trouble, whether the alleged breach of the law was criminal or otherwise. Nothing was too big or too small.

If someone was punched outside a Kings Cross nightclub by a gang member, officers from Raptor would take over the case. If gang members didn't pay their traffic fines, Raptor would follow up to ensure their driver's licences were taken away. Tips were followed up assiduously, houses and motorcycles raided for firearms and drugs. Raptor would inspect gang clubhouses and use council rules to shut them down for shoddy or unauthorised building work. If alcohol was being served, Raptor invoked archaic legislation so the gangs needed to have a liquor licence to have a beer with their mates.

Another opportunity to make life difficult for Australia's motorcycle gangs appeared just before Christmas 2014, when Immigration Minister Peter Dutton rushed through amendments to the *Migration Act* to impose a character test on visa applicants and non-citizens. Visas were automatically cancelled if an individual failed the character test – written into law as section 501 – because they had a substantial criminal record, defined as a sentence of 12 months' imprisonment or more.

Over the next five years, thousands of these so-called '501s', many of whom had lived almost their entire lives in Australia, were deported 'home' to New Zealand, where they often arrived penniless, with no long-term accommodation, employment or even family to support them.

Many had mental health issues or drug and alcohol addictions. They were vulnerable, with no one to care for them. Losers, some would say. But among the 501s was a somewhat smaller subset that posed a much greater risk to New Zealand: Australian bikies who were targeted for deportation because of their senior positions within gangs.

Both underworld figures and senior detectives here were quick to anticipate how the arrival of these brash Aussies, with their reputation for shooting first and asking questions later, would radically disrupt the gang scene forever.

* * *

As described in Chapter 1, a precarious state of peace had stayed in place between local gangs for many years. The introduction of bold new competitors in an already crowded market would soon change all that.

The Comancheros were the first of the Australian 501 gangs to officially announce their presence in New Zealand. Photographs of six imposing men wearing tight 'Comanchero New Zealand' T-shirts, hands clasped on wrists, were posted on Instagram in February 2018. Standing behind two customised, gold-plated Harley-Davidson motorcycles, the men had thick gold chains around their necks, and were wearing designer sunglasses and expensive watches.

'All done and sworn in ... welcome aboard to my brothers in New Zealand. Another Comancheros chapter opened up. We are growing stronger and stronger,' the caption said. The post went on to refer to the Australian politician who had created the harsh deportation policy: 'Fuck Peter Dutton. But you made this possible #lol.'

Detective Superintendent Greg Williams soon confirmed that the Comancheros had formed a New Zealand chapter. Williams, the head of the National Organised Crime Group, said 14 Comancheros had been deported from Australia and his staff expected the gang would attempt to establish themselves in the New Zealand drug market. 'It will be interesting,' he said, 'to see what happens.'

* * *

Abraham Tu'uheava followed the Comancheros' social media posts too. He admired their ostentatious displays of wealth and their seemingly tight bonds of brotherhood, in large part due to their members' shared Tongan heritage. Tu'uheava was Tongan too. The 28-year-old was envious, and desperate to escape the drudgery of driving trucks around industrial Auckland. Tu'uheava had experienced the gangster life before, in Australia, and longed to get back into the game.

He was born and bred in the 1990s in Mangere, at a time when that part of Auckland was the main power-base of ethnic gangs like the Mongrel Mob and Black Power. Cannabis was the drug of choice, and various Black Power chapters – like the breakaway Sindi chapter, led by the legendary Abe Wharewaka – controlled most of the tinnie houses dotted across Counties Manukau. Gangs like the Tribesmen and the King Cobras also maintained strongholds in the region.

But when methamphetamine exploded onto the scene in the early 2000s, the ethnic gangs were disorganised and slow to react compared with the likes of the Head Hunters and Hells Angels, who seized control of the best meth cooks, as well as having the best connections for sourcing pseudoephedrine in China. In those early days, gangs like Black Power and the Tribesmen were simply retailers in

South Auckland, stocking their numerous tinnie houses with a popular new product, before establishing their own manufacturing enterprises in time.

Around 2005, South Auckland also saw the emergence of another phenomenon: the ABC street gangs. Young men of mainly Polynesian heritage, disenchanted by school and family life, were drawn to one another, often simply because they lived in the same street or neighbourhood. Searching for a common bond, many felt connected with the hip-hop culture of the United States, where their heroes rapped lyrics about growing up poor, wore heavy 'bling' jewellery, glamourised street feuds and violent retribution, and sexualised women as property.

Loosely inspired by the warring Crips and Bloods gangs in Los Angeles, dozens of these street gangs popped up overnight like mushrooms, with names like Juvenile Crip Boys (JCB), Dope Money Sex (DMS) and the Ruthless Young Thugs (RYT). With many having names that could be abbreviated to three letters, the police called them 'ABC gangs'. The most infamous was the Killer Beez, whose leader was the charismatic Josh Masters. (His story is told in Chapter 10.)

The so-called ABC gangs were a disorganised rabble. The teenagers gathered in somebody's garage, then roamed around the streets, fuelled by booze and drugs, and committed petty crimes. They would steal anything from handbags to cars, but more problematic were the street brawls involving fence palings, bats and chains, which inevitably led to bodies left dead on the ground as everyone scattered and headed for home.

Established gangs like the Tribesmen and Black Power looked at the speedy rise of the LA-style street gangs and saw the potential. These rebellious young men were foot soldiers in the making, an instant army if given direction, so many of them became feeder groups for the established gangs, doing the dirty work for the older men.

* * *

The membership of RYT – the Ruthless Young Thugs – included a rather large young man by the name of Abraham Tu'uheava.

He got into a little bit of trouble as a teenager, but like many his age who were arrested by the police, or given a cuff around the ear by family members, he grew out of the phase with maturity. He met a young woman called Yolanda at her aunt's Otahuhu dairy. They were married in December 2008. Nine months later, their only son was born.

Struggling to get ahead, the young couple decided to move to Australia in 2013 for a better life. They moved in with Abraham's cousin in Sydney, who helped him get work driving trucks and then with a tree-clearing business, while Yolanda got a job at a theme park. The cousin also introduced Abraham to the Nomads motorcycle gang.

More than any other Sydney club, the Nomads were the driving force behind the transformation of the bikie scene in Australia through the recruitment of Middle Eastern and Polynesian members. They were the first gang to have a leader of Middle Eastern heritage, when Sam Ibrahim – brother of John Ibrahim, immortalised in the television series *Underbelly: The Golden Mile* for his ownership of nightclubs across Sydney's King Cross – became president of the Parramatta chapter in the late 1990s.

The imposing size of 170-kilo Abraham Tu'uheava impressed the Nomads. He was embraced with open arms by current national president Sleiman Tajjour, a close relative of the Ibrahim family. Sleiman, better known as Simon, took Tu'uheava under his wing. The pair grew so close that Tu'uheava was entrusted with the job of chauffeuring Tajjour's mother to medical appointments.

In return, Tu'uheava was rewarded with an expensive European car, and his rent on a Sydney apartment was paid for him. As a trusted member of the inner circle of one of Sydney's most influential crime families, Abraham Tu'uheava was proud of how far he'd come since roaming the streets of Mangere with the Ruthless Young Thugs.

But the trappings of success were taken away just as quickly. Simon Tajjour was arrested in August 2017 as part of a global investigation into drug and tobacco smuggling, along with members of the Ibrahim family.

Without their leader, the Nomads were rudderless. Yolanda Tu'uheava would describe the gang members as 'little lost sheep' in the absence of Simon Tajjour – her husband most of all.

Robbed of his patronage, the Tu'uheavas lost the car and the house. They moved in with another Nomad family but the relationship soon soured. When Yolanda's brother committed suicide in Sydney later in 2017, the family accompanied his body back to New Zealand for the funeral and did not return.

They were back in Mangere. Yolanda got a job in a factory. Abraham drove trucks in the industrial streets around Auckland International Airport.

It was a depressing demotion for Abraham, who yearned for the Sydney high life. He flicked through the social media feeds of the Comancheros, watching videos of them riding Harley-Davidsons in convoy behind the team bus of the Tongan rugby league team. Thousands of flag-waving Tongan fans of the giant-killing team, filled with league superstars like Jason Taumalolo and Andrew Fifita, were caught up in a wave of national pride during the 2017 Rugby League World Cup held in New Zealand and Australia. The team's motto was Mate Ma'a Tonga, or Die for Tonga. The deep-seated passion of Tonga's red army of supporters was rooted in the same loyalty demanded by the Comancheros, who now leaned on genealogy and Tongan culture to bind the gang together.

Before long, Abraham moved beyond simply scrolling the Comancheros' social media feeds to exchanging messages with members. Those messages turned into a meeting with around 10 patched members in the Auckland township of Botany, to which Tu'uheava took his two brothers for support. He was offered a Comanchero patch, but turned down the chance, as he still harboured a dream of returning to Sydney and reuniting with his mentor Simon Tajjour of the Nomads.

However, the decision to turn down a patch didn't stop Tu'uheava from doing business with them. The Comancheros had the international connections to smuggle large amounts of methamphetamine into the country, but the tight Tongan crew was still small in number. They needed a distribution network so they could sell drugs across the country, and Abraham Tu'uheava wanted a consistent supply.

He had rekindled relationships with some friends from his Ruthless Young Thugs days. RYT now called themselves Crip Family, and Tu'uheava was purchasing methamphetamine from them to sell in ounce weights. But they sometimes came up short, which frustrated Tu'uheava, who had willing buyers in Christchurch and Southland. To satisfy their needs, he needed a reliable weekly flow of drugs, which he was confident that the Comancheros could provide.

A deal was struck. It ultimately cost Tu'uheava his life.

* * *

No one is absolutely certain why the business relationship soured so dramatically. The investigation into Tu'uheava's murder – Operation Weaver – gathered evidence that suggested Tu'uheava had been passing himself off as a Comanchero while selling meth in the South Island and also undercutting the price of other dealers the gang was supplying down there.

Detectives on the case were told that the gang had begun asking hard questions when their buyers started complaining about this mysterious Comanchero. They'd settled on Tu'uheava as the most likely suspect.

Phone records revealed numerous calls and messages between Tu'uheava and a senior member of the Comancheros, whose name is suppressed, suggesting Tu'uheava enjoyed direct access to the brains trust of the gang he so admired.

This changed on 27 April 2018, when he received a text from an unknown number: 'Sup tox [Tongan slang for 'bro'], texting on behalf of the tokos ['bros'], if you need to contact them, it's going to go through me now.'

His new point of contact was Viliami Taani, also known as William, who was a patched Comancheros member. They arranged to meet in three days' time, when Abraham would return from yet another meth run in Christchurch.

They met in the carpark of a McDonald's restaurant in Manukau. The 26-year-old Taani was driving a black BMW and had his two cousins in tow, Fisilau Tapaevalu, nicknamed 'Fish', and Mesui Tufui.

After meeting Tu'uheava, Tufui overheard Taani call someone with an Australian accent and ask, 'What's the go with the Nomads?'

Later that night, the three cousins drove to meet another Comanchero at Bucklands Beach, where Taani disappeared into the dark for five minutes, while Tufui and Tapaevalu smoked cigarettes.

On his return, Taani looked over at Tapaevalu and said, 'Yeah, green light', according to Tufui. Later, they whispered,

'That's the guy that's making money off the Commos' name. We're going to put him to sleep.'

Taani sent a text message to Abraham Tu'uheava, suggesting another meeting immediately in Greenwood Road. Excited at the prospect of picking up a substantial amount of methamphetamine, Abraham woke up Yolanda, asleep on the couch, and told her to pack a bag. Their son was left asleep with family.

The plan was to meet the Comancheros crew in Mangere, then carry on driving through the night to Invercargill to sell meth. It wasn't the first time Yolanda had accompanied her husband on a 'business' trip. She just turned a blind eye, and enjoyed the perks of hotel life.

'Ofa atu dox,' Tu'uheava texted back to Taani – 'I love you brother', roughly translated from Tongan.

He was being lured to his death.

* * *

Around 5.45am, a passing motorist noticed a hulking body, lying face down in the gravel, then another smaller body motionless in the grass. The Good Samaritan called 111, and to his astonishment, the woman gasped for help. She was alive.

Police officers squeezed into the ambulance, to glean as much detail from Yolanda as possible straightaway, in case she didn't survive.

Two bullets were lodged in her brain; surgeons were able to excise one, but the second was too dangerous to remove.

Over the coming days, as she drifted in and out of sleep, Yolanda gave longer formal statements to police from her hospital bed, with a surprising level of recollection. Armed officers stood outside the door.

Piecing together her memories, along with phone records, CCTV footage, DNA and forensic evidence, Operation Weaver was able to produce a photo board of suspects. Yolanda Tu'uheava identified Fisilau Tapaevalu, Mesui Tufui and the 'main guy', Viliami Taani. The trio were charged with murder and attempted murder.

Tapaevalu and Tufui denied the charges but were convicted following a jury trial in June 2019 at the High Court at Auckland. Two months later, they were given the mandatory life sentence for murder and will be eligible to seek parole after 17 and 19 years respectively.

Taani pleaded guilty and will serve at least 17 and a half years in prison. He led a double life. Raised in a strict Christian household, he was described by those close to him as an attentive father who shielded his family from his life in the Comancheros. Taani claimed to be remorseful, saying to a probation officer, 'The Tu'uheava children will have to live without a father and I have to live with that.' (He was apparently unaware that Abraham and Yolanda had just the one child.)

Yolanda Tu'uheava has to live with it too. With a bullet lodged permanently in her brain, her vision is rapidly deteriorating and she suffers from headaches. She has trouble sleeping and has been diagnosed with post-traumatic stress disorder. She struggles to think straight, is in constant pain from her injuries, and cannot work as a result. There is just $20 left over each week after the bills are paid.

Not a day goes by when Yolanda doesn't relive the horror of what happened.

Their son, still at primary school, wears his father's clothes and looks at pictures of him at night. They're all he has left.

10

JUST THE FACTS: ATTACK OF THE KILLER BEEZ

2018–2020

EVERY CRIMINAL CASE BEFORE the courts includes a document known as the 'police summary of facts'. It sets things out in numbered points. It's a kind of crime journalism, stripped back to the bare essentials – names, places, dates. It refers only to facts that are not in dispute. When you read a summary of facts, you're reading the established truth.

> Summary of facts, March 23, 2020. Queen vs
> Akustino Tae, defendant. Offence: Wounding with
> intent to cause grievous bodily harm. Penalty:
> 14 years' imprisonment.

The Queen is very busy in Commonwealth law. All crimes are committed against the Queen; her name is a constant feature in every district court and high court the length and breadth of New Zealand. She is represented by the police and by Crown lawyers.

However, in this case, everyone – including his lawyer – spelled Tae's first name incorrectly. It's actually Okusitino.

1. The complainant in this matter is Joshua MASTERS who is a 41 year old male with extensive family connections in South Auckland.

Surnames in the summary of facts are always introduced in capitals.

2. The defendant, TAE, is a 39 year old male who lives in South Auckland.

The setting, then, is South Auckland. Tae has pleaded guilty to a charge of wounding with intent to cause grievous bodily harm. Masters is the wounded person.

And then the summary teases out a small but vital piece of information.

3. Masters and Tae are known to each other.

Actually, Masters and Tae had been close friends, almost like brothers. They had known each other since 1998, when they started selling tinnies together. Masters had been 20, Tae just 18.

They'd grown up in Otara, a suburb in South Auckland jammed up against the eastern edge of State Highway 1. The population is largely Polynesian and poor, as was the Masters family when Joshua James Masters came into the world in 1978, at a time when memories of the divisive Dawn Raids of the 1970s – when Pasifika people were targeted as overstayers by the New Zealand Government – were still raw.

He had an unsettled upbringing and education. He was passed around between family members and lived all over Otara, attending every primary school, both intermediates, and both secondary schools in the district. After repeating fifth form, Masters left school at the age of 17. He had passed some academic subjects but excelled at sport, especially rugby league.

Otara was also the home of the Tribesmen MC.

4. Tae is a patched gang member of the Tribesmen Motorcycle Gang.

The Tribesmen were an established local gang like the Head Hunters or Highway 61. They rode motorcycles, hung out at their pad and protected their turf. Their insignia is meant to be noticed: a yellow and black patch decorated with a skull and a raised middle finger.

But all around them in Otara in the mid-2000s were a new breed of wannabe gangstas who could never afford a Harley-Davidson. Or even want one. Just like Abraham Tu'uheava, many disaffected Pasifika youth felt more connected with the hip-hop street culture of the United States.

So the Tribesmen made a calculated, strategic move. They saw the potential of the rebellious young ABC street gangs in their neighbourhood and recruited an army. The Killer Beez were born.

5. Masters is the President of the Killer Beez gang. The Killer Beez has long been a feeder gang for the Tribesmen.

Masters had been eager to join the Tribesmen. He had a role model: he was following in the footsteps of the only father figure in his life, Verne Wilson, a notoriously hard Tribesman and representative rugby league player.

He rose up through the ranks of the Tribesmen alongside his friends Michael and Denis Solomon, Dion Snell – and Okusitino Tae. By the time he was 21, Masters was the president.

He and his mates were also attracted to the culture of the ABC gangs. They became founding members of the Killer Beez. Masters became the gang's charismatic leader; Tae was a staunch foot soldier.

Around the same time as the rise of the Killer Beez, other ABC gangs were developing ties with established patched gangs: the Juvenile Crip Boys (JCB) were linked with Black Power, the Red Army with the Mongrel Mob, Dope Money Sex (DMS) with the Head Hunters.

The phenomenon of the South Auckland street gangs had cropped up around 2005, but faded away within a few years, as members got in trouble with the police or their disappointed families, or simply grew up.

But the Killer Beez kept going. What made them different from the other feeder gangs was Josh Masters.

* * *

Masters was tough, strong and fearless. He was also handsome and charming, and had genuine leadership and business savvy. As an aspiring rapper who called himself Gravity, Masters appeared in music videos, and in February 2007 he set up a music label, Colourway Records, which promoted local musicians, held concerts and sold CDs, clothing and merchandise at the Saturday flea markets.

Young people were used to seeing the glamour and wealth of rap culture in American music videos on the MTV channel. But this was Otara, not Los Angeles, and Masters was a homegrown hero. His political lyrics spoke to a generation of disenfranchised Pasifika youth on the margins of society.

Masters was untouchable, the epitome of cool, and young men flocked to join his black and yellow banner. A potent combination of contemporary hip-hop culture and traditional patched gang structure, the Killer Beez became a highly marketable modern gang, the likes of which New Zealand had never seen.

Yet armies bring violence, and the Killer Beez were no different. At the start of 2008 there was a spate of attacks across Auckland, often unprovoked, sometimes against entirely innocent parties. Golf clubs, bats and even fence palings were used as weapons.

Police in Counties Manukau had no doubt that the Killer Beez were being used as cannon fodder for the Tribesmen when enforcement was required. The violence was not always random either.

In January 2008, a group of Killer Beez drove to Othello Drive, Otara, to send a message. In a scene likened by one veteran detective to the gunfight at the OK Corral, the gang members stopped outside a house and emptied their firearms into the dwelling. It was a tinnie house run by a well-known local crime family who had cut ties with the Tribesmen.

Someone inside the house fired back with a shotgun. Pellets from the blast struck Okusitino Tae in the face.

Just 27 years old at the time, Tae woke up from surgery in Middlemore Hospital to discover he'd lost his left eye. Doctors had removed two shotgun pellets from his brain.

That same month, journalist Patrick Gower wrote about the Killer Beez in the *New Zealand Herald* as the fastest-growing street gang in Auckland. It was the first time the gang had featured in mainstream media. In a string of stories, Gower linked the Killer Beez to a number of violent acts across Auckland, including several particularly sickening beatings on the North Shore in which the victims had been bashed around the head with baseball bats or a metal bar, in a rumoured 'prospecting' ritual.

Masters refused to speak to Gower. He did, however, agree to an on-camera interview with John Campbell in a primetime 7pm television slot in February 2008.

Masters was asked about his hopes for the high school students of nearby Sir Edmund Hillary College. 'For more doors to open … for opportunities to be given to the poor,' Masters said, looking straight at Campbell. 'That's the sort of backgrounds we come from around here.

'As Killer Beez, we're standing up and saying, "If you're not going to give us the options, we're going to create options for ourselves. Be the best you can be. Don't fall short. If you do, we're there to back you up."'

With remarkable sangfroid, Masters earnestly rejected any suggestion that those wanting to join the Killer Beez must commit an act of violence – 'We're disgusted by those acts and we're disgusted by the [media] coverage blaming us for doing them' – and rebuffed rumours of drug dealing. 'We're against it, we hate it,' he replied when asked about the gang's attitude towards methamphetamine.

It was a masterclass in presenting an innocent front.

Probing a little deeper in a somewhat soft interview, the host of *Campbell Live* questioned why anyone should believe Masters.

The gang boss responded, 'I have no drug convictions whatsoever. It's not because I'm good at what I do, or good at what [the police] think that I'm doing.

'I give you my word. No drugs. I'm not known for taking drugs, my family knows that, my friends know that, my boys [in the Killer Beez] know that, and now New Zealand knows that.

'I've got nothing to hide.'

* * *

Watching the television interview in growing disbelief were Detective Senior Sergeant Albie Alexander and Detective Sergeant Ross Ellwood.

To the pair of long-time Counties Manukau investigators, Masters's proclamations were more than brazen rhetoric, they were barefaced lies. Since the Othello Drive shooting in January 2008, Alexander and Ellwood had been running a covert inquiry into Masters, Colourway Records and the Killer Beez.

Operation Leo had intercepted more than 110,000 phone calls and text messages from January up until May, when Masters and 43 other members or associates of the Killer Beez and the Tribesmen were arrested. The termination of Operation Leo came just a few short weeks after the *Campbell Live* interview in which Masters had indignantly maintained his innocence, giving police the ultimate right of reply.

The Killer Beez had tried to portray themselves as 'modern-day Robin Hoods', Detective Inspector John Tims told waiting media at a press conference. 'They have attempted to achieve status through music and videos in connection with the youth of our community. Based on the evidence secured throughout this operation and today, in simple terms they are drug dealers who are causing destruction and chaos in our community by their actions.'

Police seized about $500,000 worth of meth and cannabis and $20,000 in cash. They also confiscated a large quantity of stolen property as well as motorcycles and cars, including Masters's brand-new Harley-Davidson, under the *Proceeds of Crime Act*.

Masters was denied bail, repeatedly, and remanded in custody in Mount Eden Prison for two more years until, in a late twist, he admitted all charges against him shortly before his High Court trial was due to start in 2010.

Despite pleading guilty to supplying and conspiracy to supply methamphetamine, as well as to laundering money through Colourway Records, Masters managed to drag the case out for another two years. He fired his lawyers, claiming they had given him poor legal advice, and argued over the evidence in an attempt to minimise his criminal culpability and eventual prison sentence.

Instead of a jury trial, a disputed facts hearing was held in the High Court at Auckland in July 2012, in which Justice Kit Toogood listened to the Crown evidence, as well as Masters's own explanations.

Masters signed an affidavit as well as giving evidence in the witness stand, saying that at the time of the Operation Leo surveillance, he had stepped down as the leader of the Killer Beez to concentrate on his Colourways music business. He wanted to be a role model, he said, to show others like him that there were legitimate ways to earn a good living.

Masters told the judge that while he'd been aware people around him were selling drugs, he did not approve of them. He'd done no more than put buyers and sellers in touch with one another, which was why he had pleaded guilty to the drug charges. But he denied ever handling controlled drugs himself. No trace of drugs or drug paraphernalia, such as P pipes, were ever found in his home.

In response, the Crown played to the court a series of conversations between Masters and convicted drug dealer Nguyen Ming that had been intercepted on 1 May 2008. At 5.03pm the following exchange took place:

Masters: All good for three friends?
Nguyen: Um yeah should be soon.
Masters: 9 o'clock tonight.

At 8.48pm, Masters called to ask how far away Nguyen was. Nguyen told him 15 minutes, then called back at 9.09pm to assure Masters he was only five minutes away.

When Nguyen failed to arrive, Masters called his phone again at 9.33pm. No answer. 'This fella is not usually that late,' Masters was recorded as saying, making yet another call at 9.55pm.

The reason for the disappearing act was that Operation Leo had made a tactical decision to arrest Nguyen en route to Masters's home, in order to prove that they had been talking about methamphetamine. Three 1-ounce bags of the Class A drug were found underneath the driver's seat; these were the three 'friends' Masters had referred to, according to the Crown case.

In the face of overwhelming evidence, Masters was adamant that 'three friends' was a reference to three Killer Béez who wanted to meet Nguyen. He was only facilitating a meeting, he claimed, and had had nothing to do with the drug transactions.

'I found this explanation completely lacking in credibility,' Justice Kit Toogood said in response.

In August 2012, Masters was sentenced to 10 years and five months in prison, required to serve five years and nine months before being eligible for parole.

'I accept that you have genuine leadership qualities and undoubted business acumen. It is a great shame that your obvious qualities as a charismatic leader amongst your peers were not confined to legitimate business enterprises.'

* * *

To the great satisfaction of Albie Alexander and Ross Ellwood, Operation Leo had achieved its goal of swatting Josh Masters to one side. This diminished the presence and influence of the Killer Beez on the streets of Otara, which hugely relieved local residents.

Unfortunately, though, the harsh environment of prison proved an even more fertile ground for Masters in recruiting alienated and angry young men. His army kept growing behind bars, and not just in Paremoremo prison, where Masters was serving his sentence. Inmates are often shifted around different Corrections facilities depending on security risk, court hearings or even just the availability of beds. The influence of the Killer Beez, once contained in the suburb of Otara, spread to prisons in Northland, Waikato, Taupo, Whanganui, Wellington, Christchurch and Dunedin. Once in their new homes, the Killer Beez soon earned a reputation as dangerous prisoners, carrying out brutal attacks on other inmates and prison guards.

One of the worst was the fatal 2010 assault on Jason Palmer, a former US Marine employed as a Corrections officer at Spring Hill Prison north of Hamilton. Killer Beez member Latu Kepu punched Palmer so hard that it jolted the guard's head back, and he fell backwards, hitting the concrete pavement with the back of his skull. The 33-year-old died in Middlemore Hospital the following day from severe brain injuries. He was married with two children, aged five and two.

While the assault was premeditated, the Crown could not prove murderous intent, so Kepu pleaded guilty only to manslaughter. An extra six years and four months were added to his time in prison, though the Killer Bee stood defiant and remorseless in the dock, almost revelling in the notoriety of killing a prison 'screw'.

Angry young men with little else going for them signed up to join the Killer Beez 'swarm', which came with the added bonus of safety in numbers in the dangerous prison environment. By 2015 they were the fourth-largest prison gang in the country, with 167 affiliates. (By comparison, the Mongrel Mob and Black Power – New Zealand's two largest gangs by far, with thousands of members between them – had 684 and 522 affiliates behind bars respectively.)

By now Josh Masters was eligible for early release on parole. Prison intelligence reports provided to the Parole Board showed that a mobile phone and a large quantity of drugs had been found inside his cell.

Masters 'remains involved at a high level in the Killer Beez gang', according to the reports, which stated that the mobile phone had been used to give orders to gang members outside prison.

Masters told the Parole Board the intel reports were 'a fiction'. He claimed he had retired from the Tribesmen Motorcycle Club, asking his aunt to hand in his patch, and had no association with the Killer Beez either. The first claim might have been true, but Masters was still as involved with the Killer Beez as ever.

In its decision of August 2015, the Parole Board called much of Masters's explanation for his misconduct 'disingenuous'. Panel convenor Neville Trendle wrote: 'He gave the impression of being the victim of circumstances and of prison mis-management. There was a factual basis for some of his claims but on key issues we were far from satisfied.'

Parole was declined again the following year, and Masters's behaviour in prison was described as 'confrontational and at times intimidatory'.

Meanwhile, tensions between Killer Beez inmates and Corrections staff at Paremoremo escalated in a number of violent incidents. They culminated in a bloody brawl in which both prisoners and prison guards were charged with criminal offences.

Patched Killer Beez Samuel Junior Hutchins and Trent Wellington, along with prospect Mitai Angell, ambushed prison officer Desmond Fa'afoi in April 2018. Wellington punched Fa'afoi then attacked a second guard. Hutchins and Wellington used two shanks – pieces of plastic or metal sharpened to a dagger-like point – to stab Fa'afoi in the scalp, face, arms and upper body. He started to bleed heavily from his wounds, and blood was soon smeared over the walls and floor.

Other prison guards came to the aid of their colleague and the tables soon turned, with Fa'afoi captured on CCTV cameras kicking Angell in the head three times. Fellow prison guard Wiremu Paikea was alleged to have snapped Wellington's ankle at a 90-degree angle, when the inmate was already subdued on the ground. A third prison guard, Viju Devassy, was accused of deliberately turning away the body camera on his protective vest so the actions of his colleagues weren't caught on tape. All three were acquitted at a High Court jury trial, while the prisoners all pleaded guilty to wounding with intent to cause grievous bodily harm.

The motivation for the inmates' brutal attack on Des Fa'afoi emerged only 18 months later, when they were sentenced. It was revenge, a retaliatory gang-hit just one month after a confrontation between Fa'afoi and Josh Masters.

Judge Claire Ryan: 'Mr Joshua Masters adopted a fighting stance. It was difficult to tell from the CCTV footage whether or not there was contact ... or simply threatening and menacing words.'

But nothing more could be done to Masters. He served every day of his 10 years and five months' imprisonment imposed by Justice Toogood in August 2012 (the starting point of which was backdated to his arrest in May 2008). Now 40 years old, Masters walked free from prison in

October 2018 to return to the head of a black and yellow army that was bigger than ever.

* * *

6. Tensions developed between the two gangs [the Killer Beez and the Tribesmen] after the complainant's release from prison and there were a number of connected shootings and other acts of violence between the gangs in the early months of 2019.

After his release, Masters wasted no time in flexing his muscles and claiming back what he believed to belong to him: the streets of Otara, where he'd fought his way to the top of the pile.

But in his prolonged absence, the underworld had changed. New players had emerged, such as the Comancheros and Mongol Nation, another Australian outlaw motorcycle gang.

Masters had always been arrogant. His self-importance had rubbed some people up the wrong way. And one of them happened to be standing at the Auckland Harley-Davidson service counter when Masters visited the motorcycle dealership on Friday, 26 April 2019.

7. Masters went to the Auckland Harley Davidson dealership at 521 Mount Wellington Highway to pay for repairs to his motorcycle and uplift it. At approximately 1:31pm, he put on his distinctive white leather Killer Beez President's vest and, shortly thereafter, at about 1:39pm, left the dealership on his motorcycle.
8. At approximately 1:41pm, after Masters had left the dealership, Tae and an associate arrived at the Auckland Harley Davidson dealership in a black Toyota Vitz.

9. Upon arrival at the address Tae parked his Toyota Vitz at the service entrance of the address, nearest to Niall Burgess Drive.

10. Tae exited the Vitz from the driver seat and the male passenger also exited the Vitz from the passenger side.

11. Tae and the male passenger both entered the service counter area together, and shortly thereafter walked out to the service area where they stood talking to each other.

A summary of facts can sometimes be very, very boring. But police procedure demands painstaking and pedantic detail.

12. At approximately 1:45pm the male passenger got onto a dark coloured motorbike and left the dealership. Upon leaving the driveway, he turned left onto Mount Wellington Highway.

13. Also at about 1:45pm, as the passenger left the dealership's driveway, Masters, who had ridden a short distance away, returned to the dealership. Masters had not intended on returning after he left the first time, but discovered his motorcycle's gear lever needed to be adjusted, so decided to immediately return to the dealership to facilitate this.

14. After crossing paths with Tae's passenger at the driveway entrance/exit, Masters rode his motorcycle down the driveway to the service area, arriving at approximately 1:46pm.

15. From where Tae was standing at the service counter, he had a clear view down the showroom floor to the driveway, and, through the glass store frontage, was easily able to see who was entering the driveway.

As the Killer Beez president rode down the alley beside the dealership, Tae moved quickly for a man of his size – almost 2 metres tall and nearly as wide – through the shop to the service area where Masters was headed.

16. Tae recognised it was Masters riding into the driveway, the complainant being easily recognisable due to his motorcycle and the bright white Killer Beez gang patch he was wearing.

17. As Masters rode down the side of the dealership to the service area, Tae moved towards the service entrance, producing a black semi-automatic 9mm pistol from his pocket.

18. Masters stopped his motorbike outside of the service entrance area and remained on the bike.

19. Tae immediately pointed the pistol at Masters, firing one shot. The bullet travelled through Masters' left arm, into his side and became lodged in his spinal canal. Masters fell to the ground and his motorbike fell on top of him.

20. After firing the first bullet, the pistol reloaded a second bullet into the chamber. Tae failed to recognise this and attempted to manually reload the pistol by pulling (racking) the slide back, which ejected the chambered round into the breech where it jammed.

21. Tae moved towards Masters and again pointed the gun at him. Tae pulled the trigger twice more, but the pistol failed to fire due to the jam caused by Tae racking the pistol. At this point he was only a few metres away from Masters.

22. Tae continued to walk towards Masters while again attempting to rack the top slide of the pistol. These actions caused the only remaining bullet in the pistol to

be ejected. Tae stopped walking when he was standing over Masters and pointed the pistol at his head. He then pulled the trigger again, but the pistol did not fire because there was no bullet in it.

Only sheer incompetence stopped Josh Masters's brains from being blown out at point-blank range.

23. Tae said something to Masters as he lay on the ground. Witnesses heard someone yell words to the effect of 'I told you not to come around here'. He then calmly walked to his Toyota motor vehicle and left the scene.

As Masters lay still on the ground, word of the attack spread like wildfire among the police and the media. Masters was a high-profile criminal, and had been gunned down at a motorcycle shop in broad daylight.

In some respects, it was no surprise that the simmering gang tensions in Auckland had finally boiled over. What *did* shock detectives who had been dealing with the Killer Beez for nearly 20 years, though, was who had pulled the trigger.

* * *

By the time Masters left Paremoremo, the ranks of the Killer Beez had swollen to 312 members. Once a ragtag group of childhood friends from Otara, the Killer Beez were now the fourth-largest gang in New Zealand, behind the Head Hunters, Black Power and Mongrel Mob.

It wasn't long before the trouble started.

Masters's return to Auckland's criminal underworld coincided with two interrelated phenomena that had frustrated frontline police. The first was an unprecedented explosion in the number of gang members. According to police intelligence, there were 4679 gang members as of December 2016. Four years later, the number was 7027.

The spike could not be attributed solely to the arrival of several dozen members of the Australian motorcycle gangs among the thousands of 501 deportees. Nearly all major gangs grew rapidly in size, perhaps in response to the threat of the Australian newcomers.

Many of the new recruits looked different too: young, clean-cut and muscular, with good-looking partners and children, showing off their designer clothes and expensive cars in social media posts. It was a cultural shift similar to what Australia had experienced roughly 20 years earlier.

The emergence of new Australian gangs with a take-no-prisoners mentality, coupled with the sharp intake of new recruits in local gangs, many brimming with the brash confidence of youth, meant the precarious state of peace in the gang scene was over. Alongside the huge spike in the gang population, police noticed the proliferation of pistols and semi-automatic firearms, which were being seized in routine searches on an almost daily basis. And to swing the balance of power, gang members weren't afraid to use them.

If the merciless slaying of Abraham Tu'uheava over a perceived slight to the Comancheros' reputation was seen as a stake in the ground for the Australian newcomers, so too was the spraying of the Head Hunters' pad in Ellerslie with semi-automatic rifle fire in 2019.

The warning shots were fired after a Head Hunter patched over to the Commos. The aggrieved Head Hunters were making threats and demanding financial compensation from their former member. His answer? The drive-by shooting of the Heads' pad at 232 Marua Road. In another bold power play that left police and other gang members agog, two senior members of the high-profile Mongrel Mob also joined the Comancheros.

Over the previous two years, the Waikato Mongrel Mob Kingdom chapter had captured headlines for hosting community events, establishing a separate all-female chapter, and guarding a Hamilton mosque after the 15 March 2019 Christchurch terror attacks. Their leader, Sonny Fatu, a Mongrel Mob member for 33 years, had announced on Facebook in 2018 that his chapter was walking away from the gang's national council to forge a new kaupapa (founding charter) based on empowering those marginalised by mainstream society.

Sceptical police said Fatu's rhetoric was nothing more than a PR ploy. But he was also one of the first Kiwi gang leaders to warn of the threat posed by the incoming Australian gangs. He likened the influx of 501 gang members to a 'modern day land grab', and even mooted an alliance between the Mongrel Mob and long-standing enemy Black Power to fend off the invaders.

But in a stunning defection, his own brother and nephew left the Mongrel Mob Kingdom to expand the Comancheros empire by establishing a Waikato chapter. Photographs posted on social media in April 2019 showed Dwight Fatu and his son, Sonny Fatu Junior (named after his uncle), with Comancheros president Pasilika Naufahu and treasurer Jarome Fonua. One showed Naufahu with his arms around the father-and-son duo. The caption underneath said 'Waikato Chapter is next'.

(As an aside, Dwight Fatu was the eponymous villain of *R v Fatu*, the appeal judgment mentioned way back in Chapter 2, which established sentencing guidelines for meth offences in 2005. Fatu's appeal against his nine-year lag for manufacturing and supplying methamphetamine failed, but his legal legacy far outlasted the sentence he received.)

It wasn't just the Comancheros ruffling feathers. The first New Zealand chapter of the Mongol Nation, notable for a black and white patch featuring a Genghis Khan figure riding a motorcycle, was set up in the Bay of Plenty in 2019.

The Mongols had started in California in 1969. There are now chapters in Mexico, Canada, Denmark, Germany, Indonesia, Malaysia, Singapore, Switzerland, Thailand, Australia, and of course New Zealand.

The Bay of Plenty chapter president Jim David Thacker, 'JD' for short, had been a member of the Bandidos, another international motorcycle gang, when he was deported from Australia as a 501 in August 2018. But he soon fell out with the Bandidos leadership in New Zealand.

So JD Thacker patched over, trading the Bandidos colours for those of the Mongols, along with about 20 others. Their perceived lack of respect for established gangs in the Bay of Plenty region soon rubbed these rivals up the wrong way.

First, someone torched three cars parked in the driveway of Thacker's home in Papamoa in October 2019. Security cameras outside the property captured the action, though by the time police turned up, the files had been erased.

A few months later, on New Year's Eve, someone tried to set fire to a barber shop the Mongols owned. The arson attempt failed, but someone came back a few weeks later to finish the job. This second blaze completely gutted the shop and adjoining tattoo studio in the Tauranga suburb of Greerton, which had long been the turf of the local Mongrel Mob chapter.

Retribution was swift. Early one morning in February 2020, a residential home owned by a leading Mob figure was riddled with bullets fired from semi-automatic weapons.

The scale of the shootout was unprecedented in New Zealand, with police officers picking up 96 empty bullet cases littering the street outside. Five children had been inside at the time; only good fortune had stopped an innocent life from being snuffed out by a stray bullet.

Within hours, the turf war had escalated, with reports of carloads of Mob members trading semi-automatic gunfire with Mongols at a rural address in Te Puke before the police arrived.

'This behaviour and level of violence is completely unacceptable and has no place in our communities,' said Detective Senior Sergeant Greg Turner of the Tauranga Criminal Investigation Branch. Police would seize high-powered firearms, drugs and cash from the Mongols over the coming weeks and months.

The conflict was out of control. Peace talks were set up between JD Thacker and senior representatives of the Mob. The rivals sat down on neutral ground and one Mob leader began airing his grievances. Thacker interrupted to say 'I don't give a fuck', or words to that effect.

Afterwards, tensions eased in Tauranga, although a Mongols-linked barber shop in Christchurch was also torched, and remarkably, members of the 'Quake City' Hells Angels – historically the bitter enemies of the Mongols – patched over to join JD Thacker.

This was the volatile, rapidly evolving underworld to which Josh Masters returned after his 10-year stretch. Compared with the scene he'd left, it was almost unrecognisable.

* * *

With traditional allegiances and rivalries so fluid, the police were finding it difficult to tell friend from foe. What had become clear, however, was that there was no love lost between Masters and the childhood friends who had helped him turn the Killer Beez into a powerhouse.

From a young age, he had knocked around with the likes of Okusitino Tae, Denis and Michael Solomon, and Dion Snell. But his fellow fledgling Killer Beez grew up and, perhaps somewhat disillusioned by the self-centred motivations of Masters, moved into the hierarchy of the Tribesmen.

With Masters inside prison, and supposedly having handed back his Tribesmen patch but retaining control of the Killer Beez, his former friends re-established the dominance of the Tribesmen in Otara.

Their reign was somewhat shortlived, however: it took a terminal slide into irrelevance after a Tribesmen prospect, Clayton Ratima, was beaten to death inside the gang's pad.

Standing 190 centimetres tall and weighing 130 kilograms, Ratima was an imposing figure, but a gentle giant, according to his family. When another gang prospect, heavily intoxicated, refused to fight the reluctant 24-year-old, two patched Tribesmen attacked Ratima in a drunken rage to 'harden him up'.

Punches and kicks rained down on Ratima's upper torso and head, at least 22 distinct blows according to the post-mortem examination. Wounds on his arms and hands showed that he had tried to defend himself by covering his head, but hadn't fought back, as per the rules of the Tribesmen, which say prospects are not allowed to retaliate against patched members.

Still breathing, Ratima lay on the ground for eight hours before someone took him to Middlemore Hospital, where he was declared brain-dead shortly afterwards.

The two senior members, Denis Solomon – Masters's former mate – and Vincent George, were convicted of murder and were given a life sentence by Justice Anne Hinton in December 2017; they will remain in jail for at least 10 years.

'Mr Ratima had done nothing other than to be a prospect.

He died at the very hands of the gang he was seeking to join,' said Justice Hinton.

The homicide investigation led to the demise of the Otara chapter of the Tribesmen. The gang's pad on Collett Road was cordoned off for nearly a week during the forensic examination of the scene, but afterwards, members of the Tribesmen were so paranoid that the police had bugged their headquarters that they refused to return. The intense scrutiny of a murder inquiry, combined with divided loyalties among gang members and associates over Ratima's death, meant that the Tribesmen were markedly less visible in Otara when the case was over.

Stepping into the power vacuum were the Killer Beez who had stayed loyal to Masters. Their confidence was bolstered by his return in the middle of 2018. Tensions between the two groups, once so tight they had shared members, flared in the following months as Masters reasserted himself. The innocent citizens of Otara were dragged into a string of tit-for-tat shootings and violent episodes.

They all came to a head at the Harley-Davidson dealership in Mount Wellington on a Friday afternoon in April 2019. The security cameras captured every moment in grainy detail.

Josh Masters returns to the dealership on his motorcycle; Okusitino Tae raises his pistol to fire once. Masters falls to the ground, lying prostrate under his motorcycle; Tae reloads and aims straight at Masters's head. He fires again but nothing happens. He leaves his former friend and walks calmly back to his car.

Later that evening, he does something unexpected.

24. The defendant presented himself to the Manukau
Police Station and handed over the pistol used in the
incident but declined to comment.

25. The defendant has previously appeared before the
Court.

* * *

Shortly after midnight, Tae handed himself in to waiting
police at the Counties Manukau station with his long-time
defence lawyer Lorraine Smith in tow.

She first met him as a 27-year-old, missing an eye and
handcuffed to a bed in Middlemore Hospital after the 2008
shooting in Othello Drive. Eleven years later, late at night,
the 77-year-old Smith waited for her client at a bus stop on
Queen Street before negotiating the terms of his surrender.

Tae handed the pistol over, but declined to explain anything
to police in his formal interview.

At the same time, Masters was undergoing emergency
surgery to save his life and remove the bullet from his back.
He survived, but, like Tae, never spoke to police about the
bad blood between them.

Okusitino was the Tribesmen's sergeant-at-arms,
responsible for enforcing club discipline and carrying out the
orders of the chapter president. To this day, no one is entirely
sure whether he stepped up to the plate to follow gang orders,
or whether there was a more personal feud between him and
Masters.

The day after the shooting, Tae appeared in the Manukau
District Court, dwarfing the two security guards beside him
in the dock, and was charged with attempted murder.

Despite the damning surveillance-camera footage, which
clearly showed Tae pulling the trigger three times, it was
difficult for the Crown to prove murderous intent, and Tae
pleaded not guilty. The case was heading towards a jury
trial in the High Court at Auckland in June 2020, but was

adjourned indefinitely following the nationwide lockdown during the global COVID-19 coronavirus pandemic.

Despite pleading not guilty to attempted murder, Tae had offered to plead guilty to the lesser charge of wounding with intent to cause grievous bodily harm. The deal was originally rejected by the Crown, on the ground that the question should be determined by a jury, but that decision was changed following the outbreak of the pandemic.

The maximum penalty of 14 years' imprisonment for wounding with intent to cause grievous bodily harm is the same as for attempted murder. Masters had refused to have anything to do with the investigation, or to appear as a witness. For those reasons, and to save the time and expense of a trial, the Crown accepted the offer, and Tae pleaded guilty in April 2020, almost a year to the day after he gunned down Masters.

Just four weeks later, Okusitino Tae stood in the dock at the High Court at Auckland to learn his fate. He needed to pay for what happened, he told a psychologist ahead of the hearing, but was adamant that the shooting had been opportunistic, not premeditated.

'Josh will always be my brother, I will always love him,' Tae said, according to the psychologist's report. 'He always looked after me, protected me. He had my back and I had his.' It was an unfortunate choice of words, given the spinal injury suffered by his friend.

As Justice Matthew Palmer noted at the sentencing hearing in May 2020, Tae was fortunate not to be facing a more serious charge – meaning murder. The judge was clearly puzzled as to how two close friends, who became staunch brothers in the Killer Beez and the Tribesmen, could fall out so dramatically. He'd picked up on the fact that Masters had visited Tae's home a few weeks before the shooting, a meeting from which Tae had come away fearful for the safety of his family.

Tae told the psychologist he'd assumed Masters was coming after him at the Harley dealership. He thought he saw him reaching for a gun, so reacted on impulse.

In strong advocacy on behalf of her client, Lorraine Smith revealed some curious new details that in some ways only made the picture murkier. She pointed out to Justice Palmer that within 30 minutes of the shooting, Tae had offered to turn himself into the police.

He didn't actually turn up at the station for another seven or eight hours. Why not? He spent that time meeting with representatives of both the Killer Beez and the Tribesmen: truce talks, it seems. Assurances of some kind were clearly made, although all Tae had permitted his lawyer to say was that everyone agreed there would be no trouble arising from the shooting.

Tae deserved credit for his cooperation with the police and his guilty plea, said Smith. She also spoke of mitigating factors, such as his tumultuous upbringing following the death of his mother when he was a teenager. Joining the Killer Beez and Tribesmen gangs, she said, had given Tae a sense of belonging that he had never experienced at school, in his family, or at church.

Justice Palmer agreed, and cut Tae's prison sentence from eleven years down to seven. Tae will be eligible for an early release after serving two years and three months.

'You are now at an age where you should see the downsides of continued life as a gang member and the upsides of life as a family man,' said Justice Palmer, although he was sceptical when Tae claimed he was considering leaving the Tribesmen.

Somewhat optimistically, Tae wanted to participate with Masters in a restorative justice hearing, in which the victim and offender discuss what has happened. This request was declined.

As for Masters himself – the physically powerful and charismatic leader who raised an army, was feared inside and outside of prison, and became the king of the Killer Beez – his fate is documented in the final paragraphs of the police summary of facts.

26. The complainant was treated by staff at the motorcycle store before Police and Ambulance arrived. He was subsequently transported to Hospital for further assistance.

27. The complainant sustained severe gunshot wounds as a result of the offending, the bullet piercing his left arm and left flank and entering his central spinal canal. As a result of the spinal injury suffered by the complainant, he is now paraplegic and will require caregiver assistance for the rest of his life.

11

GONE FISHING: IN THE BAY OF PLENTY OF COCAINE

2017–2020

THREE MATES APPEARED TO be heading out on a late-night fishing trip when their 5.7-metre pleasure-craft, the *Boston*, slipped into the dark water of Tauranga Harbour at 10pm on the night of Tuesday, 31 October 2017.

There are boats everywhere in the sheltered bays surrounding Tauranga. The *Boston* was just one of many when the three men quietly backed their Volkswagen Amarok ute down the concrete Whareroa Boat Ramp, tucked away near the marina on the Mount Maunganui side of the harbour bridge, and launched their craft. Nice night for it.

With long container terminals at industrial Sulphur Point lined with gantry cranes, and cruise ships docked at piers on the other side at the Mount, the Port of Tauranga had surpassed Auckland as the busiest port in New Zealand. Its ongoing prosperity, as one of the Bay of Plenty's rockstar businesses, had underpinned the region's strong economic growth and rapid population boom.

The trio motored the *Boston* a few hundred metres into the middle of the channel, dropped anchor and waited patiently in the dark. Their catch was about to arrive.

The bow of the *Maersk Antares* appeared from behind Mauao – Mount Maunganui – the iconic mountain standing guard at the entrance of the harbour, and the huge container ship slowly pulled in to dock at the Port of Tauranga.

Nearly 337 metres long, and able to carry the equivalent of 9000 containers, the *Maersk Antares* was at the end of a journey that had taken her from Mexico, through the Panama Canal to Colombia, Peru, Chile and finally Tauranga. Yet the massive vessel contained one item of cargo that *wasn't* listed on her manifest.

Up came the anchor on the *Boston* and the small boat moved closer to the rear of the container ship. With midnight fast approaching, one of the trio put down his fishing rod to don a wetsuit and pull on flippers, then dived in and swam towards the rudder of the *Maersk Antares*. Reaching the stern, he clambered up a ladder and disappeared inside the bulkhead.

For the next half-hour there was no sight or sound of him, just darkness and the gentle lapping of the waves against the hull. Then the bright glare of a single torch pierced the darkness from a beacon near the rudder. A gentle splash was made by two duffel bags thrown into the sea.

It was the signal the two men left in the *Boston* were waiting for. They motored the boat over to their associate bobbing in the water, picked him up with the two bags, and turned around to head back to the boat ramp.

Once the boat was winched back onto the trailer, they drove the VW ute back to the Valley Road Airbnb house they had rented for the night. With the ute safely parked in the garage, the men unpacked the bags. The strong smell of diesel wafted through the confined space.

They pulled out a total of 46 plastic parcels. Each weighed about a kilo and was tightly wrapped in green, silver or brown tape.

Inside each bundle was cocaine.

In scenes straight from a Hollywood heist caper, the three men had just successfully smuggled the largest ever shipment of cocaine into New Zealand.

And just like in any Hollywood crime caper, the authorities were watching, in darkness. Investigators from Customs and the National Organised Crime Group had seen the entire movie screen live, as it happened. It made for surreal viewing, and it filled them with a nervous excitement, as if they were waiting for the moment when everything went wrong.

It's not exactly typical for law enforcement to watch the illicit importation of drugs unfold right in front of their eyes. But every move had been caught on night-vision cameras as almost irrefutable evidence.

Usually drug syndicates try to conceal their illegal wares as genuine goods so they will slip through the border. But in this case, the cocaine smuggling tried to bypass border control completely. Just as remarkably, though, the joint investigation by the New Zealand Police and Customs had been able to stay one step ahead nearly the entire time.

It wasn't just dumb luck. The high point of Operation Heracles – a front-row seat at a midnight 'fishing' mission – had followed six months of hard work that had uncovered a ring of transnational organised crime groups working together to target New Zealand.

Ex-soldiers from Eastern Europe were behind this importation of South American cocaine. The men receiving it were Australians with links to 501 motorcycle gangs. There was also a separate Asian money-laundering syndicate shipping millions of dollars back overseas.

When they descended on a little country at the bottom of the world, these individuals from different parts of the globe all had the same thing on their mind: money.

* * *

In early 2017, 'sole trader' Matthew John Scott came to the attention of Detective Sergeant Andy Dunhill of the National Organised Crime Group. Scott, a 44-year-old from Perth in Western Australia, was living in a rented apartment in the Wynyard Quarter, the former industrial edge of Auckland's Viaduct Harbour, which had been redeveloped with swanky bars and restaurants for hosting fans during the 2011 Rugby World Cup.

Dunhill was surprised that Scott, without any prior connections in New Zealand, seemed to have been able to distribute significant amounts of methamphetamine, before switching to cocaine. In a town where the drug trade had been dominated by the Head Hunters for so long, it was surely nigh on impossible for someone like Scott to parachute in from overseas and immediately start selling drugs on a commercial scale.

The fact he had been able to get to work straightaway indicated a sharp ground shift within the criminal underworld. Someone like Scott would need the backing of an established gang, both as a distribution network and for his own protection.

Dunhill put it down to the influence of the 501 outlaw motorcycle gangs, which had true international connections. Scott wasn't a deportee, and had only a few minor driving convictions on his record – but police soon learned, through their Perth counterparts, that he had links to the Rebels motorcycle gang.

The Rebels were among the Australian gangs that had set up chapters in New Zealand. Some of the members had met secretly with Scott in Auckland. Police surveillance teams also spotted him fraternising with a man working for a senior Hells Angel, another of the top-tier motorcycle gangs.

It was Customs investigators who brought Scott's name to Dunhill. Their intelligence linked Scott to suspected 'catchers' who travelled to Auckland from Canada and China. The job of catchers is to provide an address for drugs to be sent to in the mail. Once the risk of being caught fades, they pass the parcel to the true intended recipient.

When Operation Heracles began in March 2017, the working theory was that Scott was acting as the conduit between the international drug syndicates importing methamphetamine, and the deported Rebels, who could distribute it. But the evidence was circumstantial. It certainly wasn't enough to allow them to lay criminal charges that would stick in court.

Dunhill and his team waited patiently, while Scott got on with his life – very happily. He seemed to be on a permanent holiday, playing the most prestigious golf courses on offer around New Zealand. His friend Benjamin John Northway, also from Perth, tagged along with him, and the pair were often seen scooting around Auckland together. It gradually became obvious that Northway was acting as Scott's assistant.

A new face appeared on 10 July 2017. Mario Habulin, a 35-year-old from Croatia, landed at Auckland International Airport on an Emirates flight from Dubai and went straight to Scott's apartment in the Wynyard Quarter. Although they'd never met – or not as far as Operation Heracles could tell – Habulin moved in. And while Scott continued exploring the country and playing golf, police surveillance revealed that his new flatmate spent more time in the apartment on Halsey Street, taking online lessons in Japanese and French.

Habulin was former soldier who had fought in the ethnic wars that broke up the former Yugoslavia in the 1990s. He kept up a disciplined regime, exercising every morning at the Les Mills gym on nearby Victoria Street. He was also fastidiously neat and tidy. The police officers conducting covert searches of the apartment were extremely careful to put everything back in its rightful place, fearful that Habulin would notice something was amiss and grow suspicious. As the police and Customs investigators would eventually learn, the Croatian's military experience and attention to detail were central to the success of the drug syndicate's audacious smuggling plans.

Operation Heracles was yet to work out how the drugs were coming into New Zealand. But police saw only too well how millions of dollars from sales were flowing out again.

On some of the busiest streets in Auckland, often in broad daylight, Scott and Habulin were both seen handing hundreds of thousands of dollars, hidden inside sports bags, to a Vietnamese woman they'd never met before. She'd flown in from Sydney, and was a representative of a completely different criminal group: a syndicate of professional money launderers, whose sole role is to move dirty money around the world for other criminals or terrorists.

Police call these independent operators 'international cash controller networks'. Their presence in New Zealand was a new development, and a stark illustration of the growing cunning and sophistication of the country's latest organised crime evolution.

Contracts were drawn up to move the money overseas. A token number – often the serial number of a banknote – was given to both parties to check before the cash was handed over. To avoid detection, the cash was split up and deposited into multiple bank accounts in amounts under $9999. Anything above that limit triggers a red flag for banks, which must report the suspicious transaction to financial intelligence police.

Once in the bank accounts, the funds don't need to be wired overseas. The international cash controller network can simply release equivalent funds via paperless transfer, from a separate pool, to the individual or group in the country the money is destined for.

Sometimes 'money mules' are used to physically carry bundles of banknotes. But that carries a greater risk in countries like New Zealand, where Customs have specially trained dogs at the airports to sniff out large sums of cash. It's easier to move money overseas through remittance or foreign exchange shops, like the one used by Tac Kin Voong that was raided in Operation Ice Age.

The Vietnamese woman seen with Habulin and Scott was Le Thi Lieu, a 52-year-old Sydney beauty salon operator. She made several trips from Sydney to Auckland that year, and took bags of cash from Scott or Habulin four times, in amounts of $394,000, $298,000, $200,000 and $398,500 respectively.

On the fourth and final occasion, Customs investigators were secretly watching when Habulin met her outside Les Mills on Victoria Street. The blue canvas bag was clearly very heavy; the surveillance team noted that Lieu struggled to lift it into the taxi she'd hailed.

One of Le's money-laundering minions, Dean Yang, picked up the cash when she wasn't available. On 20 September 2017, investigators were watching as Habulin strolled from the Halsey Street apartment he shared with Scott to the Les Mills gym, carrying a large black canvas bag. There was $500,000 inside. A small Toyota Vitz hatchback pulled into the gym carpark, and Yang emerged to open the car boot.

Habulin slung the black bag inside and Yang drove straight home to Beachhaven on Auckland's North Shore. The first person he called was the wife of Xiaolan Xiao, who was well known to the police Financial Intelligence Unit. He had 60 Suspicious Transaction Reports against his name as the director of Ping An Finance, a foreign exchange broker on Queen Street.

About a week after the $500,000 cash drop, in a separate prosecution, 61-year-old Xiaolan was slapped with a $5.3 million fine and banned from being a company director after a High Court judge found 'serious systemic deficiencies' in Ping An's compliance with anti-money-laundering laws.

The *Anti-Money Laundering and Countering Financing of Terrorism Act* 2009 requires businesses – mainly casinos and banks but also lawyers and real-estate agents – to carry out due diligence on customers, monitor transactions, keep records and report suspicious transactions.

In a landmark ruling, the Department of Internal Affairs (DIA) successfully argued that Ping An had failed to perform any of these tasks across a period of time when $105.4 million went through the company books. When the DIA asked to see Ping An's records, Xiaolan concocted a bogus story that his digital files had been erased by a computer virus and paperwork removed by a cleaner.

Xiaolan might not have known whether the money flowing through his company was criminal. But he was wilfully ignorant, and by turning a blind eye, he allowed the lifeblood of criminal enterprises – money – to flow out of New Zealand.

* * *

Habulin had to leave the country in September 2017 for a month to apply for another visitor's visa. It brought Detective Sergeant Andy Dunhill some breathing space.

Covert inquiries can't be extended ad nauseam without concrete progress. The probability of future success must be weighed up. While Dunhill's team had gathered enough evidence to lay money-laundering charges, Operation Heracles was still unable to lay credible charges relating to the drug smuggling.

But there'd been talk of another importation of cocaine – Habulin and Scott had discussed it during a bugged conversation in Scott's apartment – and that gave Dunhill enough of a reason to ask his bosses to extend the operation. He was given another six months to wrap it up. He breathed a sigh of relief.

As it turned out, he barely needed six days.

* * *

On 27 October 2017, Habulin arrived at Auckland International Airport on a flight from Doha, Qatar, with a new associate in tow. Like Habulin, Deni Cavallo, a 46-year-old Serb, was an ex-soldier who'd fought in the Yugoslav Wars.

The pair told Customs officials they were heading south to Christchurch. In fact, they headed straight into the heart of Auckland with Matthew Scott, in his brand-new Volkswagen Amarok truck.

On their behalf, Scott had rented apartment 1606 in the CityLife complex on Queen Street. Police had spent the last few days wiring it up with hidden audio and video recording devices.

Modern criminals are smart. They've known for years not to talk business over the phone, even in code, but instead communicate via an encrypted device such as a Blackberry, or common smartphone apps with end-to-end encryption like Telegram or WhatsApp.

For a while the prevalence of mobile phones in everyday life was a boon for covert surveillance, and older detectives talk fondly of the halcyon days when intercepting text messages and phone calls was like shooting fish in a barrel.

Thwarted by encrypted communications, detectives were forced to change their methods in the ongoing game of cat-and-mouse. In some cases, it was a matter of going back to the future. Bugging a home or car, like their drug squad predecessors did 20 years earlier in Operation Flower to bring down Waha Saifiti and the Head Hunters, was now far more likely to capture a suspect's conversations than any chatter on an encrypted phone.

Almost as soon as Habulin and Cavallo set foot inside the front door of CityLife apartment 1606, the hard work of the police in getting a step ahead paid off.

They started talking about '46 units' on a ship due to land in Tauranga in the next few days. Habulin showed Cavallo a picture of the vessel without mentioning it by name. He did, however, mention that the hull was light blue.

The relationship between the various incarnations of the Auckland drug squads and their peers at Customs has not always been warm. But the value of true joint investigation – with Customs officers embedded in Harlech House alongside police every day – was never clearer than when Heracles identified the *Maersk Antares* within a few hours. They did this by drawing up a list of all vessels scheduled to dock in Tauranga in the next few days, then looked at photographs of each boat. Only the *Maersk Antares* was light blue.

The team also brought in Customs staff who could speak Serbo-Croatian to listen to the bugged conversations live. It allowed Operation Heracles to make tactical decisions in real time off the back of the rough translation.

There was now clear intelligence that a package of Class A drugs was about to slip into the country. Dunhill threw out the six-month investigation plan. Whatever a 'unit' of cocaine was, it was obvious that the shipment was too large for police to let it hit the streets.

They had to move now.

* * *

While Dunhill was in the almost unique position of knowing when and where a suspected drug shipment was coming, he and his team still had no idea *how* the illicit cargo was to be smuggled into the country.

They had long suspected that the group's next cocaine importation would happen by sea. For months, Matthew Scott had been negotiating the purchase of a SEABOB submersible scooter from an Australian dealer for $16,000. He insisted that it be spray-painted black. He was desperate to get the SEABOB by the end of October, even paying another $2000 for the underwater sled to be freighted by air, but was forced to switch to Plan B when it didn't arrive.

Scott and Northway were overheard talking in the Amarok about hiring a boat for the weekend from a certain hire company. Dunhill resolved to beat them to the punch.

Deciding honesty was the best policy, he took the managers of the boat company into his confidence and told them why drug squad detectives were at their door. They were more than happy to help, even offering the GPS data to track the boat live. Dunhill declined, on the ground that he needed a High Court warrant for that type of surveillance.

Heartened by their response, he did ask for one favour, though: for Scott and Northway to be specifically told the boat was rigged with GPS, so they wouldn't suspect that police had planted it and change their plans.

At 6am on Monday 30 October 2017 – the day after Dunhill's visit to the hire company – the Australians hooked the *Boston*, a fibreglass-hulled vessel with a 150-horsepower outboard motor, onto the back of the Amarok ute and towed it to Tauranga, a two-and-a-half-hour hour journey southeast from Auckland. They had booked accommodation at Mount Maunganui through Airbnb. Cavallo and Habulin, meanwhile, caught a bus and checked into the Trinity Wharf hotel on the edge of Tauranga's waterfront.

By this point, police and Customs knew the drugs were somewhere on board the *Maersk Antares*, and that the *Boston* was involved somehow in the plan. But they still had no idea how the retrieval would happen. Would the *Boston* head into deep water and wait till a crew member threw bags of drugs overboard? Or would that happen when the *Maersk Antares* was closer to shore, near the Mount? Or perhaps even inside Tauranga Harbour?

A plan was made for every scenario. Investigators even toyed with the idea of getting a Customs boat to patrol the open water. Organising the operation was a logistical nightmare and a huge drain on resources, even though Detective Senior Sergeant Lloyd Schmid was moving heaven and earth to get what his staff needed.

In the end the decision was made to keep close surveillance on the shore crew of Habulin, Scott, Cavallo and Northway. The investigation didn't need to be in front of the quartet every step of the way; sometimes it was enough to be very close behind.

* * *

The *Maersk Antares* was due to dock at the Port of Tauranga at 11pm on Tuesday, 31 October 2017. Observation posts were set up along the shoreline all the way from the Mount to the docks, just in case anything was thrown overboard as she entered the harbour.

For the 48 hours leading up to the ship's arrival, police surveillance teams watched from a distance as Scott, Habulin and Northway took the *Boston* out onto the harbour so Scott could get used to driving the boat, or followed them into stores as they bought tools and dive gear. Cavallo, who had more of a hands-off role in the operation, stayed in his room at the Trinity Wharf hotel.

After a nervous wait, police finally confirmed the Amarok was leaving the Airbnb accommodation with the boat on the back.

It was on.

The next few hours passed like a feverish dream. Most of the inquiry team were running on adrenaline, exhausted after working 30 stressful hours straight.

And right in front of them, captured by high-definition night-vision binoculars borrowed from the Special Air Service, were surreal scenes of a mock fishing trip under moonlight, framed by Mauo in the background.

They watched Habulin, the former military man, tug on his wetsuit to swim to the *Maersk Antares* and pull himself aboard. Thirty minutes later he signalled with a flashlight to Scott and Northway, waiting on the *Boston*.

Once on dry land with the two duffel bags, the trio returned to the Airbnb rental to unload the parcels in the garage. Habulin was then dropped back to the Trinity Wharf hotel.

Just a few hours later, around 5.30am, a small team of police officers quickly and quietly slipped into Scott and Northway's Valley Road rental house. There was no need to kick the door down; police simply let themselves in with the set of keys the owners had been more than happy to hand over.

The Australians were fast asleep, Northway on the ground floor and Scott in another bedroom upstairs. Each was roused from slumber at the wrong end of a Glock pistol.

The two men were handcuffed and an officer read their rights to them while they stood in stunned silence. The seriousness of their situation slowly dawned on them. Putting aside the intercepted conversations and comprehensive video surveillance, the evidence in the rental property alone was damning enough.

As the detectives went from room to room, they found a wetsuit hanging on the shower door to drip-dry, with flippers and other dive equipment tossed on the tiles beneath. A zip-up bum bag lay in the middle of the pile, with a pair of wire cutters and a folding knife inside. They were the tools Habulin had taken aboard the *Maersk Antares* to gain access to the bulkhead, where the two duffel bags had been hidden.

Neatly stacked in the laundry cupboard of the Airbnb property was the final piece of the puzzle: a 46-kilogram stash of cocaine – at $450 a gram, worth an estimated $20 million on the street.

The following day, a search of Scott's address in Auckland produced five more 1-kilo parcels of cocaine, three wrapped in tape identical to the *Antares* shipment; a 700-gram bag of meth; and boxes of cash totalling $623,000.

It all added up to damning evidence. The four foreign nationals were refused bail when they appeared in the Tauranga District Court on 1 November 2017. But there was more work to be done.

In bugged conversations recorded in the days leading up to the ship's arrival, Habulin and Scott had discussed an earlier shipment of cocaine. Scott had been paid $5000 for each of the '30 units' he kept safe for distribution. Detectives also retrieved records that showed Habulin and Scott had checked into the Trinity Wharf hotel four months earlier, on 16 July 2017. This was just six days after the Croatian moved into Scott's apartment in Wynyard Quarter, and coincided with the arrival of the *Maersk Alfirk* – the sister ship of the *Antares* – at Tauranga, at the end of a trip from South America.

Based on this evidence, a second charge of importing a Class A drug was added to the indictment for Habulin and Scott, bringing their cocaine-smuggling tally to 76 kilograms, with a third importing charge of an unknown amount for Habulin in May 2017. That had been his first trip to New Zealand, and he had been accompanied by a mystery man, a fellow Croatian called Dragan Teslic, who had left for Bangkok the next day and never returned.

Operation Heracles also rounded up those involved in the separate money-laundering syndicate. Although her boss in Vietnam remained out of reach, Le Thi Lieu was arrested in Sydney and extradited back to New Zealand to serve a three-year prison sentence for laundering $1.29 million.

Xiaolan Xiao had already been hit with a $5.3 million fine in the separate DIA prosecution, and been left bankrupt. Now he also pleaded guilty to laundering the $500,000 cash drop. He was sentenced to six months' home detention and 200 hours of community work. His explanation was that he had been reckless, and used 'sloppy' business practices.

For 18 months, Matthew Scott, Benjamin Northway, Mario Habulin and Deni Cavallo steadfastly maintained their innocence and dragged out the proceedings against them – before pleading guilty to various drug-trafficking and money-laundering charges on the eve of their six-week trial in the High Court at Rotorua in June 2019. The fact that they'd left their admissions of guilt to the 11th hour, in the face of overwhelming Crown prosecution evidence, meant the sentencing judge cut their inevitable prison sentences only by a fraction.

In the High Court sentencing hearing in February 2020, Justice Grant Powell had no similar cocaine cases to consider in deciding the length of their sentence. All four men pleaded guilty to importing the 46 kilos that had slipped into New Zealand on board the *Maersk Antares*. On top of that record seizure, Habulin admitted to the earlier importation in July 2017, lifting his criminal culpability to a massive 76 kilos of coke.

Instead, comparisons were drawn with Operation Major, the first significant importation of methamphetamine way back in 2006. There were clear parallels, in terms of the quantity of Class A drugs brought into the country in both cases, as well as the roles of each individual within both organised criminal groups.

Northway, the lowest rung on the ladder, had assisted Scott with the third importation, arranging a safehouse in Auckland where the cocaine and cash would have been stored, as well as buying encrypted Blackberry devices so the group could communicate with one another. Justice Powell found Northway to be the least culpable, and sentenced him to 14 years and nine months in prison.

Scott, who also pleaded guilty to laundering nearly $1.2 million in just two months, and the mysterious Cavallo, who was suspected of arranging the export of cocaine from South America and communicating with the syndicate bosses overseas, were handed prison terms of 24 and 23 years respectively.

This left Habulin. He'd laundered $1.5 million in just months, and was up to his neck in all three imports uncovered by Operation Heracles. He narrowly avoided becoming the first person in New Zealand to receive a life sentence for cocaine offences. His last-minute guilty plea brought his final prison term to 27 and a half years.

It's expensive to keep someone in prison: about $100,000 every year. There's every likelihood that the four men will be released by the Parole Board after serving the mandatory one-third of their sentence and deported immediately.

While Justice Powell dismissed Habulin and Scott's claims that they were low-level pawns or 'hired help', it was clear that both men, although working for different organisations, answered to someone called 'Mastermind'. The police never came close to identifying this person, or even what country he or she was living in. But it was clear that Mastermind pulled the strings on the import business through Habulin, and distribution on the ground through Scott.

Just like the ever-increasing size of meth shipments, Heracles had exposed the growing demand for cocaine. Science confirms it. Wastewater analysis by ESR scientists at 38 sites across the country – described as 'one large urine test' – has provided a reliable picture of New Zealand's drug habits. Methamphetamine is still the drug of choice, but there's been an increase in the popularity of both ecstasy and cocaine.

Every time Habulin landed a shipment, there was a corresponding increase in the amount of cocaine detected by ESR in the wastewater. In one intercepted conversation, Habulin promised Scott he could obtain between 30 and 40 kilograms every month. 'You could sell 500 [kilograms] now,' replied Scott, 'everyone here just wants it.'

Ten years ago, the total amount of cocaine seized in a year was 3 kilograms. But a year before Operation Heracles, 35 kilograms were found hidden inside a diamante-encrusted horse and 24 kilograms were picked up inside a cruise passenger's luggage in Northland. Just a month after Operation Heracles, Customs and police stopped 24 kilograms, again in Northland.

While the weights were relatively small by international standards, a gram of cocaine here sold for around four times what Americans paid. With methamphetamine also fetching sky-high prices, New Zealand was starting to catch the attention of the most powerful and dangerous drug traffickers in the world.

Enter the Mexican cartels.

12

NZ *NARCOS*: THE CARTELS ARRIVE IN NEW ZEALAND

2018–2020

WE ALL KNOW THE stock scene from a thousand TV shows: a room full of cops, their shirtsleeves rolled up, gathered around a whiteboard with a single photograph pinned to it. One of the detectives will say, 'That's all we've got to go on.' Maybe another one will say, 'Let's go to work.' And the cops will look at the face of the villain in the photo, and wonder where their investigation will lead …

In the summer of 2018, the Harlech House cop shop was quiet, close to empty, as National Organised Crime Group (NOCG) staff took annual leave over the Christmas and New Year break. Detective Sergeant Damian Espinosa was tidying up paperwork from a Head Hunters meth operation when he was called into his boss's office and shown a single photograph.

There had been a changing of the guard at Harlech House. After a stellar career of close to 40 years, Detective Inspector Bruce Good had decided to call it a day in 2016. He was widely respected within the drug squads, seen as someone who was willing to take calculated risks, backed his staff to the hilt, and shielded them from any politics coming out of Wellington. His retirement had left big shoes for his successor to fill, but Detective Inspector Paul Newman wasn't scared to step into them.

Although he didn't have much of a background in covert policing, Newman was an experienced detective who had for years run gritty homicide inquiries and cold cases. He was calm and methodical, and importantly, he had integrity. Cops can sniff out a management fraud, someone promoted beyond their abilities, but Newman soon proved he wasn't out of his depth.

He was also smart enough to put his faith in his senior staff to get on with the job, or help him in making the big calls. John Sowter and Mike Beal had each been awarded the Meritorious Service Medal, one of the highest police honours, while Colin Parmenter and Lloyd Schmid had both been promoted to detective inspector.

At the same time, Newman encouraged the younger guys who were coming through, like Andy Dunhill, Jason Hunt, Andrew Stevenson and Damian Espinosa. They had all worked for the senior figures in the past, but now had their own squads to run.

It was Colin Parmenter who showed the single photograph to Damian Espinosa in January 2018. The photo was literally all that police had to go on. Most drug investigations begin with some intel from fizzes – criminal informants – or perhaps a drug importation picked up by a suspicious Customs officer at the border. But this was a completely cold start. All police knew was the names of the two men featured in the photo.

The names of the Naufahu brothers, Pasilika and Vetekina, meant nothing to Espinosa. The brothers were 501s, deported to New Zealand despite having lived in Sydney for nearly their whole lives. Their frustration at being kicked out of their home had boiled over less than 24 hours after they stepped off the plane at Auckland International Airport. The brothers were soon embroiled in a drunken street fight outside a bar.

'I don't want to be here. I'm forced to call this country home. I gave 27 years to Australia,' Pasilika Naufahu told a reporter from Television New Zealand.

'What can I say, the night just went bad. I apologise to all the staff members there and anyone who got hit.'

He went on to warn others deported from Australia under the tough immigration law that they could be forced into a life of crime.

But there wasn't anything to say the brothers *themselves* might be committing crimes in New Zealand. Not yet.

* * *

The Naufahu brothers had been senior members of the Comanchero gang in Sydney. Pasilika Naufahu had been the sergeant-at-arms, regarded by Sydney police as a larger-than-life character. The guy was a gym junkie with huge arms; he also had acumen and a keen appreciation of business. He was among the new breed of Comancheros who had moved the gang forward from the bearded, scruffy white bikies of yesteryear.

He had been one of the earliest candidates considered by Strike Force Raptor in New South Wales for deportation under the new section 501 of the Australian *Migration Act*. Police were desperate to rid Sydney of an influential gangster. He was the first of 14 Comancheros forcibly sent across the ditch.

Operation Nova, the new investigation headed by Espinosa, was in no doubt that Pasilika Naufahu's presence would lead to the setting up of a new Comancheros chapter in New Zealand. He was a heavy hitter, charismatic and cocky, with a small band of reinforcements eager to live up to the Comanchero name.

That a chapter of Australia's most dangerous motorcycle gang would establish itself in New Zealand was inevitable, and imminent. And while Operation Nova knew little about the Naufahu brothers, Espinosa and his team had read all about their brethren across the Tasman. The turf wars, the firebombings, the shootings, the all-in brawl at Sydney Airport, the birth of Strike Force Raptor ... Nobody was in any doubt that the arrival of the Aussies was bad news. But no one could claim to foresee how quickly the Comancheros would change the gang scene.

Espinosa and his team of five detectives got to work. They had only the photograph and some basic details, so they set about building an intelligence profile of Pasilika.

What was his daily routine? Where did he go? Who did he meet with? Who was in the Comancheros' inner circle in New Zealand?

The Commos were a small, tight-knit group who kept to themselves and were constantly looking over their shoulders. Their counter-surveillance techniques were like nothing Espinosa, a veteran of nine years in the drug squad, had ever seen before. Every half-decent criminal knows not to talk business on the phone, but Pasilika and his friends communicated with one another using Ciphr devices with end-to-end encryption. These sophisticated phones, which cost thousands to run each year, were well known in organised-crime circles overseas, but it was the first time they'd been seen in New Zealand.

This criminal tradecraft was a step up from the run-of-the-mill gangster, and the challenge was more than a little daunting for Espinosa and his squad. He reminded everyone to focus on the job at hand, chipping away a little more each day, and to not be distracted by the end goal. If Operation Nova kept working hard, they'd eventually get a break. Like

John Sowter always said, an investigation team needed to get lucky only once.

While the covert surveillance was tricky, every now and again a piece of valuable intelligence fell into their laps. As mentioned in Chapter 9, a few hastily snapped photos of Pasilika Naufahu and five others wearing 'Comanchero New Zealand' T-shirts cropped up on social media in February 2018. It was clear that the Comanchero 501s had now formed a local chapter. The Instagram shots of six strapping Comancheros were soon to be made infamous in a *Herald on Sunday* scoop.

Alongside Pasilika and Vetekina Naufahu was the tall figure of Tyson Daniels, who turned out to be the chapter's vice president, as well as senior members Pomare Pirini and Seiana Fakaosilea – the younger brother of Selaima and Ulakai, who featured in Chapter 8 as part of the 500-kilo meth circus in Northland.

You could argue that Pirini was partly to blame for the fact that all of them were deported. He had been one of the gang members brawling alongside Mick Hawi, the Comancheros' Australian president, at Sydney Airport in 2009. Pirini pleaded guilty to the manslaughter of Anthony Zervas, the Hells Angel associate whose brutal death had triggered the setting up of Strike Force Raptor and eventually the creation of the 501 immigration clause.

Just 22 at the time, Pirini had been sentenced to six and a half years in prison, and came back to New Zealand a convicted killer. Not long after the photograph of the New Zealand chapter was published online, Pirini's old mate Mick Hawi was gunned down in his car in broad daylight by two masked men in Sydney. It was the gangster's circle of life.

The final figure in the Instagram post was a rather hefty fellow, sitting on a gold-plated Harley-Davidson on the left of the picture.

On the day the *Herald on Sunday* published its exclusive on the new gang chapter, a rather hefty fellow did a burnout on the rather distinctive Harley on the main street of Mount Maunganui. The incredibly expensive bike was impounded, and its owner, Jarome Fonua, arrested.

He was the club treasurer, responsible for handling the finances. There was a lot of money floating around, too: a lifestyle of long lunches, gold bling and designer clothes.

Operation Nova's picture of the Comanchero hierarchy was complete.

* * *

Not long after this, Abraham Tu'uheava turned up dead, with seven bullet holes across his arm, head and back. He'd seen the ostentatious spending on social media, admired the Comancheros and wanted to work with them. His execution, and the miraculous survival of his wife Yolanda, led to a crossover between Operation Weaver, the homicide inquiry detailed in Chapter 9, and Operation Nova.

Surveillance footage showed one of the killers, Fisilau 'Fish' Tapaevalu, being handed his prospect's colours at a ceremony at a park beside the Panmure Basin, possibly as a reward. The gathering was just a stone's throw from the Head Hunters' pad in Ellerslie, which some detectives saw as a metaphorical middle-fingered salute to what was once the dominant gang in Auckland.

Whether the choice of location was symbolic or coincidental, the ruthless shooting of Tu'uheava – ostensibly for besmirching the good name of the Comancheros – could not be mistaken for anything less than a clear message. The Comancheros were brazenly stepping into Auckland, undaunted by established local rivals with much larger memberships.

The hard surveillance work of Operation Nova was starting to pay handsome dividends. Unfamiliar faces kept popping up, which the team scrambled to identify. One of them belonged to Valovalo Peter Vaiusu, an associate of Pasilika Naufahu living in Sydney who was making regular trips across the Tasman to Auckland. Returning from one of these trips in June 2018, the 34-year-old was dramatically arrested by Strike Force Raptor officers after stepping off the plane at Sydney Airport. He was involved in a scuffle with police from the specialist unit, breaking free as he was being handcuffed to take a swing at a television camera crew, presumably tipped off about the arrest.

New South Wales police alleged Vaiusu was connected with a storage unit where suitcases of cash totalling AU$2.5 million, 13 firearms and several kilograms of cocaine and methamphetamine had been discovered. Five of the illegal firearms were AR-15 semi-automatic rifles: the weapon of choice in mass shootings around the world, including the 15 March 2019 Christchurch terror attacks.

There was nothing new about gang members with guns, but it gave the New Zealand police a stark illustration of the firepower available to the Comancheros. And incidents like the Tu'uheava shooting showed that they weren't afraid to pull the trigger.

Ongoing surveillance of the Comancheros pulled up another new face: a 'cleanskin', as police call an individual without any criminal convictions. Having a friendly cleanskin, a presentable face that can come and go without raising suspicion, is useful for organised crime groups. The real name of this particular cleanskin cannot be published for legal reasons, but let's call him 'Ronnie'.

Ronnie the Cleanskin had a brother based in Sydney – let's

call him 'Reggie' – who travelled back and forth to Auckland frequently during the course of 2018.

The police theory was that the brothers were acting as a conduit between the Comancheros and their drug suppliers, arranging deals and handling cash on the gang's behalf, which allowed gang members to keep their distance and keep their hands clean.

With limited surveillance resources at his disposal, Espinosa decided to keep a close eye on Ronnie and Reggie and see where the brothers would lead him and his team. The tactic led to a lucky break. On 19 September, Nova detectives watched as Reggie – who'd flown in from Sydney the day before – had a rendezvous with a slightly built Asian man.

Sha He, a 33-year-old Sydney hairdresser, had flown into the country on 15 September and told Customs officers he was in New Zealand to visit friends and have a holiday.

Some holiday.

After making introductions and small talk, Sha and Reggie spent the rest of the day driving around Auckland. The next day, Reggie picked Sha up in the same vehicle, a white Great Wall ute.

What they didn't know was that just hours before, police had broken into the ute and planted a covert listening device that would capture all their conversation. Blithely unaware, Reggie and Sha negotiated a deal throughout the afternoon for $1 million worth of pseudoephedrine.

Pseudo was a surprise to police; it was a throwback to a different age in organised crime. Most groups had switched to bringing in ephedrine – which required one less step to convert into methamphetamine – or simply imported finished meth from South East Asia. But there was no doubt that the deal was about multiple kilograms of pseudoephedrine, as that was what Sha (speaking English) called it outright.

He was overheard speaking to someone on his phone in Mandarin, saying, 'If you stand them up again … can't stand them up, must do it today.' Reggie and Sha each had 'runners' on standby, waiting for the pseudoephedrine and cash so they could take it to the rendezvous point where the exchange would take place.

At about 3.50pm, the Comancheros' runner, a patched member who cannot be named for legal reasons, arrived at the rendezvous point on the side of a busy road in Papakura carrying $1 million in a bag. Sha had a quick look to inspect the cash, but soon afterwards received a message from his 'boss'. No one was bringing the pseudoephedrine. The deal was dead, for now at least.

To the Operation Nova team, it didn't matter that the transaction had fallen through. Nine months into the investigation, they now had concrete evidence implicating members of the Comancheros in a large-scale drug conspiracy. The meeting with Sha He was a heartening breakthrough, a fillip that reinforced the fact they were on the right track.

A month later, another bit of good fortune. Ronnie the Cleanskin's discipline slipped and he was caught talking on the wire, albeit in a guarded fashion. The mystery caller on the other end of the line said: 'You're going to start off with a nice number with two zeros. I'm going to land it between you and me … [I'll give you] all the fucken work you can handle. We're going to land it there [in New Zealand].'

Translation? Police theorised the unknown caller was promising to send an amount of methamphetamine weighing at least 100 kilos – 'a nice number with two zeros' – and the two men agreed on the rather cheap wholesale price of $120,000 per kilogram. The price per kilo had once been around $300,000, but had dropped markedly in the past few years. Even so, the usual price was around $180,000; $120,000 was a bargain designed to undercut the competition.

'A nice number with two zeros' meant a huge amount of meth. But 'zero' also summed up exactly how much Espinosa and his team knew about the mystery individual making the deal: nothing, nada. Yet again, a new face and name had cropped up in the investigation. They had no idea who had made the call – only where he was at the time: Mexico.

There were a few clues to follow up, though. Working with international partner agencies, Operation Nova soon identified the mystery man as Tallat Rahman. He was a 60-year-old Fijian-Indian, with dual Fijian and Canadian citizenship, who lived in Suva and travelled regularly to Canada, the United States and Mexico.

There was lots of talk between Rahman and Ronnie the Cleanskin, but nothing came of the promised 100-plus-kilo shipment.

Everything went quiet – until Rahman flew into Auckland International Airport in December 2018, and checked into a hotel on Queen Street, the Four Points by Sheraton.

Three days later, Rahman's son Joshua checked into the same hotel and met someone else who cannot be identified for legal reasons. Let's call him 'the Mexican'.

Two days before Christmas, Tallat Rahman departed New Zealand and left his son and the Mexican behind, but not before receiving a backpack full of cash. The Mexican was waiting for a package to arrive in Auckland from the United States, but when the Mexican called the freight company to inquire as to its whereabouts, he was told the consignment hadn't been cleared because of a missing tax invoice.

In actual fact, the consignment – a kitchen stovetop – had been seized by Customs and examined. There was nearly 5 kilos of methamphetamine inside.

The Mexican was overheard talking about previous methamphetamine imports, money they were owed, and the need to create professional-looking false invoices so future consignments wouldn't be delayed. Operation Nova heard every last detail of his chats, via an listening device hidden in their hotel room.

While Tallat Rahman had boasted of landing a big shipment of at least 100 kilos, it seemed his buyers preferred to receive smaller amounts on a more frequent basis. It meant less risk for everyone – less risk of getting caught bringing the gear in, and less risk that word would get out about a massive stockpile and the drugs would be ripped off by rivals or seized by the police. It might take three months to organise 500 kilos, but just three days to arrange 5 kilos. And if you have a regular supply of 5 kilos of meth every week or so, the quantity quickly adds up over the course of a year.

Two separate consignments from the United States – a waffle maker and coffee brewer – were stopped at the border by Customs in February 2019, with each piece of kitchen equipment containing 2.9 kilos of methamphetamine.

Customs let Tallat Rahman in, though. Espinosa couldn't believe his luck. The 60-year-old returned in time for the termination of the first phase of Operation Nova (which had targeted the importation side of the business). Rahman was arrested together with the Mexican and a 33-year-old Chinese man named Wang Hui, who was called 'the Wire Guy' because he laundered hundreds of thousands of dollars in cash via wire transfers overseas.

A search was also carried out at the home of Joshua Rahman in Suva in February. Fijian police discovered 39 kilos of cocaine at the property, presumably destined for the Australian and New Zealand markets. The haul was worth about $20 million. Joshua Rahman was charged with unlawful possession of the drug and will stand trial in Fiji.

When brought in for questioning by police, Tallat Rahman lied through his teeth. He denied knowing Ronnie the Cleanskin and the Mexican, claiming to be in New Zealand on holiday. When told that an audio device had been covertly installed in the Mexican's hotel room, Rahman said, 'Oh, shit.'

* * *

Oh, shit indeed. His goose was cooked. But in the understated, robotic language that only a press release from the police can achieve, reducing the riveting to the really mundane, news of the arrests barely caused a ripple in the 24/7 news cycle.

'This investigation shows the strength of New Zealand working with its close partners in the Pacific region to combat transnational organised crime groups intent on supplying methamphetamine and cocaine into the New Zealand markets,' the 22 February 2019 statement quoted Detective Inspector Paul Newman as saying. 'It is well understood that these illicit drugs are the cause of significant social harm to our communities.'

No further comment could be made, the press statement concluded, as the matter was before the courts and the police investigation was ongoing. 'We cannot rule out further charges being laid.'

For obvious reasons, there was no mention of the Comancheros. Two months later, though, on 11 April 2019, the name of the motorcycle gang was front and centre when NOCG head Greg Williams and Financial Crime Group head Iain Chapman announced the termination of the second phase of Operation Nova, which had targeted the Comancheros themselves. Now they had *everyone's* attention, with reporters and videographers from every news organisation heading to Harlech House for the obligatory show-and-tell press conference.

Among those arrested were gang president Pasilika Naufahu and vice president Tyson Daniel, who were charged alongside other members and associates with a variety of offences, including money laundering and participating in an organised criminal group.

Pasilika Naufahu was also charged with conspiracy to import a Class A drug and conspiracy to supply a Class B drug: the aborted pseudoephedrine deal. He was also charged with unlawful possession of a pistol found in his Bucklands Beach home during the raids, but the charge was later dropped – the gun was a fake, although the ammo was real.

Otherwise, the charges laid against Pasilika Naufahu and Tyson Daniels were all about money.

Among the $4 million of assets seized in the raids under the *Criminal Proceeds (Recovery) Act* 2009 were the two gold-plated Harley-Davidsons the Comancheros had proudly displayed in their Instagram posts, as well as a Rolls-Royce Wraith valued at nearly $500,000. A trio of late-model Range Rovers worth $150,000 each were also towed away on the back of a truck, and the homes of Naufahu and Daniels in the plush eastern Auckland suburbs were frozen by the High Court order as well.

The ostentatious wealth was a marketing tool to recruit members, said Chapman and Williams at the press conference, which took place on the same day as the raids. They emphasised that stripping the Comancheros of their status symbols was just as important as the criminal prosecution.

Williams then made a headline-grabbing claim. The methamphetamine allegedly distributed by the Comancheros had been sent by the Sinaloa Cartel – the ruthless drug empire established by the notorious Joaquín 'El Chapo' Guzmán.

* * *

The Mexican Sinaloa Cartel is considered one of the most dangerous criminal syndicates in the world, responsible for smuggling hundreds of tonnes of drugs at a time and carrying out thousands of murders over the decades since El Chapo came to power. But what would Sinaloa – a name most New Zealanders had only ever heard in movies or the Netflix series *Narcos* – want with a little country at the bottom of the South Pacific Ocean?

As always when it comes to organised crime, the answer is money. Methamphetamine is dirt cheap in Mexico, where Tallat Rahman was a regular visitor.

In a landmark case heard in the Court of Appeal in April 2019 (more on that in the Epilogue), Detective Superintendent Greg Williams submitted an affidavit that revealed more about the Comancheros' connections with the Sinaloa Cartel. The Mexican methamphetamine seized in Operation Nova had been purchased for as little as $5000 per kilo. So even when the meth was sold for the relatively cheap wholesale price of $120,000 a kilo, the cartel would make $575,000 profit on a small 5-kilo shipment like the one found inside the kitchen stove in December 2018.

'The Sinaloa example significantly undercut other importing syndicates by selling at a reduced price. Competition by importers bringing the drug into New Zealand is seeing the wholesale price of methamphetamine dropping,' Williams wrote in his affidavit, to explain the wider context of the meth market to the Appeal Court judges.

'This is concerning because it means that retailers can lower the price at the retail point, thus expanding their markets to include lower socio-economic areas and vulnerable communities.'

The police were now able to estimate exactly how much methamphetamine was being consumed around the country. The ESR's 'one large urine test' shows that nearly 2.3 kilograms of meth are smoked, snorted or injected in New Zealand each and every day. At the rough street price of $500 a gram, that's $1.15 million in cash, daily.

As we've seen, the prices for methamphetamine and cocaine in New Zealand are among the highest in the world, adding up to big profits even if the economies of scale are smaller than elsewhere. If there was any doubt that the Mexican drug lords had now joined the Asian syndicates as a major supplier of drugs to our shores, it was dispelled with the announcement that the Drug Enforcement Administration (DEA) was opening an office in New Zealand.

The DEA is the lead anti-drug-trafficking agency in the United States. These are the guys who took down El Chapo, and Pablo Escobar before him. Just like organised drug crime, the DEA has gone international.

While intelligence has long been shared between members of the Five Eyes alliance – New Zealand, Australia, Canada, the United Kingdom and the United States – the relationship between Australasia and the DEA has become much tighter in recent years, with liaison officers working closely with local drug police on Pacific operations. In 2018, the US Congress voted to approve funding to permanently station DEA agents in Auckland and Wellington to work side by side with NOCG investigators as Mexican syndicates like Sinaloa and rival Jalisco New Generation Cartel ply their trade here.

'If you were to ask any significant trafficker what is the best market for meth and coke in the world, they would say Australia and New Zealand,' Kevin Merkel, the DEA attaché for Australia, New Zealand and the Pacific Islands, once told me. 'The same people that are pumping drugs out to the

United States are the same ones that are pumping out drugs here. If they see potential to make more money, they're going to do it.'

* * *

If you're making millions of dollars from drugs, you'll need help to hide it. While the Sinaloa connection hogged the headlines, another important detail was listed in the charging documents laid against the Comancheros and their associates in the Auckland District Court.

Among those charged was a surprising name. Andrew Neill Simpson of Lynfield, 40 at the time of his arrest, was charged with 13 counts of money laundering. Occupation: lawyer.

'Follow the money' has been a mantra for law enforcement everywhere for decades. While organised crime figures are able to distance themselves from illegal products through the use of lieutenants and foot soldiers, it's far more difficult to disguise the fruits of their labour. Money is, after all, the driving factor behind their criminal enterprises.

Since stronger measures came into force in 2018 under changes to the *Anti-Money Laundering and Countering Financing of Terrorism Act* 2009, real-estate agents, accountants and lawyers have been required to report suspicious transactions. Police have long been aware that white-collar professionals have often acted as 'enablers' for organised crime – setting up trusts and accounts, moving money offshore, and purchasing assets in someone else's name.

Now they had a lawyer caught dead to rights handling money for the Comancheros, and they were going to make an example of him.

Just like Sha He, the pseudoephedrine dealer, and Tallat Rahman, the meth importer, Operation Nova found Andrew

Simpson by following Ronnie the Cleanskin. He took them right to the door of Simpson's law practice, at the Mount Roskill end of Dominion Road.

No one who knew Simpson, a happily married father of five actively involved in his church and community, could fathom what had happened over several months in 2017 and 2018.

On 1 November 2017, Simpson had created the Kea Trust for Pasilika Naufahu and the Kiwi Trust for Tyson Daniels. Cash deposits had then been made into the trust account of Simpson's law firm, either by Simpson himself or by Ronnie the Cleanskin, nearly always under the $10,000 limit, which triggers a mandatory Suspicious Transaction Report by the bank to the police's Financial Intelligence Unit.

There was also a transfer of $32,000 from Australia, deposited into the law firm's trust account by Valovalo Peter Vaiusu, the alleged Sydney drug dealer linked to the storage unit containing the drugs and guns and $2.5 million in cash.

Between November 2017 and August 2018, associates of the Comancheros deposited a total of $1,269,067.10 into Simpson's trust account. The lawyer then shifted different amounts into the Kea and Kiwi Trusts, or bought expensive property and vehicles on behalf of patched Comanchero members. He kept only $18,384.33 as payment for his services.

When police interviewed Simpson after the termination of Operation Nova in April 2019, they could immediately tell he was no hardened criminal. Instead of exercising his right to silence, Simpson 'coughed' and made some partial admissions.

Explaining his out-of-character deeds, Simpson told detectives he had become suspicious about the source of the funds after the second or third large cash deposit. Ronnie the Cleanskin had assured him that everything was above board.

Well, not exactly above board, but Simpson was led to believe that the deposits were cash payments to a concreting business.

He assured police he thought he was helping his clients avoid tax, not launder drug money. Their conversations about their shared Christian faith and love of basketball had pulled the wool over Simpson's eyes. It was only later, around November 2018, when Simpson searched the internet, that he realised his clients moved in Comanchero circles.

By then, it was too late. He was over a barrel, and the gang knew it.

His arrest in Operation Nova brought shame, but also a sense of relief. He pleaded guilty to the money-laundering charges and was sentenced in the High Court at Auckland in February 2020.

Standing next to him in the dock was Tyson Daniels. What a couple. The 30-year-old Daniels was tall and strong, powerfully built across the chest and shoulders, his frame covered in a tight-fitting designer Versace top in his gang colours of black and gold. The bespectacled 42-year-old Simpson, bookish and slender, wore a bland grey suit, blue shirt and tie. The vice president of the Commos drove a fleet of luxury sports cars. Simpson drove a seven-seater van to ferry his family around.

The two men had almost nothing in common – except that they were about to be sent to prison for laundering the vast profits creamed by the Comancheros through commercial-scale drug importation and distribution.

'It is perplexing,' said Guyon Foley, Simpson's lawyer, in trying to explain his client's fall from grace to Justice Gerard van Bohemen.

Friends, family and clients wrote 20 letters of support for Simpson, all of them shocked and dismayed by his offending, which was labelled 'completely out of character'. Words like honourable, respectful, humble and patient were used to describe Simpson, who sometimes would not charge clients who couldn't afford his services. If they needed help, he'd just do the work anyway.

'He was known as a good lawyer, an honest man, who consistently placed the interests of his clients ahead of his own,' said Foley. 'He asks for mercy.'

The judge said there was little doubt that Simpson was 'at least naïve and incredibly foolish', but noted the disgraced lawyer's own words that he had turned a blind eye to the source of the funds. That was reckless, said Justice van Bohemen, and made the point that Simpson had used his skills, knowledge and membership of a professional body to set up the money-laundering scheme.

'You made it work … even when your suspicions were raised, you not only placed your personal gain above your duties as a lawyer but you risked bringing your profession into disrepute.'

At this point in the proceedings, it was clear that Simpson was going to prison. What kind of message would it send if a lawyer who'd laundered millions of dollars for criminals were to serve his sentence in home detention?

Even taking into account his early guilty plea, genuine remorse and previous good character, Simpson was sentenced to two years and nine months in prison.

'I deeply regret a father being separated from his young family … sadly, that is the consequence of your decisions, Mr Simpson.'

One of the clients whose interests Simpson had placed above his duties as a lawyer was the man next to him in the dock, Tyson Daniels. It was a surprise when the senior Comanchero pleaded guilty to nine charges of money laundering, and one of participating in an organised criminal group. He was recently married, and now a stepfather. Perhaps it was because putting his hand up – and receiving a generous discount for the early admission – would mean he would be reunited with them faster.

The money-laundering offences related to Daniels's purchase of an almost unbelievable swag of expensive vehicles. There were four Range Rovers – with price tags of $175,000, $255,000, $218,000 and $280,000 respectively – a $200,000 Mercedes-Benz, a Lamborghini for $285,000, and two Rolls-Royces that had respectively cost $364,000 and $595,000.

The entire fleet was seized in April 2019 when Operation Nova ended. Yet just one month after his arrest, Daniels arrogantly purchased another Mercedes-Benz for $215,000 while on bail. The police grabbed that too, as well as the extra $247,000 cash found in his home.

While Daniels faced no drug-dealing charges, Justice van Bohemen was under no illusions as to how he had afforded such a lavish lifestyle. His case was compared with that of William and Beverley Wallace, the couple we met way back in Chapter 1. The original commercial meth cook and his wife were among the first people charged with money laundering in New Zealand, in relation to over $1 million in unexplained wealth. Mrs Wallace argued that she didn't know where the money came from, although the Court of Appeal inferred that she did.

Daniels's offending was far worse than the Wallaces', said Justice van Bohemen. 'You clearly knew that the money was derived from a significant drug importation and supply operation by the group of which you are a member and Vice President,' the High Court judge said, in sentencing Daniels to four years and eight months in prison.

'Your place in the Comancheros hierarchy means you were one of the directors of this serious offending, which exemplifies how organised criminal groups can obtain significant financial benefit from offending without putting themselves directly at risk.'

The remarks of the judge succinctly assessed the evolution of gangs and drugs in New Zealand over the past 20 years. While Operation Nova started with just one photograph, another image sums up what organised crime in New Zealand is all about right here, right now: a nerdy lawyer and a macho gangster standing side by side in the dock.

EPILOGUE

IF YOU WANT METHAMPHETAMINE, you can get it quickly and efficiently, anywhere in New Zealand. The drug is now cheaper and easier to score than ever before, especially in our poorer provincial communities. Supply is at an all-time high, and it's driven down prices. On the streets, a gram will cost you around $350 – down from $600 to $800 just a few years ago. Higher up the food chain, a kilo of meth sells for around $150,000 now, roughly half of what the wholesale price used to be. Shipments of 100 kilos or even more have become routine. Long gone are the days when a single kilogram bust was newsworthy; even street dealers will have more meth than that stashed away.

This book has charted the growth of New Zealand's criminal underworld since meth first appeared on the local scene in the mid-1990s. Gangs and their cohorts have followed an escalating evolutionary curve. And we've just reached the top of yet another curve, with the arrival of the 501s and the emergence of the Mexican cartels.

The arrival of the Australian gangs has introduced two new threats to the police and general public: corruption and firearms.

For many years, New Zealand has had a reputation for being largely free of corruption. But since the start of 2019, law enforcement bodies have detected a number of disturbing incidents, referred to as 'insider threats'.

An entire shipping container disappeared from the Ports of Auckland on the back of a truck in July 2019, with the help of a long-serving worker at the port. The police found $90,000 in a shoebox in her home, but she refused to talk, claiming she had been intimidated into silence.

Several men who worked at Auckland International Airport, with access to planes and baggage, were prosecuted in May 2020 for importing Class A drugs by allegedly circumventing border security.

Perhaps most insidiously, an Auckland police constable was caught in March 2019 leaking sensitive material to a gang. Vili Taukolo had used his position to search the police National Intelligence Application (NIA) for details about a $50 million importation of methamphetamine from Mexico. He spent hours reading files while working a late shift, then printed out 17 restricted documents, as well as searching the NIA for details about certain police officers.

When Taukolo was apprehended, police found $30,000 in cash in his bedroom drawer. All up, he was paid $70,000: not bad money for a rookie cop. He was jailed in December 2019 for two years and two months.

Within a few months of Taukolo's guilty verdict, the police set up a National Integrity Unit, comprised of senior detectives, to investigate and root out bent cops. One of their first targets was a new recruit who was introduced, through wider Tongan family ties, to members of the Comancheros.

They had a fun night out partying in Auckland: harmless to start with, but then the constable made the foolish error of accepting an offer of cocaine. The snorting of Class A party drugs was filmed by one of the gang: surely the perfect leverage for extorting a little favour from a young police officer. And then a bigger favour, and so on. Once you cross that line, they've got you by the balls.

Wads of cash, gangster glamour, a friendly face at first then intimidation later, if necessary ... Members of the New Zealand Police, or anyone in the public service or transport industries, can no longer afford to be naïve about the dangers of being groomed by organised criminals.

But while having dirty colleagues among their ranks naturally erodes public trust and confidence in police, there's a far more lethal threat faced by officers every single day.

More and more illegal firearms are being found in raids on drug dealers and gang members – particularly military-style semi-automatic weapons such as the AR-15. Firearms have always featured in the gang and drug scene in New Zealand, as both insurance and intimidation, but now there are more than ever on the streets. They are more lethal, and also more likely to be drawn and fired to prove a point, or exact revenge.

The problem is that no one really cares when criminals shoot at one another. Not until an innocent person is caught in the crossfire.

'We're seeing guns every day,' one organised crime detective told me over coffee in June 2020. 'It's only a matter of time before one of us gets killed.'

Three days later, Constable Matthew Hunt was fatally shot during a routine traffic stop in West Auckland.

* * *

A week or so after I put the final touches on this book, the National Organised Crime Group raided 10 homes across the Bay of Plenty and arrested the senior leadership of the Mongols Australian bikie gang (discussed in Chapter 10).

More than 200 criminal charges were laid in the covert operation led by Detective Sergeant Nigel Grey: participating in an organised criminal group, money laundering, conspiracy to deal methamphetamine, supplying cocaine, and unlawful possession of firearms and explosives. Police seized 19 vehicles – five motorcycles, one light truck, one heavy truck, seven cars, four utes and a quad bike – as well as Molotov cocktails, ammunition, cannabis, methamphetamine and cash. Eight firearms were found during the search warrants, including two AK-47s and two military-style semi-automatic rifles.

Detective Superintendent Greg Williams said the Mongols had been involved in six shootings with other gangs – that police know of – since JD Thacker established their chapter in Te Puke, near Tauranga. 'The ongoing violence between this organised crime group and other local gangs is simply about controlling a share of this drug market, and all these gangs have made it clear that they are prepared to use violence to protect their share.'

Williams referred to an incident in June 2020 in which Thacker, the national president of the Mongols, was arrested after a loaded .357 Magnum pistol was allegedly found in the car he was travelling in. Police claim Thacker was on his way to visit the home of a member of the Greazy Dogs, a rival gang in the Bay of Plenty, allegedly to exact retribution, in broad daylight. (This followed tit-for-tat shootings involving the Mongrel Mob chapter in February 2020, detailed in Chapter 10.)

This is suburban Tauranga, not Kings Cross in Sydney. It's crazy stuff.

Just a day after Operation Silk locked up the Mongols' hierarchy, NOCG arrested a senior patched Comanchero, a close Comanchero associate, and a car dealer. The trio were charged with money laundering, and five expensive cars were seized, including a $250,000 limited-edition Mercedes-Benz.

I can't help but wonder if the madness will ever end. With so much money at stake, no doubt there's much, much more to come.

By the time you're reading this, the fate of Pasilika Naufahu and the other Comancheros locked up in Operation Nova (Chapter 12) will have been settled in a High Court trial, scheduled for September 2020. On the eve of the hearing, the Naufahu brothers Vetekina and Pasilika, as well as the gang's treasurer Jarome Fonua followed Tyson Daniels's lead and pleaded guilty to money laundering and participating in an organised criminal group. But Pasilika Naufahu steadfastly maintained his innocence of the more serious charges of conspiracy to import methamphetamine, and conspiracy to supply pseudoephedrine. Will the verdict of the jury be 'Guilty' or 'Not guilty'?

And what of Wayne Doyle, the Head Hunters' president whose $6 million worth of assets were frozen in Operation Coin (Chapter 7)? Will he get his family homes back, or will the gang's pad be sold?

Not to mention the serious organised crime charges against JD Thacker and the Mongols.

Those are stories that must be told – another day.

* * *

Prosecutions like these, past, present and future, are something of which all those involved should be proud. The work of police – and Customs staff at our borders – is immense, and ingenious. They love the thrill of the chase and the satisfaction of a bust. But these dogged investigators must feel like they've got their finger in the dyke, when the dam has already burst.

Even the police admit we can't arrest our way out of the problem. There's no point in locking up the end user; what they need is help with their addiction.

And addiction levels are off the charts. Meth addiction is a serious social ill, inextricably linked with poverty, unemployment, and unacceptable housing standards, family violence levels and suicide rates. The cost to this country is in the billions of dollars. You can't even put a figure on the damage that P will end up causing to generations of families already at the bottom of New Zealand's socioeconomic heap – the dispossessed and the uneducated, Maori, Pasifika and white, struggling to get by in towns where gangs have massive power and influence.

Successive governments were slow to react to the warnings of frontline police officers in the early 2000s about the perils of methamphetamine, the vast amounts of profit to be made, and the drug's potential to transform organised crime in this country. Their dire predictions fell short of the mark; it's worse than anyone ever imagined.

So, what comes next? And is there a solution in sight?

When it comes to the decision-making of governments faced with this problem, the basic economic law of *supply and demand* seems to have been forgotten. Time and effort are poured into tackling the *supply* of drugs. But there's very little attention paid to addressing *demand*.

It's a point that was recognised by the Court of Appeal in 2019, when a senior panel of judges revised the sentencing guidelines for meth offences. The guidelines had been in place since the judgment of *R v Fatu* in 2005, which led to the first sentences of life imprisonment for meth offences, imposed on the masterminds in Operation Major (as detailed in Chapter 2). As revealed in Chapter 10, *Fatu* was Dwight Fatu, the Mongrel Mob member who joined the Comancheros:

another link that illustrates the two degrees of separation within the New Zealand underworld.

That judgment stood in place for nearly 15 years, before being replaced by *Zhang v R* in 2019. Judges will still be able to throw the book at anyone cooking massive amounts of meth, or those involved in the more recent trend of smuggling large shipments from Asia or Mexico. But the courts will now have more discretion in determining sentences. Crucially, they will now be based not just on the weight of the methamphetamine involved, but also on the *role* of the offender.

A wide spectrum of meth-related offences comes before our courts each year. 'At one end lies ... the "head of the snake", often beyond the jurisdiction of New Zealand authorities, masterminding manufacture or importation, and distribution,' wrote Justice Stephen Kos, in the *Zhang* decision. 'At the other end lies a solo mother in a provincial town, given free methamphetamine by a gang member to addict and in-debt her, who is then forced herself to deal the drug to get by.'

The new guidelines issued in *Zhang* give judges more scope to make the right call. Before the 2019 ruling, all those caught with 500 grams or more of methamphetamine were lumped in together, regardless of whether they were a mastermind or a pawn, and faced a starting point of at least 10 years in prison.

The *Zhang* ruling allows judges to consider addiction as a mitigating factor, if – and it's a big if – the accused can show that their addiction was the root cause of their drug dealing.

Under the new guidelines, meth dealers will now be able to shave up to 30 per cent off their sentence if they can prove their own struggles with addiction were the cause of their crime.

On the back of this, Justice Kos urged lawyers and judges to take advantage of a little-used clause in the *Sentencing Act* 'tailored' to drug dealers whose crimes have been caused by drug addiction.

The judgment dovetails with the Labour government's recent law change, giving police more discretion in relation to drug arrests. Because of the *Misuse of Drugs Amendment Act* 2019, anyone caught in possession of small amounts of Class A drugs can be prosecuted only if there is a clear public interest in doing so.

It's a health-based approach. But if we're no longer sending people to prison for low-level drug offences, they'll need to be sent somewhere else for more appropriate and effective help. Counselling and rehab centres are jam-packed, and their waiting lists are long. In July, the government promised an extra $20 million in funding for regional treatment programs across the country, but it's a drop in the ocean. Those in frontline social and health services say much more is needed – and urgently – to curb the seemingly insatiable appetite for methamphetamine.

Yet strangely enough, the idea of spending hundreds of millions of taxpayers' dollars on better-resourced rehabilitation centres and counselling services is unlikely to be a vote-winner for politicians at the ballot box. So it probably won't happen any time soon.

Instead, all that money will continue to go down the drain … to pay for overcrowded prisons, clogged courtrooms and a straining social welfare system.

It's the ambulance at the bottom of the cliff. And so many New Zealanders keep falling off the top.

ACKNOWLEDGEMENTS

When it came to writing this book, there are so many people whose influence and contributions need to be recognised. It's hard to know where to start, so it may as well be at the beginning.

As a baby reporter at the *Herald on Sunday* newspaper, I was in absolute awe of the crime reporting of my senior *HoS* colleague David Fisher as well as Patrick Gower and Phil Taylor, who were both investigative reporters at the *New Zealand Herald*.

They were quick to realise the criminal underworld was rapidly changing, and their meticulous reporting on gangs and methamphetamine stands the test of time 15 years later. In particular, Paddy's reporting on Waha Saifiti and the Head Hunters laid the groundwork for my own research in writing Chapter One of this book.

I joined the *Herald* to replace Paddy when he moved to Wellington to write about other unsavoury characters – as a member of the press gallery at Parliament – and somehow picked up where he left off reporting on the fascinating world of organised crime. Cheers Paddy!

If those three journalist peers planted the seed which sprouted into a tree, it's another cherished colleague who helped prune the branches.

A massive thank you to Steve Braunias, a fellow *Herald* writer and HarperCollins author, for spending hours and hours improving this book. I don't consider myself a great writer, and suffered a great deal of Imposter Syndrome at the thought of taking on a book project. Steve was hugely encouraging and made the incredibly generous offer to knock my copy into shape, before I submitted the manuscript to HarperCollins for final editing.

I'm so grateful for his deft work, and I suspect the team at HarperCollins would be too. I'd also like to acknowledge Alex Hedley, Emma Dowden and Lachlan McLaine at HarperCollins. The final product is so much better because of your hard work, and to push me to go a little further.

Of course, a journalist is only as good as their sources. There are many I'd like to thank but as I've undertaken to keep their names out of print, I'm sure they'd rather stay anonymous. But given Bruce Good is retired now, after so many years running Auckland's drug squads, I'm sure he won't mind me publicly acknowledging him. I rang Bruce nearly every month or so, for a decade. I never got a decent story out of him, but anytime someone doesn't hang up on a journalist is a win.

Having that relationship meant Bruce agreed to sit down to help me research a few of the older cases for this book. We raked over some of his career highlights, some of the best investigations ever run in New Zealand. Ever humble, Bruce gave all of the credit to his talented and hardworking detectives. That's the kind of guy he is.

Finally, a big thank you to the many other sources who helped me but can't be named: detectives, Crown prosecutors, defence lawyers, court staff, criminals. You know who you are.